The European Union in the Asia-Pacific

Manchester University Press

The European Union in the Asia-Pacific

Rethinking Europe's strategies and policies

Edited by
Weiqing Song and Jianwei Wang

Manchester University Press

Copyright © Manchester University Press 2019

While copyright in the volume as a whole is vested in Manchester University Press, copyright in individual chapters belongs to their respective authors, and no chapter may be reproduced wholly or in part without the express permission in writing of both author and publisher.

Published by Manchester University Press
Oxford Road, Manchester M13 9PL

www.manchesteruniversitypress.co.uk

British Library Cataloguing-in-Publication Data
A catalogue record for this book is available from the British Library

ISBN 978 1 5261 3185 0 hardback
ISBN 978 1 5261 6388 2 paperback

First published 2019
Paperback published 2022

The publisher has no responsibility for the persistence or accuracy of URLs for any external or third-party internet websites referred to in this book, and does not guarantee that any content on such websites is, or will remain, accurate or appropriate.

Typeset
by Toppan Best-set Premedia Limited

Contents

List of tables	*page* vii
List of figures	viii
Notes on contributors	ix
Preface	xii
List of abbreviations	xiv

Introduction: The European Union's Asia-Pacific strategies and policies at the crossroads *Weiqing Song and Jianwei Wang*	1

Part I: General strategic context

1 The European Union in the Asia-Pacific: strategic reflections *Michael Reiterer*	17
2 A European pivot towards Asia? Inter-regionalism in a new era *Julie Gilson*	39

Part II: Major issues and themes

3 European Union security policy and initiatives in the Asia-Pacific *Fulvio Attinà*	59
4 Assessing the European Union's economic relations with the Asia-Pacific *Miguel Otero-Iglesias*	73
5 Public diplomacy of the European Union in East Asia *Suetyi Lai and Li Zhang*	96
6 The European Union's approach to human security: lessons from the Asia-Pacific *Evangelos Fanoulis*	120

Part III: Selected countries and groups

7 The European Union's partnership with China: navigating between trouble and promise *Gustaaf Geeraerts*	145
8 Shifting constraints, evolving opportunities and the search for the "strategic" in the European Union and Japan bilateral partnership *Elena Atanassova-Cornelis*	164

9 The European Union's security strategy in the ASEAN
   region   *Reuben Wong*   184
10 The European Union in Australia and New Zealand
   Nicole Scicluna   200

Index   217

Tables

5.1	The EU's public diplomacy in Asia, sources of empirical data	*page* 105
5.2	News outlets monitored in the research projects	106
5.3	Respondents' ranking of their country's most important partner, March 2012	113
5.4	Respondents' choice of adjective to describe the EU, 2012 and 2015	114
6.1	The EU's strategic partnerships in Asia	125
6.2	EU–ASEAN collaboration on security questions	127
6.3	EU delegations in the Pacific	128
6.4	Disbursements of ODA managed by DG DEVCO to the Pacific countries, 2010–15	131
6.5	Societal sectors benefiting from the tenth EDF	132
6.6	Eleventh EDF commitments towards Pacific countries	133
6.7	EU humanitarian aid and civil protection assistance to Pacific countries, 2010–15 (major cases)	134
6.8	Disbursements of DG ECHO funds to Pacific countries, 2013 and 2014	135

Figures

4.1	Percentage share of South Korean imports, 1995–2016	page 81
4.2	Percentage share of ASEAN imports, 1995–2016	82
4.3	Main EU countries' exports to South Korea, 1995–2016	82
4.4	Main EU countries' exports to ASEAN, 1995–2016	83
4.5	ASEAN trade with main trading partners, 1995–2016	84
4.6	Percentage share of ASEAN commerce with main trading partners, 1995–2016	85
5.1	Monthly average of EU-related news items in each location per newspaper	107
5.2	Monthly average of EU-related news in prime-time TV news bulletins	108
5.3	Centrality of the EU's actions in the collected EU-related news	109
5.4	Comparison of visibility of EU communal institutions and EU member states in the 2015 media analysis dataset	110
5.5	Respondents' awareness of EU institutions, March 2012	111
5.6	Respondents' frequency of hearing or reading about the EU, August 2015	112
5.7	Respondents' conception of the EU as a partner to their country, surveyed in August 2015	113
5.8	Evaluation of the EU by the general public, 2011 and 2015	115
5.9	Evaluation of media reportage of the EU, 2006–15	116

Contributors

Atanassova-Cornelis, Elena: Lecturer in East Asian Politics at the Department of Politics, University of Antwerp, and at the School of Political and Social Sciences, Catholic University of Louvain, Belgium. Her research interests and expertise include Japanese and Chinese foreign policy, US regional strategy and alliance politics in Asia, maritime security and regional co-operation in Asia, as well as EU–Asia relations. She has published more than thirty academic articles, book chapters, briefing papers and reports.

Attinà, Fulvio: Professor of Political Science and International Relations, and Jean Monnet Chair Ad Personam at the University of Catania. He served as former Chair of the Italian Association of Political Science and also served in the governing bodies of ECPR, ISA and Italian ECSA. Currently, he does research on the EU's role in multilateral security, humanitarian and emergency actions, and the management of the migration crisis.

Fanoulis, Evangelos: Lecturer in International Relations at the Department of International Relations, Xi'an Jiaotong – Liverpool University. He was previously postdoctoral researcher at Metropolitan University, Prague, lecturer in Politics at Leicester University and fellow at Essex University. He has done research and published on security governance, democracy and populism in Europe, EU–China relations and post-structuralist international relations theory.

Geeraerts, Gustaaf: PhD in Political Science, is currently Distinguished Professor at the School of International Relations and Public Administration, Fudan University, China. He is Emeritus Professor of Vrije Universiteit Brussel and founder of the Brussels Institute of Contemporary China Studies, Belgium. His research interests focus on contemporary China, international relations theory, China's foreign policy, global governance and EU--China relations.

Gilson, Julie: Reader in Asian Studies at the University of Birmingham, UK. Author of *Japan and the European Union* and *Asia Meets Europe*, she has also written journal articles on East Asian regionalism, civil society in Asia and transnational advocacy networks.

Lai, Suetyi (Cher): Lecturer at Guangdong University of Foreign Studies, China, researching and teaching China–EU relations. She finished her doctoral studies in National Centre for Research on Europe, University of Canterbury, New Zealand, in 2012. She has published on Asia–Europe relations, China–Europe relations and Asia Europe Meeting.

Otero-Iglesias, Miguel: Senior Analyst in International Political Economy at the Elcano Royal Institute and Professor at IE University in Spain and Research Fellow at the EU–Asia Institute at ESSCA School of Management in France. He is interested in international and European monetary affairs and the EU's economic diplomacy vis-à-vis China and Asia at large. He has published more than a hundred articles in peer-reviewed journals and international media.

Reiterer, Michael: studied law at the University of Innsbruck (Dr. juris) and holds diplomas in international relations from the Johns Hopkins University/Bologna Centre and the Graduate Institute of International Studies in Geneva; since 2005 Adjunct professor for international politics, University of Innsbruck. As an official of the EU, he is presently EU Ambassador to the Republic of Korea. He specialises in EU foreign policy, EU–Asia relations, human rights, regional integration and new forms of diplomacy, on all of which areas he has published extensively.

Scicluna, Nicole: Visiting Assistant Professor of Political Science and International Relations at the University of Hong Kong, China. She received her PhD in International Relations from La Trobe University, Melbourne, Australia, in 2013. Her teaching and research interests include European integration, EU politics and the effect of international law on international relations.

Song, Weiqing: associate professor of international relations and holder of a Jean Monnet Chair in European Politics at Department of Government and Public Administration, the University of Macau, China. He received a PhD degree in political science from University of Siena, Italy. He has research interests in Chinese foreign policy, global governance, EU studies, and the post-socialist regime in China.

Wang, Jianwei: received his PhD in political science from the University of Michigan, US. He is currently Professor of International Relations and Director of the Institute of International and Public Affairs, University of Macau, China. His teaching and research interests focus on East Asia politics and security affairs, Chinese politics and foreign policy, Sino-American relations, Sino-Japanese relations, UN peacekeeping operations and American politics and foreign policy.

Wong, Reuben: holds the Jean Monnet Chair at National University of Singapore and is Director of Studies at the College of Alice & Peter Tan. He earned an MPhil in European Politics at Oxford, and a PhD in International Relations at the LSE. He is the author of *The Europeanization of French Foreign Policy* (2006); *National and European Foreign Policies* (co-edited with Christopher Hill, 2011); and refereed articles in the *Cambridge Review of International Affairs, Politique Européenne, Asia Europe Journal*, and *European Foreign Affairs Review*.

Zhang, Li: Associate Professor in the School of Journalism and Communication, Tsinghua University, China. She holds a PhD from the University of Leeds, UK. Her research interests fall on International Communication, Political Communication and Public Relations, particularly with a focus on relations between the European Union and Asia.

Preface

Through all its ebbs and flows, the European Union (EU) has grown resiliently to become an international player with a global vision. Its strategic outreach has extended as far as the Asia-Pacific region. About two decades ago, the EU officially embarked upon its strategic march to the Asia-Pacific region, thereby going far beyond its traditional focus of external relationships with its immediate neighbours and with the African, Caribbean and Pacific (ACP) countries that were formerly European colonies. This courageous move was driven by its ambition to implement its embryonic yet high-profile EU foreign policy, and by the increasing appeal of the rapid development of the Asia-Pacific region. Since the mid-1990s, this region has been identified as one of its key strategic targets in its ambitions to become a truly global leader. The EU has since made consistent efforts to implement strategies, policies and activities in the Asia-Pacific region and to develop relationships with various countries and organisations in the region.

Because more than twenty years have elapsed, the EU is due to reflect on its presence in the Asia-Pacific region and rethink its interests, roles and policies towards this region for the years to come. This is crucial given the major challenges and opportunities that the EU currently faces on various fronts, particularly with respect to its internal crises of financial debt, the Brexit vote and refugees. With the rapid development of the Asia-Pacific region in recent decades, the world is witnessing a dramatic shift in power. This shift is coupled with unprecedented forces and trends unleashed by globalisation. It is not an exaggeration to say that the Asia-Pacific region is gradually replacing the trans-Atlantic region as the centre of gravity of global economics and politics, which has an immediate and significant influence on the relationship between Europe and the Asia-Pacific region and on the EU's foreign policy. Against this backdrop, the EU has been forced to redefine its strategies and policies in the Asia-Pacific region.

From the perspective of international relations and foreign policy analysis, this collection provides cutting-edge analyses of the EU's foreign policy in the Asia-Pacific region. In contrast to much of the existing research on comparative regionalism or inter-regional relations on Europe and Asia, this edited volume is written from the perspective of the EU, which is conceptualised as a strategic player in the international arena. Individual chapters are devoted to discussion of the EU's roles, interests and policies with respect to a specific area, an individual country or a group of countries. The issues and countries selected are all important to the EU's external strategy, with reference to the Asia-Pacific region. However, this collection of individual discussions will constitute an updated and systematic anatomy of the EU's policy in the Asia-Pacific region. The research findings are expected to provide valuable contributions to our understanding of the EU as an international player and to the relations between the EU and the Asia-Pacific region. This book will mostly appeal to scholars and students as a reference guide and will generally serve as a textbook of EU studies, Asia-Pacific studies, foreign policy analysis and international relations. It will also appeal to policy-makers and other readers who are interested in the EU, the Asia-Pacific region, global governance and international relations.

The editors are indebted to a long list of people who were helpful, in one way or another, in completing this book. First, we wish to thank the European Union Academic Programme Macao, a joint initiative of the EU and the University of Macau, which aims to disseminate knowledge and raise the visibility of the EU in the region, and the Institute of European Studies of Macau (IEEM), a government-sponsored organisation specialising in teaching and conducting research on Europe-related topics in Macao. We not only appreciate their generous financial sponsorship, but also their very objectives, which have spurred our immediate inspiration and motivation for this book project. We also thank the team of academic colleagues who accepted our invitation, joined us from Europe and the Asia-Pacific region and have worked with us to complete this enterprise. Last, but not least, we wish to thank a group of managerial leaders, administrative staff and graduate assistants at the University of Macau and the IEEM, particularly Rui Martins, José Luís de Sales Marques and Rui Flores, for their indispensable advice, support and assistance in this book project and beyond.

Abbreviations

ACP	Africa, Caribbean Sea, Pacific
ADIZ	Air Defence Identification Zone
ADMM+	ASEAN Defence Ministers Meeting Plus
AEC	ASEAN Economic Community
AfT	Aid for Trade
AIIB	Asian Infrastructure and Investment Bank
APEC	Asia-Pacific Economic Co-operation
APT	ASEAN Plus Three
ARF	ASEAN Regional Forum
ASEAN	Association of Southeast Asian Nations
ASEM	Asia–Europe Meeting
BIA	Bilateral Investment Agreement
BRI	Belt and Road Initiative
BRICS	Brazil, Russia, India, China and South Africa
CAP	Common Agricultural Policy
CFSP	Common Foreign and Security Policy
CSCAP	Council for Security Co-operation in the Asia-Pacific
CSCE	Conference on Security and Co-operation in Europe
CSDP	Common Security and Defence Policy
DG CLIMA	Directorate-General for Climate Action
DG DEVCO	Directorate-General International Co-operation and Development
DG ECHO	Directorate-General for European Civil Protection and Humanitarian Aid Operations
DIPECHO	Disasters Preparedness ECHO Programme
EAS	East Asian Summit
EC	European Community
ECSC	European Coal and Steel Community
EDF	European Development Fund
EEAS	European External Action Service
EEC	European Economic Community

Abbreviations

EIDHR	European Initiative for Democracy and Human Rights
EOM	Election Observation Missions
EPA	Economic Partnership Agreement
ESDP	European Spatial Development Planning
ESDP	European Security and Defence Policy
ESPO	European Sea Ports Organization
ESS	European Security Strategy
ETS	Emissions Trading Scheme
EU	European Union
EUCPM	EU Civil Protection Mechanism
EUGS	EU Global Strategy for Foreign and Security Policy
FDI	Foreign Direct Investment
FPA	Framework Participation Agreement
FPDA	Five-Power Defence Arrangements
FPIs	Foreign Policy Instruments
FTA	Free Trade Agreement
FTAAP	Free Trade Area of the Asia-Pacific FTIA Free Trade and Investment Agreement
GCF	Green Climate Fund
HR	High Representative for Foreign Affairs and Security Policy
HRVP	High Representative for Security and Defence Policy / Vice President of the European Commission
HSRF	Human Security Response Force
IFP	Investment Facility for the Pacific
IfS	Instrument for Stability
IMF	International Monetary Fund
NAPCI	North East Asia Peace and Cooperation Initiative
NAS	New Asia Strategy
NATO	North Atlantic Treaty Organisation
NDPG	National Defence Programme Guidelines
NPE	Normative Power Europe
NSS	National Security Strategy
NTS	Non-Traditional Security
ODA	Official Development Assistance
PCAs	Partnership and Co-operation Agreements
PRC	People's Republic of China
SAARC	South Asian Association for Regional Cooperation
SAR	Special Administrative Region
SDF	Self-Defence Forces
SDG	Sustainable Development Goals
SLOCs	Sea Lines of Communications
SPA	Strategic Partnership Agreement
TAC	Tactical Air Control

TAC	Treaty of Amity and Co-operation in Southeast Asia
TPP	Trans-Pacific Partnership
UNFCC	UN Framework Convention on Climate Change
WTO	World Trade Organisation

Introduction: The European Union's Asia-Pacific strategies and policies at the crossroads

Weiqing Song and Jianwei Wang

The EU's global reach to the Asia-Pacific region

Europe is an old player in the Asia-Pacific region because several European states have substantial links with the region, mostly due to their colonial histories. Meanwhile, Europe is also a new player in the region, because the EU has had substantial ties with the region only for about two decades. The EU officially embarked upon its global adventure as an international player after the inauguration of the Common Foreign and Security Policy (CFSP) by the Maastricht Treaty in 1993. The Asia-Pacific region has since become a major target of the EU's global outreach, driven by its economic motivations and political ambitions. This is marked by the issuance of the European Commission's communication to the Council of the EU, proposing a "New Asia Strategy" in 1994. This was a big step in the history of the EU, because the EU moved far beyond its traditional scope of external relations with the Asia, Caribbean, Pacific (ACP) countries, its immediate neighbours and trans-Atlantic partners. Rather, it began to target a diverse group of countries in the faraway and volatile Asia-Pacific region. This move was made when the EU was optimistic about its new creation and the attractiveness of Asia's economic potential. Around two decades after the EU's global outreach with the Asia-Pacific region, it has gained valuable experience with respect to its foreign policy practices. Through its Asia-Pacific policies, the EU has exhibited notable qualities of an international player, such as proficiency in strategic and policy planning, projection of resources and capabilities, and policy results and outcomes.

In its policy on the Asia-Pacific region, the EU has displayed some competence in strategic and policy planning, including defining its own interests, policy objectives and overall strategy. It can be noted that the EU's interests and objectives in the Asia-Pacific region are pursuant to and in conformity with the major objectives of the CFSP: to preserve peace, reinforce international security and promote international cooperation, democracy, the rule of law, respect for human rights and fundamental freedoms. These objectives have been documented in the 1994 strategy paper, with a focus on "strengthening the Union's economic presence in Asia". The EU's new Asia strategy in 1994 was clearly driven by its self-interest against the backdrop of the rise of Asia in the world economy. In addition, the creation of the EU provided the momentum for a more ambitious global objective to "maintain the Union's leading role in the world economy". To this end, the EU has adopted an engagement strategy that aims to implement its own foreign policies in the Asia-Pacific region through contacts, exchange and co-operation. By adopting a comprehensive approach, the EU plans to cover political, economic and co-operation aspects of its policy on the Asia-Pacific region: to focus on political dialogue in both bilateral and multilateral settings; to open up markets; to help integrate Asian countries into the open, market-based world trading system; and to conduct joint programmes of poverty alleviation in relevant Asian countries.

Beginning with its first Asian strategic paper in 1994, the EU has reviewed and updated its strategic plans pertaining to its Asia policy by considering changes and developments in Asia, Europe and the rest of the world. The first comprehensive policy review led to the Commission's Communication "Europe and Asia: A Strategic Framework for Enhanced Partnerships" in 2001. Comparing the 1994 and 2001 documents, it can be observed that the EU has redefined its concept of the Asia-Pacific region and accordingly readjusted its objectives and policies on the region (Murray, 2008: 190). It is true that definition of the Asia-Pacific region is elusive, given its tremendous heterogeneity in terms of scope, social and economic development, political systems and values, culture and religion. In the 1994 strategic paper, the EU included in the region of Asia 26 countries in Northeast Asia, Southeast Asia and South Asia. This definition has been expanded to cover Australasia in the 2001 document to reflect the substantial and intensified social, economic and political links between Oceania, particularly Australia and New Zealand, and East Asia proper. Aware of the differences in sub-regions in the Asia-Pacific, the 2001 strategic paper distinguishes between "action points for the region as a whole" and "action points for the different regions of Asia". An adjustment was also made in strategic priorities. Although an engagement strategy was adopted in the 1994 paper to strengthen the EU's economic presence in the region, the 2001 document widens the scope of strengthening both the political and economic presence of the EU across the Asia-Pacific and broadening its engagement with the region. Furthermore, the 2001 paper mentioned "joint efforts" with Asian countries on global governance issues such as environment and security. This strategic review is attributable to the EU's deepened understanding of the Asia-Pacific region, development of its foreign policy competences and its ability in related strategic and policy reflections on past experiences.

The EU has been quite proactive in implementing its own foreign policies in the Asia-Pacific region, which includes countries in the region and the region as a whole. Over the years, the EU has proved itself to be a qualified global power with respect to the Asia-Pacific region. Although it is not always successful, its ability in policy projection is relevant and notable. In general, the EU has several resources and capabilities at its disposal, including strategic partnership, inter-regional co-operation, economic statecraft and public diplomacy. These instruments are not designed specifically for the Asia-Pacific region, but are tools of its global engagement policy. The EU's diplomacy with the Asia-Pacific region is characterised by a combination of bilateral and inter-regional approaches. In addition to traditional bilateral relations, the EU has been a major player in promoting inter-regional diplomacy in different parts of the world. The Asia-Pacific region is a major target. It has a long history of conducting inter-regional co-operation with the Association of Southeast Asian Nations (ASEAN) and has expanded to the wider region since the mid-1990s. The Asia–Europe Meeting (ASEM) has been acclaimed as a major achievement of the EU's effort in implementing inter-regional diplomacy. The ASEM is an informal process of dialogue and co-operation, addressing political, economic and cultural issues, in a spirit of mutual respect and equal partnership. Thus far, the process has drawn together almost every country in the two regions. The instrument of a strategic partnership stands out because it highlights the EU's ambition to become a major international player vis-à-vis other key powers around the world. As part of its global strategic partnership diplomacy, the EU has established high-profile bilateral strategic partnerships with several key players in the region, including Japan in 2001, China in 2003, India in 2004, and South Korea in 2010. In addition, another strategic partnership with the ASEAN as a bloc is under consideration. Four of its ten officially claimed strategic partners worldwide are within the Asia-Pacific region. This fact alone suggests the importance of the region to the EU and the EU's devotion to the region. The EU attempts to establish long-term relationships with major players in the Asia-Pacific region by setting long-term goals and commitments and by promoting its interests and values at the global level. It is no exaggeration that strategic partnership diplomacy consumes much of the EU's energy in its Asian policy.

As a global player, the EU's policy outcomes are achieved at practical, perceptual and strategic levels. At a practical level, the EU has established working ties with interlocutors and partners in the Asia-Pacific. The ties are institutional, both formal and informal, and substantive across various areas. Through strategic partnership diplomacy, the EU's relations with major Asian countries are substantiated with a series of events such as annual summits, political dialogue and co-operation programmes. Similar institutional links are established with the ASEAN and, to a lesser extent, with Australia and New Zealand. The EU's ties with countries in the region are substantive, covering a range of policy sectors, including trade and economic, political and security matters, public diplomacy, development assistance, democracy and human rights promotion and global governance issues. This is particularly noteworthy in trade and economics. The EU and Asian countries are amongst each other's most important trade partners. In 2015, the Asian partners, defined as Asian members of the ASEM, accounted for about 46 per cent of EU imports and about 29 per cent of its exports. Of the top ten EU trading partners, four are in the Asia-Pacific, with China as its second-largest partner. Free trade agreements were concluded with South Korea in 2011, Singapore in 2012 and Vietnam in 2016. Another agreement was expected soon with Japan, and negotiations were under way with Thailand, Malaysia and India. At a strategic level, the EU's strategic partnership diplomacy has produced some modest results because relations with the most important Asian countries are institutionalised and generally stabilised. Apart from its economic presence, the EU has been trying to increase its political presence in the region. This is exemplified by its participation in the ASEAN Regional Forum (ARF). Its recent public show at the Shangri-La Dialogue is a modest step towards its role in Asian security. Furthermore, its strategic co-ordination with the United States in the region is noteworthy, at least rhetorically. In 2012, on the side lines of the ARF, the then US Secretary of State, Hillary Clinton, and the then EU High Representative of the CFSP, Catherine Ashton, issued a joint statement declaring that the two should conduct 'closer consultation' on their 'common objectives' in a wide array of issues in the Asia-Pacific, including peace and security, sustainable development, and trade and economics.[1] At the perceptual level, it is evident that the EU has been recognised as a meaningful international player. Empirical studies suggest that images of the EU's international leadership and great power status are highly issue-specific and country-specific (Chaban et al., 2013). However, it has been almost unanimously recognised as an economic and diplomatic power, with a leadership role in trade and economics, political and diplomatic areas, and development and normative areas.

Challenges of the dynamic Asia-Pacific region

It has been widely acknowledged that the Asia-Pacific region is one of the most dynamic and volatile regions in the contemporary world. Asia is not simply one (Acharya, 2010). The region is heterogeneous, in terms of both material and ideational aspects. It is a collection of countries that are massively different in terms of physical size, socio-economic development, civilisational tradition and political and normative aspirations. The density of divergence within the more or less arbitrarily defined region has posed serious challenges not only to international relations of the region itself but also to relevant outside players. The EU is such an outsider, far away, yet with strong motivation and stakes in the region. In fact, this is particularly the case with the EU now, owing to some of its most pressing internal crises. All factors combined, the EU's policy on the Asia-Pacific region is facing various challenges in the political, economic and normative spheres.

First, the EU has been challenged as a political and security power in the Asia-Pacific. Its core objective is to strengthen its political and economic presence in the Asia-Pacific region. To this end, it should work to "contribute to peace and security in the region" through engagement and to "build global partnerships and alliances" with Asian countries to address issues of global governance (European Commission, 2001: 15). However, the EU's political engagement with the region is becoming increasingly difficult to attain. The political and strategic horizon of the Asia-Pacific has undergone dramatic changes over the past two decades. This includes the redistribution of power, gravitating towards major emerging powers such as China and India. More acutely, the region has several dangerous flashpoints of the contemporary world, particularly territorial disputes over the South China Sea, the Sino-Indian border and the North Korean nuclear crisis. The tense security situation has been further complicated by the participation of other inside and outside players. This is most exemplified by the United States' strategy of "pivot" or "rebalancing" for Asia under the Obama Administration and then increasing uncertainty under the Trump Administration. The security uncertainty is further complemented by the Sino-Japanese geopolitical rivalry and growing China–India strategic suspicion and competition. All this has imposed a big challenge for the EU's role as a political and security player in the Asia-Pacific. Admittedly, the EU is not well prepared to take on these intensifying challenges. For example, there was no coherent position on the EU's part to respond to the US's pivot/rebalance strategy in Asia earlier, and it is now even more difficult to co-ordinate with its US ally on a concerted strategy for the region. Although the EU has devoted the bulk of its Asia-Pacific policy to China, it continues to be deeply divided on China. Moreover, it has made limited commitments with respect to the rest of Asia, a situation which is sometimes exacerbated by diverging interests and priorities. The EU's underperformance has exposed its perennial weakness: the lack of unified and sufficient capabilities in the political and security spheres. It is true that the time that the EU could be qualified as a real foreign policy player remains in the distant future (Krotz, 2009). However, the challenges of the Asia-Pacific region demand that the EU should work out a feasible option to bring about the effective implementation of its international leadership, with instruments such as rule-based multilateralism, inter-regional co-operation and normative engagement. Otherwise, its international credibility will be severely undermined.

Meanwhile, the EU has also been challenged as an economic power in the Asia-Pacific region, although it has for long been proud of itself as a global economic giant. Since the very beginning of its Asia policy, the EU has prioritised strengthening its economic presence in the Asia-Pacific region. This core objective is detailed to further improve its "mutual trade and investment flows" with Asia. The overall context has transformed dramatically over the past twenty years. The Asia-Pacific region has apparently become the most dynamic part of the global economy, if one considers its economic vitality and resilience, particularly during a global economic slowdown. After decades of rapid economic growth, the region is now home to a group of newly emerging global economic powers, joining the ranks of some of its traditionally powerful counterparts. In fact, six of the Group of Twenty (G20) members have been drawn from the region. The aggregate economic size has been coupled with active economic initiatives occurring in parallel. The United States again plays its pivotal role in the region, leading the negotiations on the Trans-Pacific Partnership (TPP), although its future is gloomy due to the Trump Administration's strategic U-turn on the issue. Rivalled by the United States, China is unhappy with the stalemate of talks on the Regional Comprehensive Economic Partnership. It has exhibited its global ambition by launching its own projects, notably, the "One Belt, One Road" initiative; the Brazil, Russia, India, China and South Africa (BRICS) co-operation; and related concrete projects such as the Asian Investment Infrastructure Bank (AIIB) and the 16 + 1 framework with Central and Eastern European countries. The EU largely remains an observer because it is not party to any of these most important multilateral economic negotiations. This absence is in complete contrast to its huge stakes in the region and even in Europe itself. Moreover, it is still embroiled in its internal inability to reach agreement, owing to issues such as the Euro debt crisis and the lack of co-ordination on global economic strategy, the massive influx of refugees from neighbouring countries and the rise of political populism. In the case of its China policy, the EU is working hard with China on a bilateral investment agreement, but a future free-trade agreement is still a distant dream. The member states are deeply divided in recognising China's market economy status, and there is no co-ordinated approach to China's proactive initiatives such as the AIIB and the 16 + 1 process.

In a related, but more profound, development, the EU has been increasingly challenged as a normative power in recent years. Its clear objective is to promote its values and norms globally, including the Asia-Pacific region, which is evident from its intent 'to contribute to the spreading of democracy, good governance and rule of law'. The EU's normative power is derived from its economic might, political influence and soft power. However, the appeal of its normative power is on the decline owing to internal weaknesses demonstrated by the Euro debt crisis, the challenges of its welfare models and the more recent Brexit issue. Furthermore, the rise of emerging powers and the overall weight of the Asia-Pacific region have strengthened the confidence of the countries in the region to stand up to traditional Western powers. Led by countries like China, some of the Asian countries pose challenges to the existing global order and values in which the EU and its members are mostly beneficiaries and strong supporters. These countries are very suspicious of the EU style of regional integration, which is essentially promoted by the EU itself in its inter-regional diplomacy with many parts of the developing world. They are not content with the formula of major international institutions, in many of which the EU is over-represented. In fact, the EU also faces the Global South challenges to the so-called Western-dominated "rule-based multilateralism". The EU has declared, in its most recent global strategy paper, its objective to promote democracy and other values; a rule-based global order with multilateralism as its key principle (European Union, 2016: 15). This goal is yet to be supported by sufficient means to cope with these new challenges, among others.

In its most recent guidelines on global strategy, the EU declared that its focus is on developing relations with "a connected Asia" (European Union, 2016: 37–8) However, it is not clear how the EU will try to make progress amidst the major challenges and setbacks in its Asia policy. It claims that "unity", "engagement", "responsibility" and "partnership" will be upheld as key principles in its external policy (European Union, 2016: 16–18). For those observing the case of the Asia-Pacific region, several questions remain unanswered about how the EU will implement its acclaimed principles. The first question concerns the prioritised partner or target country in the region. There has been much criticism that the EU has attached too much importance to China and neglected the rest of Asia. Given the rising importance of China and its strong stakes in the Asia-Pacific, it is not a matter of choice for the EU, but rather a difficult task of selection and balance between different targets in the Asia-Pacific region. Another major issue is maintaining a difficult balance between two major policy objectives: the pursuit of economic and practical interests and the pursuit of normative values. On quite a few occasions, the EU and its member states have sacrificed their moral values in pursuit of pragmatic benefits, particularly in their relations with major Asian powers such as China. In all probability, this "principled pragmatism" will guide the EU's external action in the years ahead, compromising the Scylla of isolationism and the Charybdis of rash interventionism. However, analysts predict that pragmatism will most likely precede principles when the two are contradictory. The third major question is a perennial one, concerning co-ordination between the EU and the member states and between the member states themselves.

Moment for strategic reflections

About two decades ago, the EU officially embarked on its strategic outreach to the Asia-Pacific region. It went far beyond its traditional focus of external relations with its immediate neighbours and the ACP countries, which are mostly former European colonies. This courageous move was driven by its ambition to implement its embryonic, yet high-profile European Union foreign policy and by the increasing appeal of the rapid development of the Asia-Pacific region. Since the mid-1990s, the Asia-Pacific region has been identified as one of its key strategic targets on its ambitious road to becoming a truly global player. The EU has since made consistent efforts to implement strategies, policies and activities in the Asia-Pacific region and to develop relations with various countries and organisations in the region.

In recent decades, extensive changes have taken place in both regions and in the world at large. It is about time that the EU's performance with respect to its Asian policy is evaluated, and, if necessary, its interests and roles redefined, and its strategies and policies re-examined. In fact, the EU is at a crossroads on its Asia-Pacific policy. Its hesitation and indecision are vividly evidenced by the fact that the two top EU leaders made almost contradictory remarks simultaneously on the role of the EU in the region, in 2012.[2] The 2016 EU Global Strategy for its foreign and security policy stresses the importance of a "connected Asia" as a direct link between European prosperity and security in Asia (European Union, 2016: 37–8). However, this brief statement does not provide a detailed plan of its Asian strategy and policies. Given the major challenges and opportunities that the EU now faces on various fronts, some strategic rethinking, with a focus on policy reflection and adjustment, is not only necessary but also crucial. The rapid development of the Asia-Pacific region in recent decades is well under way, and, in turn, the world is witnessing a dramatic shift in power redistribution. This is coupled with unprecedented forces and trends, unleashed by the process of globalisation. It is fair to say that the Asia-Pacific region is gradually replacing the trans-Atlantic as the centre of gravity of global economics and politics. Equally pressing is the fact that the EU is embroiled in a series of internal crises, particularly its financial debts crisis, the refugee crisis and the upcoming Brexit. This has all had an immediate and significant effect on EU's foreign policy and its relationship with the Asia-Pacific. Therefore, the EU has been forced to redefine its strategies towards the Asia-Pacific, in terms of its interests, roles and policies.

Since the end of the Cold War, world politics has undergone unprecedented transformations on various aspects. Regional integration in Europe and the rise of the Asia-Pacific region are two of the major developments in this context. The subject area of this book is the interactions of the two regions in contemporary international relations, with the focus on the EU as an emerging global player in the emerging Asia-Pacific region. With the exception of several books on inter-regional relations between Europe and the Asia-Pacific region, no book specifically addresses the EU's foreign policy in the Asia-Pacific region. More particularly, this book attempts to elaborate the EU's strategic and policy rethinking, at a time when it is at critical crossroads with its foreign policy. We aim to fill this gap by

The EU's Asia-Pacific strategies and policies

producing an updated and high-quality study on this increasingly important topic of contemporary international relations. This study is intended to be a major volume edited in the Asia-Pacific region, by bringing together a mixed group of established and younger scholars from Europe and the Asia-Pacific region.

From the perspective of international relations and foreign policy analysis, this edited book aims to provide a collection of cutting-edge analyses on the EU's external relations and foreign policies in the Asia-Pacific region. It addresses the following questions:

- What are the effects and implications of globalisation and changes in the world order on the EU's relations with the Asia-Pacific region? The emphasis here is also on the role of the United States and the increasing influence of China and other emerging powers in the region.
- What are the effects and implications of the EU's internal challenges and developments in its relations with the Asia-Pacific region?
- What are the main processes and characteristics of the EU's presence, policies and activities in the Asia-Pacific region, with reference to specific sectors or individual countries in the region and to the internal dynamics of EU institutions and member states?
- How can we evaluate the major achievements of and setbacks in EU policies, with reference to specific sectors or individual countries in the region and to the internal dynamics of EU institutions and member states?
- What are the EU's main challenges and opportunities when developing its relations within the region?
- What are the perceptions and responses of Asia-Pacific countries towards the EU?
- How can the EU redefine and readjust its interests, roles and policies regarding the Asia-Pacific region, with reference to specific sectors or individual countries and to its overall external strategies?

Compared with existing books on similar topics, this book stands out in terms of three major aspects. First, it comprehensively covers the EU's foreign policy in the Asia-Pacific region, in terms of its general strategic context, a selected number of major issue areas and target countries or country groups. Second, it is more systematic, with a clearly defined overarching conceptual framework of the EU as a global strategic player. Third, it is solid in its empirical analysis, by drawing together a group of scholars in EU studies and international relations. It is expected that this book will serve as a comprehensive and valuable resource in terms of empirical knowledge and conceptual and theoretical understanding of EU studies, and its relations with the Asia-Pacific. It could also serve as a research-based textbook on the EU and Asia-Pacific studies. Therefore, this book will appeal to a wide range of readers, including scholars; students; and analysts and practitioners of international relations, European studies, and Asia-Pacific studies.

Organisation of the book

This book consists of three parts. The Introduction and the two chapters in Part I contextualise the EU's policies and relations with the Asia-Pacific region. It sets the scene for the empirical chapters that follow, each of which addresses a specific aspect of the topic. The book further provides more empirical analyses in the second and third parts. The second part is composed of four chapters on major themes and issues of the EU's policies towards the Asia-Pacific, including traditional hard security, economic and trade issues, public diplomacy and issues of human security. The third part includes four chapters that cover the EU's policies towards the selected countries and groups of countries in the Asia-Pacific region, including China, Japan, the ASEAN countries, and Australia and New Zealand.

This Introduction provides the background, rationale and objectives of the edited project. With an introduction to the EU's presence in the Asia-Pacific in recent decades, it discusses the challenges and opportunities that the EU currently faces in the region and raises several issues and questions that will urge the EU to rethink its strategic priorities and policies in the region. Michael Reiterer's chapter studies the issue of the general strategic nature of the topic: the EU's strategic reflections towards the Asia-Pacific region. It contends that although the EU maintains strategic partnerships with several Asian partners, there are doubts in Asia about whether it can be a genuine strategic partner. Reviewing the generally unimpressive performance of the EU in the region, the chapter draws on the EU's New Global Strategy, officially published in June 2016, as a moment for strategic reflection of the EU's approach to the Asia-Pacific. It explores the possible consequences of this new approach, with specific reference to its strategic partnership diplomacy in the region. It argues that in line with the changed circumstances, the partnership diplomacy will have to be cross-sectoral, that is, across institutions, governments and peoples. It is further suggested that in Asia, which is undergoing profound changes, investment in regional security and strengthening of global governance in the twenty-first century will be essential features of this overhauled strategic partnership diplomacy. Julie Gilson's chapter presents a provocative argument that the EU is adopting a strategic pivot to the Asia-Pacific. It interrogates this apparently renewed European approach to Asia, within the context of inter-regional relations through the ASEM framework, and as a European tool for the collective management of external relations with Asia. The chapter contends that weak institutional structures combine with a rise in the number of bilateral agreements and contentious intra-regional dynamics within Asia and Europe, to dilute the relevance of any EU pivot. It proposes that we should regard inter-regionalism as an issue-led and process-led form of managing foreign policy, rather than as an overarching narrative for understanding relations among regions today.

The second part consists of four chapters on the major thematic issue areas of the EU's policy towards the Asia-Pacific. Fulvio Attinà contributes a chapter on the EU's security policy and initiative in the Asia-Pacific, amidst the current trends of international security in the global system and of the role the EU plays in such scenarios. This chapter first attempts to explain why EU policy-makers expect to also have an influence on the management of security in the Asia-Pacific region, through regional initiatives such as the co-management of security issues, the growth in the number and effectiveness of multilateral security negotiations and the progression of the non-proliferation of nuclear and mass destruction armaments. It then goes on to explain the security culture of the European and the Asia-Pacific nations, which are useful to assess the possibility of a sound security dialogue between the EU and the Asia-Pacific nations. Finally, the present state of the EU foreign policy apparatus is analysed in depth to assess the possibility of the further involvement of the EU as a united block of countries in the Asia-Pacific security process. Miguel Otero-Iglesias's chapter analyses the EU's economic and trade policy. It is generally acknowledged that, although the EU is an established global economic power, its presence is less palpable in the Asia-Pacific region, which is currently the world's most dynamic region. In contrast, this chapter first maps out the general patterns of the EU's economic and trade presence and policies in the region and then assesses whether the EU is, in fact, under-represented. It argues that the EU has neglected the Asia-Pacific region for several primary reasons: too much focus on the Atlantic, the distance, cultural differences, overemphasis on China, the lack of strategic presence and vision, and internal problems. Suetyi Lai and Li Zhang's chapter presents a systematic study of the EU's public diplomacy in the region, with a focus on East Asia proper. In the beginning, the chapter provides key contextual information on the EU's public diplomacy, which appeared much later than its traditional diplomacy, and its role and significance in the Asia-Pacific has been less prominent compared to unitary great powers. This chapter is devoted to examining the public diplomacy programme of the EU in East Asia to determine how it has (or has not) contributed to the EU's rapprochement with the region. Given the limitation of time and space, this chapter particularly focuses on the EU's public diplomacy in the ASEAN+3 group countries since the mid-1990s when the EU announced its first Asian strategy. Evangelos Fanoulis examines the EU's role as a provider of human security in the Asia-Pacific region. This chapter claims that studies on the EU as a foreign policy player neglect this area. It first briefly presents the concept of human security and its perception in EU circles. It proceeds to conduct a systematic empirical analysis of the means that the EU employs in the Asia-Pacific to offer human security. In this regard, foreign policy instruments, development, trade, humanitarian aid and global health and environmental instruments are assessed. It concludes with a discussion about how the EU's presence in the Asia-Pacific as a human security provider may shed new light on the debate around the EU's role in the international arena.

The third part of the book is composed of four chapters on the EU's policies towards individual countries or country groups in the Asia-Pacific. Gustaaf Geeraerts's chapter addresses the EU's relations with China and claims that the EU and China have steadily built a partnership, which probably constitutes one of the most structured relationships between two global powers in the contemporary world system. As the world's major trading entities, China and Europe affect each other deeply and their policies beyond their borders. At the same time, however, China's re-emergence and mounting influence also pose a challenge to Europe's very identity and governance outlook. Although they have many interests in common, they are also competitors – and increasingly so. It concludes that the future relationship between the EU and China is bound to be a difficult balancing act between competition and co-operation. Elena Atanassova-Cornelis contributes a chapter on the EU's relations with Japan. Interestingly, she argues that Japan represents the most institutionalised bilateral link in Europe's relations with the Asia-Pacific region. On the basis of the shared values of freedom, democracy and the rule of law, the EU's relations with Japan have steadily evolved since the early 1990s. This chapter examines the evolving EU–Japan strategic partnership by focusing, in particular, on the politico-security dimension. To this end, the discussion explores the motivations of both sides for strengthening ties, the factors that further and inhibit co-operation and the main joint initiatives and policies. On the one hand, it demonstrates that "new" opportunities for co-operation have emerged, in particular, in the maritime security domain, whereas some of the "old" constraints have receded. On the other hand, the geopolitical environments in both Europe and the Asia-Pacific are undergoing major shifts. All this suggests that the search for a more effective and genuinely strategic partnership is positioned to continue, whereas the outcome remains more, rather than less, uncertain. Reuben Wong's chapter analyses the EU's policies towards the ASEAN countries, with a focus on security matters. It argues that the EU has long receded from Southeast Asia as a serious security player, with the completion of the decolonisation process. However, it can make, and has made, a difference in civilian missions of the European Security and Defence Policy since 2000, notably in the Aceh Mission of 2005–6. The EU's main interests in the ASEAN region continue to be trade and investment over its own self-proclaimed normative goals of human rights and democracy promotion, with individual member states competing for a share of the growing market in the Asia-Pacific region. Nevertheless, its human security interests, especially in development and counter-terrorism, have begun to overlap with the priorities of countries in Southeast Asia, giving the EU much scope to play a role in the Asia-Pacific region. This chapter suggests that these goals must be strategised and prioritised with reference to the EU's larger goals in the Asia-Pacific, which have hitherto been dominated by its relations with China and the United States. Nicole Scicluna's chapter deals with the EU's relations with Australia and New Zealand. It aims to explicate the EU's relations with two "Western" countries in the Asia-Pacific region, highlighting major points of both commonality and contention between the two sides. To this end, it focuses on certain key policy areas. First, trade, which continues to define the relationship, but which, nevertheless, has produced significant disputes over EU agricultural subsidies. Second, climate change, one of the most pressing global challenges of our time and an area in which the EU's leadership aspirations and agenda have been frustrated by the recalcitrance of major energy exporters such as Australia. Third, security, an area in which Western states have significant imperatives for co-operation and in which engagement with Australia and New Zealand may feed into the EU's broader regional strategy. Fourth, human rights, another realm in which "soft power Europe" seeks to provide global leadership. The picture that emerges is one of a relationship that is strong, but not unproblematic; both historically rooted and of great contemporary resonance.

Notes

1 US–EU Statement on the Asia-Pacific Region, www.state.gov/r/pa/prs/ps/2012/07/194896.htm, accessed online on 12 August 2016.
2 Patryk Pawlak and Eleni Ekmektsioglou, "Can EU Be Relevant for Asia?", *The Diplomat*, 11,June 2012, http://thediplomat.com/2012/06/can-eu-be-relevant-for-asia/, accessed online on 12 August 2016.

References

Acharya, Amitav (2010). "Asia Is Not One", *Journal of Asian Studies* 69 (4): 1001–13.
Chaban, Natalia, Elgström, Ole, Kelly, Serena, and Suetyi Lai. (2013). "Images of the EU beyond its Borders: Issue-Specific and Regional Perceptions of European Union Power and Leadership", *Journal of Common Market Studies* 51 (3): 433–51.
European Commission. (1994). "Towards a New Asia Strategy", *Communication of the Commission to the Council*, Com (94) 314 final, Brussels http://aei.pitt.edu/2949/, accessed online 4 September 2016.

European Commission. (2001). "Europe and Asia: A Strategic Framework for Enhanced Partnerships", *Communication from the Commission*, COM (2001) 469 final. Brussels. http://eur-lex.europa.eu/legal-content/EN/TXT/?uri=celex:52001DC0469, accessed online 4 September 2017.

European Union. (2016). "Shared Vision, Common Action: A Stronger Europe", *A Global Strategy for European Union's Foreign and Security Policy*. http://europa.eu/globalstrategy/en, accessed online 12 August 2017.

Keukeleire, Stephan, and Hooijmaaijers, Bas. (2014). "The BRICS and Other Emerging Power Alliances and Multilateral Organizations in the Asia-Pacific and the Global South: Challenges for the European Union and Its View on Multilateralism", *Journal of Common Market Studies* 52 (3): 582–99.

Krotz, Ulrich. (2009). "Moment and Impediments: Why Europe Won't Emerge as a Full Political Actor on the World Stage Soon", *Journal of Common Market Studies* 47 (3): 555–78.

Murray, Philomena. (2008). "European Perspectives on Engagement with East Asia", in Philomena Murray (ed.), *Europe and Asia: Regions in Flux*, Basingstoke and New York: Palgrave Macmillan, pp. 188–209.

PART I

General strategic context

1 The European Union in the Asia-Pacific: strategic reflections

Michael Reiterer

Introduction

Although the EU maintains four (China, Japan, Republic of Korea, India) out of its ten strategic partnerships with Asian partners (Reiterer, 2013a) and is contemplating adding a fifth (with the Association of Southeast Asian Nations, ASEAN), doubts are harboured in Asia whether the EU can be a genuine strategic partner. Perceptions may not match: the EU has over the years developed policy papers dealing with Asia in general (*Europe and Asia: A Strategic Framework for Enhanced Partnerships* (European Commission, 2001)) or with sub-regions, for example *Guidelines on the EU's Foreign and Security Policy in East Asia* (Council of the EU, 2012), the 2015 Communication *The EU and ASEAN: A Partnership with a Strategic Purpose* (European Commission 2015), or with specific countries like the 2016 China Strategy (European Commission, 2016a) while on the Asian side only China has so far published two policy papers on the EU in 2003 (Ministry of Foreign Affairs of PRC, 2003) and in 2014 (Ministry of Foreign Affairs of PRC, 2014).

The perceived missing link in the Europe–US–Asia triangle led in 1996 to the creation of the Asia–Europe Meeting (Reiterer, 2002) on the joint initiative of France and Singapore. Following the year-long blockade over the political situation in Burma/Myanmar after the military junta took over, the EU intensified its dialogue and cooperation with the Association of South East Asian Nations (ASEAN), signed the Treaty of Amity and Co-operation in 2012, and intensified its engagement in the ASEAN Regional Forum (ARF) in order to demonstrate its comprehensive interest in Asia. "Comprehensive" means, firstly, in the sense of the EU's comprehensive approach to foreign policy and, secondly, underlines the political and security dimension (Reiterer, 2014a) in addition to the well-known economic and trade dimension. In terms of security Asian partners still demand more "proof" of the EU's engagement as they perceive the EU primarily as an economic force to reckon with but less of a political and security player: thus, perceptions do not match.

On the basis of the Treaty of Lisbon, which entered into force in 2009, the EU is in a position to become a more active foreign policy player. Additional tools, like the High Representative for Security and Defence Policy / Vice President of the European Commission (HRVP) and the European External Action Service (EEAS), the diplomatic service of the EU, were added and the principles of the EU's foreign policy defined in the Treaty. However, at the time history was not waiting for the EU to set up the new framework with ease – soon the neighbouring area was in flames (Arab Spring), Russia invaded and annexed the Crimean Peninsula, terrorism globalised further and found in the so-called Islamic State a new incarnation. Terrorism firmly arrived at the heart of Europe, refugees and immigrants swept over Europe's border straining the principles of European integration like solidarity and all that on top of the financial and debt crisis since 2008.

In parallel we witness a power shift from West to East, economically and politically (Reiterer, 2015a). Asia became the economic engine largely built on China's economic growth which in turn led to a shift in the political and power relationships in the region as well as globally. The latter aspect led the Obama Administration to underscore its Pacific vocation in "pivoting" to Asia, not least to counterbalance China's political rise and endeavour to regain its position as a regional power (Reiterer, 2013a). Thus, the "return of geopolitics" (Mead, 2014) and the danger of the Thucydides trap (Allison, 2015) entered the political discourse.

Taking the 2003 European Security Strategy (Council of the European Union, 2003), as the point of departure, the EU has embarked since 2014 on an overhaul of its foreign policy. Mandated by the European Council (2015), the HRVP has developed a new "Global Strategy for the European Union's Foreign and Security Policy" (EUGS) (European Union, 2016) in order to position the Union as a global player, taking into account on the one hand the new level of ambition for its foreign policy and on the other hand the changes in international politics which have occurred since 2003. In 2003 *A Secure Europe in a Better World* indicated a world of optimism – after the fall of the Berlin Wall and other fences, but also after 9/11 and the first Iraqi War. The "end of history", the peace dividend characterised then the political discourse. In contrast, today's world is more contested, complex and connected, requiring a new approach and making use of the toolbox of the Treaty of Lisbon.

Within a decade the strategic environment of the EU has changed; the election of the novice politician Donald Trump in the United States became another watershed requiring further adaptations and a hitherto unknown striving for more autonomy in EU foreign relations.[1] After the "end of history" illusion in the 1990s, security takes centre stage again, however, without the traditional separation of domestic and international aspects. Today's challenges need a response that combines aspects of internal and external policies; foreign policy and security start at home but are entangled with international developments. Centre stage also means that citizens are directly concerned and expect protection and solutions by their governments and the EU.

Recognising these changes, the EUGS responds: "The European Union will promote peace and guarantee the security of its citizens and territory ... Internal and external security are ever more intertwined" (European Union, 2016: 14). The European Commission translated this proposition into an Implementation Plan on Security and Defence (European Commission, 2015) which led to Council Conclusions in 2017 on Security and Defence in the Context of the EU Global Strategy (European Council, 2017). It had also rekindled the discussion about a European army by Commission President Juncker in 2015[2] or a "defence capacity" by the HRVP Mogherini;[3] EU foreign and defence ministers in November 2016 did not decide in favour of an army as the HRVP clearly stated but agreed to push ahead with co-operation on security and defence matters. In order to be successful this task needs to be a comprehensive approach to security and to crisis management through a "whole-of-EU approach" (Faria, 2014).

Published only a few days after the Brexit decision, the EUGS develops a collective sense of direction for the EU: it needs to appear united on the world stage to keep its citizens safe, preserve its interests and uphold its values. To this end, the EU needs to become a strong(er) power in order to become a security provider.

The EUGS sets out the EU's core interests, priorities and principles for engaging in the world. Built on an analysis by EEAS (European Eexternal Action Service, 2015; also Missiroli, 2015) of the changes since 2003, the EUGS aims to clarify the EU's values and the ensuing goals, and spells out what it wants to achieve (priorities) while respecting and realising its core interests. Core interests are security and prosperity of the EU and its citizens living in a democratic system which in turn has a rules-based system as its environment. The EU's priorities are its security, societal resilience inside the Union and in particular in its southern and eastern region, an integrated approach to conflicts and crises, helping to set up co-operative regional orders while contributing to sustainable global governance.

Strategic autonomy in relation to security, although it had already been discussed for a long time, gets new traction, leading to a discussion on how best to strengthen the European structures and make them resilient and complementary to the North Atlantic Treaty Organisation (NATO) in the overall context of the trans-Atlantic partnership. All this should lead to a more credible, more responsive and better co-ordinated Union. In view of the election victory of Donald Trump and his professed intention to engage allies and partners more, financially and materially, in security and defence while sowing doubt on continued US engagement, this option turns into a necessity.

In order to translate this "shared vision" as mentioned in the EUGS subtitle into action (Reiterer, 2017a), follow-up processes have been initiated immediately in close co-operation with member states, the European Commission and European Parliament. Therefore the EU Foreign Minister concluded only four months after the adoption of the EUGS on 17 October 2016 that the EU expects the implementation to focus on the following priority areas during the next two years:

- resilience building and integrated approach to conflicts and crises
- security and defence
- strengthening the nexus between internal and external policies
- updating existing or preparing new regional and thematic strategies
- stepping up public diplomacy efforts

Therefore, the EUGS sets out global ambitions, core interests and principles for engagement in different geographic regions, in a principled manner thereby leaving the necessary room for individualisation through regional or horizontal strategies.

Furthermore, the EU's approach to foreign and security policy needs to change from ad-hoc reaction to strategic planning, from words to deeds, from putting out fires to securing the environment (Reiterer, 2016a). In daily policy-making and the need to react to immediate challenges one can easily lose sight of long-term goals and interests. A common strategy will be instrumental in preparing scenarios and related toolboxes, first to plan ahead to prevent crises or where this is no longer possible to react quickly and effectively to prevent escalation; second, to induce member states and other European institutions, primarily Commission services but also the European Parliament, to buy in to strategies and policies and to engage; this should lead to co-ownership of the external action. To be able to mobilise the required resources and instruments in the sense of the mentioned "whole-of-EU" approach is not just a noble principle but a necessity.

Given the nature of the EUGS, which follows primarily a functional approach, the implementation process will be on two levels: first, clarifying and developing further concepts used, e.g. resilience, higher level of ambition for security and defence, and, second, applying the overall concept globally, not according to one-size-fits-all but individually to regions and sub-regions with a view to helping to establish "cooperative regional orders" (European Union, 2016: 32).

Thus, the EUGS deals more with horizontal issues, policy areas and thematic aspects which are important to the EU: resilience, security and defence, sanctions, development policy, sustainable development goals, human rights, migration, countering violent extremism, global governance, energy and climate and cyber security to name just a few. "Human rights, as well as women, peace and security and gender equality and women's empowerment" remain important issues which "will continue to be mainstreamed in all external EU policies" (Council of the European Union, 2016d). Migration is rightly identified as one of the problems in need of particular and urgent attention: "The EU will support different paths to resilience, targeting the most acute cases of governmental, economic, societal and climate/energy fragility, as well as develop more effective migration policies for Europe and its partners" (European Union, 2016: 9). Migration stands at the intersection of internal and external policies. Implementing the Valletta Action Plan (Council of the European Union, 2015c), which aims to get to the root causes of migration, will be important in addressing pull and push factors. Adding a European economic (Imberteu, 2017) and cultural diplomacy (Council of the European Union, 2017a; European Commission, 2016a; Reiterer, 2014b) to the toolbox is another example of the new comprehensive and integrated approach which was translated into action rather speedily.

The EU as a specially qualified non-state actor with institutional limitations has to calibrate its policy to play a role which can be decisive in its core areas of competence, in particular its smart power anchored in economic power with strategic and security implications. Hence a joined-up approach, leveraging in particular the EU's trade and development policies, while creating synergies between internal and external policies, has the potential to strengthen the EU's role as a security actor and security provider beyond crisis and conflict management.

A particular challenge is posed by the EU's inclination to seek solutions in line with effective multilateralism, working with international institutions and the United Nations in particular. While this approach fosters international governance and the rule of law, the EU still has to establish itself as a full multilateral partner, as it often is not a member of international organisations such as the UN. While in the latter case a specific solution could be found, albeit with difficulties, other institutions which are of particular importance for international governance still pose problems (Organisation for Economic Co-operation and Development, Food and Agriculture Organization of the United Nations World Bank, International Monetary Fund and so on). This is also reflected in the fact that all ten strategic partnerships of the EU (Reiterer, 2013b) are with states, not multilateral or with regional institutions. There is a Catch-22-like situation: in order to establish itself as an international actor, the EU has to prove itself in the bilateral context, which in turn would strengthen its role in multilateral organisation while the reverse is hardly possible. The mediation in the Iran nuclear case with the international community based on a UN mandate is a notable exception.[4] The latter and the need to tackle transnational problems multilaterally should also induce the EU member states to stay united (European

Union, 2016: 17) and to enable the EU to play a larger and more effective role multilaterally in the overall EU interest.

In order to translate the EUGS swiftly into action a Roadmap[5] with time lines on the follow-up to the EU Global Strategy was established and synchronised with the Commission Work Programme 2017, which carries the fitting programmatic title *Delivering a Europe that Protects, Defends and Empowers* (European Commission, 2016c). The EUGS has an anticipated lifeline of about five years; in June 2017 the first yearly implementation report (Mogherini, 2017d) was already published and discussed by member states in the Council (Council of the European Union, 2017b). Speed was important in order to be able to present to citizens a "Europe of results" and not only a "Europe of intentions" to regain confidence because of the wide scope of urgent concerns covered by the EUGS. Striking a balance between a realist view on the EU's capacities and its normative aspirations, and an "idealistic aspiration to advance a better world" (European Union, 2016: 8), the EUGS adopts "principled pragmatism" as its guiding principle for the EU's external action. This acknowledges Europe's limited enforcement capability, while upholding its values and legal obligations.

In the following sections two of the main concepts, resilience and the security and defence nexus, will be briefly discussed, followed by an overview of the main lines of action in the Asia Pacific.

"Resilience": a core concept to be further developed

Resilience is one of the key terms of the EUGS and appears often and in different contexts – with politics, institutions/states, infrastructure and societies in and around Europe, from Central Asia to Central Africa.

In relation to democracy, resilience encompasses the EU's values such as respect for and promotion of human rights, fundamental freedoms, the rule of law in general. In addition, a resilient civil society has a greater chance in succeeding to hold governments accountable through democratically elected bodies as well as a vibrant civil society: "A resilient state is a secure state, and security is the key for prosperity and democracy" (European Union, 2016: 23). Material resilience refers to critical infrastructure, networks and services, and reducing associated crimes such as cybercrime (European Union, 2016: 22). Energy and environmental security are further facets of resilience. Resilience is also invoked in terms of security in relation to NATO, cybersecurity, conflicts and their prevention or awareness, and finally global governance in general.

Among them, societal resilience "is a broader concept, encompassing all individuals and the whole of society. A resilient society featuring democracy, trust in institutions, and sustainable development lies at the heart of a resilient state" (European Union, 2016: 24). Therefore resilience is also part of the enlargement process and a strategic priority in the neighbourhood where the EU "will pursue a multifaceted approach to resilience" (European Union, 2016: 25) as fragility at its borders and beyond threatens the vital interests of the EU. This includes work on resilience with countries of origin or transit of migrants and refugees (European Union, 2016: 27).

Resilience also links up to culture in international politics as recognised in a recent policy paper (European Commission, 2016a) in deepening "work on education, culture and youth, to foster pluralism, coexistence and respect" (European Union, 2016: 26); this recent recognition of the importance of culture in international politics provides the basis for an active cultural diplomacy which complements the traditional approach to diplomacy (Reiterer, 2014b).

Resilience can also serve as a bridge to the Sustainable Development Goals (SDG) in terms of energy and environment or development in general. EuropeAid has its own definition of resilience: "Resilience is the ability of an individual, a household, a community, a country or a region to withstand, cope, adapt, and quickly recover from stresses and shocks such as violence, conflict, drought and other natural disasters without compromising long-term development" (European Commission, 2016d). Furthermore, the 2012 Communication *The EU Approach to Resilience: Learning from Food Security Crises* (European Commission, 2012), an *Action Plan for Resilience in Crisis Prone Countries 2013–2020* (European Commission, 2013), aiming at bringing together humanitarian action, long-term development co-operation and ongoing political engagement, as well as the 2014 *Resilience Marker* (European Commission, 2014) offer further insights in the development nexus.

Action instead of status quo without over-ambition

Achieving resilience implies that some actions are required. Therefore it is a term indicating activity, not contentment with the status quo: "Resilience – the ability of states and societies to reform, thus withstanding and recovering from internal and external crises" (European Union, 2016: 23) has an inherent long-term perspective. Resilience is meant to meet anxiety, concern, insecurity, to turn the situation round and to achieve stability, thereby meeting major requests and expectations by European citizens.

At the same time, resilience applied to a concrete situation on either the national or the regional level has to be in line with the capabilities at the disposal of the entity which is or wants to become "resilient", adding to credibility. Measures have to be individualised, which leads to co-ownership. This also signals the end of the policy to simply export the EU model, as "[r]egional orders do not take a single form" (European Union, 2016: 32). Pledging support for co-operative regional orders and governance which allow people "to reap the economic gains of globalisation, express more fully cultures and identities, and project influence in world affairs" (European Union, 2016: 10) is also in line with the EU's own development. Most importantly, this policy is geared towards concrete and manageable actions on the ground, not towards a grand design or lofty ideas to which people cannot relate to.

Need for operationalisation

The challenge is to operationalise such an encompassing notion, to avoid it becoming an empty catch-all phrase which primarily serves to get various differing stakeholders on board.

Therefore the EEAS in co-operation with Commission Services and the member states published a joint communication on resilience, published in June 2017 (European Commission, 2017a). While there is a focus on the EU neighbourhood, the HRVP underlined the global element: "One fourth of the world's population lives in fragile States or societies. We want to prevent these fragile situations from turning into new wars, new humanitarian catastrophes, or new refugee crises. This is what we call resilience" (Mogherini 2017a).

The Communication develops the concept of resilience along three strands: first, support for weak states to become more resilient in rendering societies more participatory and democratic, overcoming long-lasting crises and fostering crisis prevention; second, sharing experience in addressing complex domestic policy challenges, such as energy security and climate adaptation, economic and social policy or addressing global health risks; third, addressing internal and external security together in order to face up to hybrid threats, cybersecurity, the security of critical infrastructure, terrorism and violent extremism.

Security and defence and the security and development nexus

"In this fragile world, soft power is not enough: we must enhance our credibility in security and defence" (European Union, 2016: 44) is the new leitmotif signalling one of the bigger changes in conceptualising the EU and changing policies accordingly. HRVP Mogherini is clear about this change: "I know that the Defence part of the Strategy is the one that attracts the most of the public attention. Maybe it is because Europe is always perceived as a soft-power, when we actually have also some degree of hard-power. Very few people know that we have already as the European Union seventeen – civilian and military – operations around the world supporting peace, like the United Nations have peacekeeping operations" (Mogherini, 2016a). This despite the fact that this issue has been under discussion since the creation of the European project: "some sixty years ago, the founding fathers and mothers of our European Union believed that a united Europe had to be built on two pillars: a European Economic Community, and a Defence Community" (Mogherini 2016a).

This change has gained additional importance as President Donald Trump exhorted allies and partners in his campaign to contribute more, to shoulder a larger part of the burden. Advocating that "Europeans must be better equipped, trained and organised to contribute decisively to such collective efforts, as well as to act autonomously if and when necessary" (European Union, 2016: 19), the EUGS has anticipated this exhortation. The EUGS outlines five lines of action: security and defence; counter-terrorism, cybersecurity; energy security; and strategic communication to rebut factual disinformation. Experts have already provided analysis (European Union Institute for Security Studies, 2016). However, as foreign and defence policy are the prerogative of member states, the joint development of policies is essential for success. On the other hand, this clear competence does not allow member states to escape from their responsibility in referring back to "the EU" which is playing its role in making proposals. Three strings need to be brought together now: "First, the implementation of the Global Strategy, with the Implementation Plan on security and defence, second the European Defence Action Plan, and third the follow-up to the Joint EU–NATO Declaration that we signed in Warsaw last July" (Mogherini 2016a).

The Foreign Affairs Council on 14 November 2016 was held as a joint meeting with defence ministers to discuss the security and defence aspects of the EUGS. Taking into account the European Defence Action Plan (European Commission, 2016e) prepared by the European Commission as well as the Joint declaration of the EU and NATO in Warsaw (European Commission 2016f), the Council conclusions define the level of ambition (Biscop and Coelmont, 2016) in the area of security and defence in formulating three main aims for the European Union: readiness to face international conflicts and crisis; preparing for these cases through building security; and defence capacities within the Union and with partners, in order to meet the citizens' request for comprehensive security. To this end ministers welcomed the Implementation Plan in the Conclusions (Council of the European Union, 2016a).

The stakes are high as expectations have been raised. Therefore the HRVP, while talking of a "qualitative leap" in the EU's defence and security policy, clarified from the outset what the Conclusions do not provide for: no European army, no duplication of SHAPE (Supreme Headquarters Allied Powers Europe), no territorial defence, no competition and or duplication with NATO (Mogherini, 2016b). However, as a small step along this road and meeting expectations, defence ministers agreed for the first time in six years on a small increase of the European Defence Agency (Mogherini, 2016c).

The European Council in dealing with the EUGS as well as defence aspects, endorsed the conclusions in December 2016 and specifically underlined that "Europeans must take greater responsibility for their security"; it also endorsed the above-mentioned "Council conclusions of 14 November and 17 October 2016 on implementing the EU Global Strategy in the area of Security and Defence which sets the level of ambition of the EU". The Council welcomed "the Commission's proposals on the European Defence Action Plan as its contribution to developing European security and defence policy 'while inviting the Commission' to make proposals in the first semester of 2017 for the establishment of a European Defence Fund" (European Council, 2016). This window of opportunity for action and not just theoretical discussion led to the publication of the *Reflection Paper on the Future of European Defense* by the European Commission in June 2017 (European Commission, 2017b) as well as to the agreement of the requested European Defence Fund of €5.5 billion per year (European Commission, 2017c).

The June 2017 European Council welcomed the establishment of the European Centre of Excellence for Countering Hybrid Threats in Helsinki, called for rapid agreement on the proposal for a European Defence Industrial Development Programme and joint procurement of capabilities within the European Defence Fund, and agreed on the on the need to launch an inclusive and ambitious Permanent Structured Co-operation (European Council, 2017).

On the latter the European Council delivered in 2018 (Flott, Missirolli and Tardy 2018), following on the steps of the Military Planning and Conduct Capability, the European Defence Fund, the Co-ordinated Annual Review on Defence represents a series of actions taken within the EU in unprecedented speed. "The Union is ... taking steps to bolster European defence, by enhancing defence investment, capability development and operational readiness. These initiatives enhance its strategic autonomy while complementing and reinforcing the activities of NATO, in line with previous conclusions" (European Council, 2018b). Furthermore, the UK has clearly signalled that in foreign policy and security matters close co-operation should continue beyond Brexit. As a first step, France, Germany, Belgium, Denmark, the Netherlands, Estonia, Spain, Portugal and the UK agreed in June 2018 to establish a European rapid military crisis intervention force – outside the EU framework and in addition to the existing (on paper) EU battle groups in order to allow British participation beyond Brexit.

The development and security nexus

The development and security nexus plays an important role in helping countries which are the origin of refugees or migrants as well as transition countries to become (more) "resilient". Incorporating this nexus into policy-making and aligning it with the EU's strategic goals is therefore essential, as is the reconfirmation of the "collective commitment to achieve the 0.7% ODA/Gross National Income target in line with DAC [Development Assistance Committee] principles" (European Union, 2016: 48).

When aligning the EUGS with the 2030 Agenda for Sustainable Development in implementing the SDG, these Goals serve as a guideline for the EUGS as well as for the design of the post-Cotonou partnership. They will "drive reform in development policy, including the EU Consensus on Development" (European Union, 2016: 40). Thus, the new Consensus on Development (Council of the European Union. 2017c), adopted in June 2017, contributes to implement the EUGS (Council of the European Union, 2015a), providing also for more policy coherence and flexibility of financial instruments. "Moreover, implementing the SDGs will require change across all internal and external policies, galvanising public-private partnerships, and leveraging the experience of the European Investment Bank in providing technical assistance and building capacities in developing and middle income countries" (European Union, 2016: 40). Concrete outputs communications on the Agenda 2030 and on Sustainable Development are planned. Furthermore, the coherent implementation of the EUGS will involve revising existing regional strategies as well as devising new ones.

The Asia-Pacific region

In light of the economic weight that Asia represents for the EU – and vice versa – the EUGS emphasises that peace and stability in Asia are a prerequisite for the EU's prosperity: "There is a direct connection between European prosperity and Asian security. In light of the economic weight that Asia represents for the EU – and vice versa – peace and stability in Asia are a prerequisite for our prosperity. We will deepen economic diplomacy and scale up our security role in Asia" (European Union, 2016: 37). Therefore the EU will scale up its security role in Asia. The EUGS sets out the objective to develop a more politically rounded approach to Asia, seeking to make greater practical contributions to Asian security.

The EU will also deepen its economic diplomacy in the region, also working towards ambitious free trade agreements with Japan, India and ASEAN member states. The provisional conclusion of the double package with Japan, a Free Trade Agreement (FTA) and a Strategic Partnership Agreement, in July 2017 was an important political signal for free and fair trade under the multilateral rules of the World Trade Organisation, as President Trump pulled out of the Transpacific Partnership Agreement, which is presently seeking a life beyond the US under Japanese leadership.

This in turn offered China the possibility to present itself as a champion of free trade in pushing its own schemes, the Regional Comprehensive

Economic Partnership and the Free Trade Area of the Pacific. The US exodus strengthens China and allows it to assert a stronger rule-setting function in international trade. This underscores the EU's strategic interest in enhancing its own trade policy agenda, especially in the multilateral field, to protect its economic interests and to introduce a robust interest-centred economic diplomacy.

The EU will continue to support state-building and reconciliation processes in Afghanistan together with its partners. In East and Southeast Asia, the EU upholds freedom of navigation, stands firm on the respect for international law and promote non-proliferation in the Korean peninsula. It will support an ASEAN-led regional security architecture. In Central and South Asia, the aim is to deepen co-operation on migration, trafficking and counter-terrorism.

The EU will engage China on the basis of respect for rule of law, both domestically and internationally. The EU will pursue a coherent approach to China's connectivity drives westwards starting with a mapping exercise in order to be able to make efficient use of the Connectivity Platform already established. To this end, the EU has adapted its policy towards China through its new China Strategy which was confirmed by the EU member states in the 2016 Council Conclusions (Council of the European Union, 2016b).

The Korean peninsula and Northeast Asia more generally is one of the regions where the EUGS label "most divided" (European Union, 2016: 32) certainly applies and where regional co-operation has become only a weak option to form a co-operative regional order: the trilateral co-operation between China, Japan and South Korea goes up and down but its Trilateral Co-operation Secretariat[6] in Seoul and the low-key negotiations of a regional FTA serve as an institutionalised platform for exchanges. Former President Park had at the beginning of her term initiated *"truspolitik"* with the Northeast Asia Peace and Co-operation Initiative (NAPCI) (Reiterer, 2015b) as its backbone, which stalled because of non-engagement of the Democratic People's Republic of Korea and the disaccord on how to deal with the latter. The invitation of the EU to join NAPCI as a dialogue partner is however an indication that the EU's experience in overcoming the legacies of the past and in using integration as a tool to this end bodes well with Asian partners. It also offers the EU a foot in the door in the region should the talks restart, either in the form of the Six Party Talks, stalled since 2009, or in any new format (Reiterer, 2017b) which might succeed.

In response to the escalating tensions in 2017 and to the invitation of the new Korean President Moon Jae-in, the EU got more strongly involved in the Korean peninsula in updating its policy vis-à-via North Korea (Council of the European Union, 2017d) and in taking a clear position in favour of a diplomatic resolution based on the twin approach of strong international sanctions and critical engagement; both are not ends in themselves but means to reach the final goal of denuclearisation of the peninsula (Mogherini, 2017b).

In line with the above-mentioned 2015 Communication on ASEAN, the EU's ambition is to intensify its co-operation with the ASEAN-led institutions (Raine, 2016; Reiterer, 2016b). Therefore, celebrating ASEAN's fiftieth birthday and forty years of dialogue between the EU and ASEAN (European External Action Service 2017a) set another milestone in adopting the 2018–22 EU–ASEAN Plan of Action (European External Action Service, 2017b). This could lead to the first strategic partnership with an association and to the envisaged participation of the EU in the evolving system of the East Asia Summit (EAS).[7]

In competition with the ARF, the EAS is increasingly becoming the leading forum for strategic discussions and co-operation in the region, with Australia, China, India, Japan, New Zealand, Russia, South Korea and the United States as members, but not yet the EU. In its Conclusions on EU–ASEAN relations adopted on 22 June 2015, the Foreign Affairs Council "reiterated the EU's offer to contribute substantially to policy and security/defence related fora led by ASEAN, including the East Asia Summit" (Council of the European Union, 2015b). The invitation to join the EAS in Manila in November 2017 as the guest of the Chair (Mogherini, 2017c) – despite EU criticism of President Duterte's human rights violations in pursuing his fight against drugs – was an important step towards this goal, a reward for years-long efforts supported by ASEAN's endeavour to broaden its base for co-operation in light of mounting US disinvestment and isolationist tendencies.

Within the EAS system, security and defence policy are increasingly handled by the ASEAN Defence Ministers Plus platform which brings together the defence ministers of ASEAN and the eight dialogue partners to strengthen security and defence cooperation for peace, stability and development in the rgion.

Not least prompted by the surge of tensions on the Korean peninsula in 2017, the Foreign Affairs Council took a strong interest in the security situation in Asia and expressed this clearly in the 2018 Conclusions on Enhanced EU Security Co-operation in and with Asia (European Council 2018a):

> The Council recognises the increasing importance of Asian security for European interests and emphasises that Asian countries, regional organisations and platforms, such as the Asia Europe Meeting (ASEM), are crucial to help secure a more stable and peaceful world. The Council stresses that efforts to enhance EU–Asian security cooperation and Euro-Asia connectivity should be mutually reinforcing.

The long-simmering tensions in the South China Sea led to the rendering of an award by an international Arbitral Tribunal,[8] initiated by the Philippines which China rejects and in turn led the EU to publish two statements focusing on the need to respect and promote the rule of law (Council of the European Union, 2016c; European External Action Service, 2016).

Conclusions

Contrary to former policy papers, the Global Strategy does not look at the world as the EU would like it to be, but how the world is. This leads to what is called "principled pragmatism": the EU will try to combine interests with values, realism with idealism and – most important for credibility – match words with deeds. This means for instance not striving to export the EU model, but supporting good governance through differentiated, tailor-made approaches and fostering multilateralism, thereby contributing to global governance.

The latter could come under further stress if multilateralism is questioned. Therefore preserving two of its major success stories for which the EU has worked hard for years, the International Criminal Court and the Paris Agenda 21 Agreement, is necessary to avoid their unravelling. In light of the President Trump's decision to withdraw the US from the Paris Agreement, this turns into the test case for resilience, EU resilience as well as resilience of global governance. As one of the few remaining bastions of multilateralism the EU might have to change gear from supporting and advocating to fighting to make global governance resilient. This will imply making choices, concentrate forces in order to be successful and credible – doing less may be doing more.

When implementing the EUGS a joined-up approach is essential – member states, the European institutions guided by the High Representative supported by the EEAS have to effectively work together. The Treaty of Lisbon is the basis and provides the guidelines which are useful to recall in times when common values and solidarity become precarious (Article 21.1) sets out the content which the EUGS seeks to translate into action through the described follow-up process. Furthermore, Art. 23.3 states clearly that "The Member States shall work together to enhance and develop their mutual political solidarity. They shall refrain from any action which is contrary to the interests of the Union or likely to impair its effectiveness as a cohesive force in international relations."

However, the present political climate makes the implementation more difficult: Losing a strong element in the EU foreign policy through Brexit, the trend to renationalisation and striving populism come at a moment when more co-operation is necessary but is facing a strong headwind. Paradoxically, but confirming the experience that the EU gets stronger when challenged, the EU27 move closer together, backed by their populations.[9] Therefore, putting the interest of citizens first, putting human security in the centre, working for societal resilience, transforming the Europe of crises into a "Europe of results" is the recipe to win over a hesitant or even hostile European public opinion.

Stepping up public diplomacy to explain, to present the need for common endeavours, and to present results achieved has been identified as one of the five priority areas. Public diplomacy needs results, otherwise it is propaganda; therefore the aforementioned "Europe of results" is so important and results are needed particularly in those areas, where the citizens expect them. Migration-related fears are very high or even on top of this list. Belittling or ignoring these and other fears turns people against what they see as "establishment". Therefore there is an urgent need for resilient politicians who take up the concerns and counter insecurity through concrete actions.

Outside pressure like President Trump's putting into doubt the alliance system and US security guarantees contributes to the urge to do more not only in security but also in showing leadership, especially as the US turns more isolationist (US First). Collective efforts should be built on a genuine understanding and ensuing commitment that the EU has an international role to play, to take on responsibilities commensurate with its power resting on being the largest economy, the largest trader, the largest investor, the largest provider of development and humanitarian aid. Any other political actor would reel in these leading positions, while the EU has difficulties in turning these factors of power into a source of confidence and motivation and leveraging them. Implementing the EUGS could become a game changer if all European players are on board and work in the common European interest which is more than the sum of the national interests. Results achieved would reflect back on the member states, make them stronger and more resilient as parts of the whole and thereby reassure European citizens.

In the context of Asia, finding a common ground with ASEAN could lead to a strategic partnership as foreshadowed in the EU's ASEAN policy paper which in turn could be translated into stronger and more efficient strategic partnership diplomacy. The ASEAN chairmanship of the Philippines was expected to mark progress in realising this goal as the EU and the Philippines were working hand-in-hand to foster the rule of law in the South China Sea dispute. However, President Duterte and his war on drugs leading to thousands of extra-judicial killings which was criticised by the EU Parliament[10] led to a cooling of the relationship which had put the invitation at risk. Nevertheless, the EU–ASEAN 2017 Ministerial Meeting in Manila produced the anticipated step forward when the invitation was finally extended to the EU to attend the EAS as the guest of the Chair. In addition, agreement was reached to accelerate common projects like an inter-regional FTA and a common aviation agreement.

Political and security developments in Northeast Asia challenge the attention paid to ASEAN as it is not only home to the three of the four largest economies of Asia, China, Japan and Korea, but has turned into one of the major hotspots of international politics. The competition of the major powers crystallises on the Korean peninsula. As security has become indivisible the EU is drawn into this triangle. Furthermore, the EU has to intensify its outreach to the third largest economy, India. In pursuing its strategic partnership diplomacy with the four Asian partners and the three other strategic partners with strong interest in the region, China, Russia and the US, enhancing and upgrading the strategic partnership policy in line with the Global Strategy has become a major challenge for the EU.

Notes

1 The EU was alarmed by this election at an early stage: At an informal dinner EU foreign ministers dealt with the prospects for co-operation with the incoming Trump Administration and confirmed the will to continue the strong EU-US partnership while strengthening European policies and actions in an independent manner. They underlined the need to maintain multilateralism, for instance by implementing the climate change agreement, maintaining non-proliferation and the Iranian nuclear deal and keeping the open trading system. Remarks by High Representative/Vice-President Federica Mogherini at the end of the informal dinner of the EU Foreign Ministers, Brussels, 13 November 2016, https://eeas.europa.eu/headquarters/headquarters-homepage/14697/remarks-by-high-representativevice-president-federica-mogherini-at-the-end-of-the-informal-dinner-of-the-eu-foreign-ministers_en, accessed online 20 May 2018.
2 "Jean-Claude Juncker Calls for Creation of EU Army", *Financial Times*, 8 March 2015, www.ft.com/content/1141286a-c588-11e4-bd6b-00144feab7de, accessed online 2 August 2017.
3 'EU Reveals Plans for Military Cooperation Following Brexit Vote', *The Guardian*, 8 September 2016, www.theguardian.com/world/2016/sep/08/european-union-plans-military-battlegroups-after-brexit-vote, accessed online 8 April 2017.
4 Therefore the Iranian deal is a multilateral and not a bilateral one which in theory cannot be unilaterally terminated by one party. However, the Trump Administration announced in May 2018 that the US is withdrawing from the agreement.
5 See http://club.bruxelles2.eu/wp-content/uploads/2016/09/feuilleroute-strategie globale@ue160922.pdf, accessed online 19 May 2018.
6 See http://tcs-asia.org/, accessed online 19 May 2018.
7 The East Asian Summit is run by national Ministries of Foreign Affairs with Senior Official Meetings meeting held twice a year. The EAS has six Expert Working Groups working on (1) Regional economic and financial integration, (2) Education, (3) Disaster response, (4) Energy and Environment, (5) Health and Pandemics and (6) Connectivity.
8 See https://pca-cpa.org/wp-content/uploads/sites/175/2016/07/PH-CN-20160712-Award.pdf, accessed online 19 May 2018.
9 According to the Eurobarometer of the European Parliament survey, a majority of 57 per cent of the population in the EU wants more EU intervention in foreign policy, 68 per cent in security and defence policy, 70 per cent in border

protection, and 73 per cent in promotion of democracy and peace worldwide as well as in migration issues. Eurobarometer of the European Parliament April 2017, www.europarl.europa.eu/atyourservice/en/20170426PVL00115/ Two-years-until-the-2019-European-Elections, accessed online 19 May 2018.

10 The EP "Urges the Philippine Government to condemn the actions of vigilante groups and to investigate their responsibility for the killings; urges the Philippine authorities to conduct an immediate, thorough, effective and impartial investigation in order to identify all those responsible, to bring them before a competent and impartial civil tribunal and to apply the penal sanctions provided for by the law", 14 September 2016, www.europarl.europa.eu/sides/getDoc.do?pubRef=-//EP//TEXT+MOTION+P8-RC-2016-0990+0+DOC+XML+V0//EN, accessed online 19 May 2018.

References

Allison, Graham. (2017). "The Thucydides Trap: Are the US and China Headed for War?", *The Atlantic*, 24 September, p. 4. www.theatlantic.com/international/archive/2015/09/united-states-china-war-thucydides-trap/406756/, accessed online 1 September 2018.

Biscop, Sven, and Joel Coelmont. (2016). "The EU Global Strategy and Defence: The Challenge of Thinking Strategically about Means", *Egmont Security Policy Brief* No. 78 (October), http://egmontinstitute.be/wp-content/uploads/2016/10/SPB78.pdf, accessed online 17 August 2017.

Bouyala Imbert, Florence. (2017). *EU Economic Diplomacy Strategy*. Brussels: European Parliament. http://europarl.europa.eu/RegData/etudes/IDAN/2017/570483/EXPO_IDA%282017%29570483_EN.pdf, accessed online 1 September 2018.

Council of the European Union. (2003). *European Security Strategy: A Secure Europe in a Better World*. General Secretariat of the Council, Rue de la Loi 175 B-1048 Brussels.

Council of the European Union. (2012). *Guidelines on the EU's Foreign and Security Policy in East Asia*, Brussels, 15 June, 11492/12.

Council of the European Union. (2015a). *A New Global Partnership for Poverty Eradication and Sustainable Development after 2015*. Council conclusions, 9241/15.

Council of the European Union. (2015b). *Council onclusions on EU–ASEAN relations*, PRESS RELEASE, 487/1522/06/2015.

Council of the European Union. (2015c). *Valletta Summit on Migration, 11–12 November 2015 – Action Plan and Political Declaration, Statements and Remarks* 809/1512/11/2015.

Council of the European Union. (2016a). *Council Conclusions on Implementing the EU Global Strategy in the Area of Security and Defence*, Press Release, 657/1614/11/2016.

Council of the European Union. (2016b). *EU Strategy on China - Council Conclusions* (18 July), 11252/16.

Council of the European Union. (2016c). *Declaration by the High Representative on Behalf of the EU on Recent Developments in the South China Sea*, Press Release, 126/1611/03/2016.

Council of the European Union. (2016d). *Council Conclusions on the Global Strategy on the European Union's Foreign and Security Policy* - Council conclusions (17 October), 13202/16.
Council of the European Union. (2017a). *Draft Council Conclusions on an EU Strategic Approach to International Cultural Relations*, Brussels, 5 April (OR. en) 7935/17.
Council of the European Union. (2017b). *European Council Conclusions on Security and Defence*, Press Release, 403/1722/06/2017.
Council of the European Union. (2017c). *European Consensus on Development*, 9459/17.
Council of the European Union. (2017d). *Council Conclusions on the Democratic People's Republic of Korea*, Press Release, 485/17, 17/07/2017.
Council of the European Union. (2017e). *CFSP/PESC 413*, http://consilium.europa.eu/en/press/press-releases/2017/05/18-conclusions-security-defence/, accessed online 19 August 2017.
Council of the European Union. (2018a). *Enhanced EU Security Cooperation in and with Asia*, 25 May. www.consilium.europa.eu/media/35456/st09265-re01-en18.pdf, accessed online 1 September 2018.
Council of the European Union. (2018b). *The European Council on 28 June adopted conclusions on: migration, security and defence, jobs, growth and competitiveness, innovation and digital, and on other issues*, 28 June. www.consilium.europa.eu/en/press/press-releases/2018/06/29/20180628-euco-conclusions-final/pdf, accessed online 1 September 2018.
European Commission. (2001). *Europe and Asia: A Strategic Framework for Enhanced Partnerships*, Communication from the Commission, Brussels, 4.9.2001 COM(2001) 469 final.
European Commission. (2012). *The EU Approach to Resilience: Learning from Food Security Crises*, Communication from the Commission to European Parliament and the Council, Brussels, 3.10.2012 COM(2012) 586 final.
European Commission. (2013). *Action Plan for Resilience in Crisis Prone Countries 2013–2020*, Commission Staff Working Document, Brussels, 19.6.2013 SWD (2013) 227 final.
European Commission. (2014). *Resilience Marker, General Guidance, Humanitarian Aid and Civil Protection*, Ref. Ares (2014)3883617 – 21/11/2014.
European Commission. (2015). *The EU and ASEAN: A Partnership with a Strategic Purpose*, Joint Communication to the European Parliament and the Council, Brussels, 18.5.2015, JOIN(2015) 22 final.
European Commission. (2016a). *Towards an EU Strategy for International Cultural Relations*, Joint Communication to the European Parliament and the Council, Brussels, 8.6.2016, JOIN(2016) 29 final.
European Commission. (2016b). *Elements for a New EU Strategy on China*, Joint Communication to the European Parliament and the Council, Brussels, 22.6.2016, JOIN(2016) 30 final.
European Commission. (2016). *Juncker Commission Presents Third Annual Work Programme: Delivering a Europe that Protects, Empowers and Defends*, Press release, IP/16/3500.
European Commission. (2016d). *Building Resilience: The EU's Approach*, Factsheets, http://202.171.253.70:9999/ec.europa.eu/echo/files/aid/countries/factsheets/thematic/resilience_en.pdf, accessed online 19 May 2018.

European Commission. (2016e). *European Defence Action Plan: Towards a European Defence Fund*, European Commission – Press release, http://europa.eu/rapid/press-release_IP-16-4088_en.htm, accessed online 19 May 2018.

European Commission. (2016f). *Joint Declaration by the President of the European Council, the President of the European Commission, and the Secretary General of the North Atlantic Treaty*, European Commission – Statement, http://europa.eu/rapid/press-release_STATEMENT-16-2459_en.htm, accessed online 19 May 2018.

European Commission. (2017a). *A Strategic Approach to Resilience in the EU's External Action,* Joint Communication with HRVP to the European Parliament and the Council, Brussels, 7.6.2017, JOIN(2017) 21 final.

European Commission. (2017b). *Reflection Paper on the Future of European Defense*, European Commission, COM(2017) 315 of 7 June.

European Commission. (2017c). *A European Defence Fund: €5.5 Billion per Year to Boost Europe's Defence Capabilities*, Press release, http://europa.eu/rapid/press-release_IP-17-1508_en.htm, accessed online 19 May 2018.

European Council. (2015). *European Council Meeting (25 and 26 June 2015) – Conclusions*, Brussels, 26 June 2015 (OR. en) EUCO 22/15.

European Council. (2016). *European Council Meeting (15 December 2016) – Conclusions*, EUCO 34/16.

European Council. (2017). *European Council Meeting (22 and 23 June 2017) – Conclusions*, EUCO 8/17.

European External Action Service (EEAS). (2015). *The European Union in a Changing Global Environment: A More Connected, Contested and Complex World*, EEAS Strategic Planning, https://europa.eu/globalstrategy/en/strategic-review-european-union-changing-global-environment, accessed online 19 May 2018.

European External Action Service (EEAS). (2016). *Declaration by the High Representative on behalf of the EU on the Award Rendered in the Arbitration between the Republic of the Philippines and the People's Republic of China (15/07/2016)*, http://eeas.europa.eu/archives/delegations/china/press_corner/all_news/news/2016/2016071502_en.htm, accessed online 19 May 2018.

European External Action Service (EEAS). (2017a). *Joint Statement on the 40th Anniversary of the Establishment of ASEAN–EU Dialogue Relations*, Brussels, 06/08/2017 – 15:52, UNIQUE ID: 170806_2, https://eeas.europa.eu/headquarters/headQuarters-homepage/30785/joint-statement-40th-anniversary-establishment-asean-eu-dialogue-relations_en, accessed online 19 May 2018.

European External Action Service (EEAS). (2017b). *ASEAN–EU Plan of Action 2018–2022*, https://eeas.europa.eu/headquarters/headquarters-homepage/30780/asean-eu-plan-action-2018-2022_en, accessed online 19 May 2018.

European Union. (2016). *Shared Vision, Common Action: A Stronger Europe, a Global Strategy for the European Union's Foreign and Security Policy*, European External Action Service, June 2016 (EUGS). https://eeas.europa.eu/archives/docs/top_stories/pdf/eugs_review_web.pdf, accessed online 1 September 2018.

European Union Institute for Security Studies (EUISS). (2016). *After the EU Global Strategy: Consulting the Experts Security and Defence*, www.iss.europa.eu/sites/default/files/EUISSFiles/After_Global_Strategy_online.pdf, accessed online 1 September 2018.

Faria, Fernanda. (2014). "What EU ComprehensiveApproach". European Center for Development Policy Management (ECDPM), Maastricht, Netherlands, Briefing Note 71. https://ecdpm.org/wp-content/uploads/BN71-What-EU-Comprehensive-Approach-October-2014.pdf, accessed online 3 September 2018.

Flott, Missirolli, Tardy (eds). (2017). *Permanent Structured Cooperation: What's in a Name?* Chaillot Papers, ISS; p. 5. www.iss.europa.eu/content/permanent-structured-cooperation-what%E2%80%99s-name, accessed online 1 September 2018.

Imberteu, Florence. (2017). *EU Economic Diplomacy Strategy*, European Parliament, Brussels, http://europarl.europa.eu/RegData/etudes/IDAN/2017/570483/EXPO_IDA%282017%29570483_EN.pdf, accessed online 9 August 2017.

Mead, Walter Russel. (2014). "The Return of Geopolitics", *Foreign Affairs* 93 (69). www.foreignaffairs.com/articles/china/2014-04-17/return-geopolitics, accessed online 12 August 2017.

Ministry of Foreign Affairs of PRC. (2003). *China's EU Policy*, www.fmprc.gov.cn/mfa_eng/topics_665678/ceupp_665916/t27708.shtml, accessed online 18 May 2018.

Ministry of Foreign Affairs of PRC. (2014). *China's Policy Paper on the EU: Deepen the China–EU Comprehensive Strategic Partnership for Mutual Benefit and Win-win Cooperation*, www.fmprc.gov.cn/mfa_eng/wjdt_665385/wjzcs/t1143406.shtml, accessed online 18 May 2018.

Missiroli, Antonio (ed.). (2015). *Towards an EU Global Strategy: Background, Preferences, References*, European Union Institute for Security Studies, www.iss.europa.eu/sites/default/files/EUISSFiles/Towards_an_EU_Global_Strategy_0_0.pdf, accessed online 19 May 2018.

Mogherini, Federica. (2016a). *Opening speech by High Representative / Vice-President Federica Mogherini at the 2016 EDA Conference "The Industrial Evolution or Revolution in Defence"*, Brussels, 10 November 2016, https://eeas.europa.eu/headquarters/headquarters-homepage/14585/opening-speech-by-high-representativevice-president-federica-mogherini-at-the-2016-eda-conference-_en, accessed online 19 May 2018.

Mogherini, Federica. (2016b). *Remarks by High Representative / Vice-President Federica Mogherini at the Press Conference Following the Foreign Affairs Council*, Brussels, 14 November 2016, https://eeas.europa.eu/headquarters/headquarters-homepage/14821/remarks-by-high-representativevice-president-federica-mogherini-at-the-press-conference-following-the-foreign-affairs-council_en, accessed online 19 May 2018.

Mogherini, Federica. (2016c). *Remarks by Federica Mogherini at the Press Conference Following the Foreign Affairs Council (Defence)*, Brussels, 15 November 2016, https://eeas.europa.eu/headquarters/headquarters-homepage/14963/remarks-by–federica-mogherini-at-the-press-conference-following-the-foreign-affairs-council-defence_en, accessed online 19 May 2018.

Mogherini, Federica. (2016d). *EU as a Global Actor*. Brussels: European Commission, https://eeas.europa.eu/headquarters/headquarters-homepage/11588/speech-by-federica-mogherini-at-the-public-seminar-eu-as-a-global-actor_en, accessed online 19 August 2017.

Mogherini, Federica. (2017a). EU *Presents Its Strategy for More Resilient States and Societies Around the World*, European Commission, Press release, 7 June, http://europa.eu/rapid/press-release_IP-17-1554_en.htm, accessed online 19 May 2018.

Mogherini, Federica. (2017b). *Statement by HR/VP Federica Mogherini on the Situation on the Korean Peninsula*, Brussels, 14/08/2017 – 23:00, UNIQUE ID: 170814_7, https://eeas.europa.eu/headquarters/headQuarters-homepage_en/31084/Statement%20by%20HR/VP%20Federica%20Mogherini%20on%20the%20situation%20on%20the%20Korean%20Peninsula, accessed online 19 May 2018.

Mogherini, Federica. (2017c). *Opening Remarks by High Representative / Vice-President Federica Mogherini at the EU–ASEAN Post-Ministerial Conference*, https://eeas.europa.eu/headquarters/headquarters-homepage/30827/opening-remarks-high-representative-vice-president-federica-mogherini-eu-asean-post_en, accessed online 19 May 2018.

Mogherini, Federica. (2017d). *The EU Global Strategy–Year 1*. Brussels: European Commission, https://europa.eu/globalstrategy/en/vision-action, accessed online 7 August 2017.

Raine, Sarah. (2016). *A Road Map for Strategic Relevance: EU Security Policy Options in Southeast Asia*, International Institute of Strategic Studies, www.iiss.org/en/events/events/archive/2016-a3c2/june-4a2d/launch—a-road-map-to-strategic-relevance-98c1, accessed online 19 May 2018.

Reiterer, Michael. (2002). *Asia-Europe: Do They Meet?: Reflections on the Asia–Europe Meeting (ASEM)*. Singapore: Asia-Europe Foundation – World Scientific.

Reiterer, Michael. (2013a). "Great Power Competition in Asia", in *The 7th Berlin Conference on Asian Security*, http://swp-berlin.org/fileadmin/contents/products/projekt_papiere/BCAS2013_Michael_Reiterer.pdf, accessed online 17 April 2017.

Reiterer, Michael. (2013b). "The Role of 'Strategic Partnerships' in the EU's Relations with Asia", in T. Christiansen, E. Kirchner and P. Murray (eds), *The Palgrave Handbook of EU–Asia Relations*. London: Palgrave Macmillan, pp.75–89.

Reiterer, Michael. (2014a). "The EU's Comprehensive Approach to Security in Asia", *European Foreign Affairs Review* 19 (1): 1–21.

Reiterer, Michael. (2014b). "The Role of Culture in EU–China Relations", *European Foreign Affairs Review* 19 (3): 135–53.

Reiterer, Michael. (2015a). "The NAPCI in the Volatile Security Environment of North-East Asia: Which Role for the European Union?", *European Foreign Affairs Review* 20 (4): 573–89.

Reiterer, Michael. (2015b). "Will the Rise of Asia Lead to Europe's Decline – Lessons to Be Learnt", in L. Brennan and P. Murray (eds), *Drivers of Integration and Regionalism in Europe and Asia: Comparative Perspectives*. London and New York: Routledge, pp. 385–404.

Reiterer, Michael. (2016a). "Asia as Part of the EU's Global Strategy: Reflections on a More Strategic Approach", in *Dahrendorf Forum*. London: London School of Economics, p. 62, http://lse.ac.uk/IDEAS/publications/reports/pdf/Changing-Waters-LSE-IDEAS.pdf, accessed online 17 April 2017.

Reiterer, Michael. (2016b). "Regional Security Architecture in the Asia-Pacific: What Role for the European Union?", in *The Asan Forum*, www.theasanforum.org/regional-security-architecture-in-the-asia-pacific-what-role-for-the-eu/, accessed online 17 April 2018.

Reiterer, M. (2017a). *Supporting NAPCI and Trilateral Cooperation: Prospects for Korea–EU Relations*. Rome: Istituto Affari Internazionali (IAI), http://iai.it/sites/default/files/iaiwp1701.pdf, accessed online 17 Mar. 2017.

Reiterer, Michael (2017b). "Die Globale Strategie der Europäischen Union – den Visionen Taten folgen lassen", in *The Global Strategy of the European Union – Vision needs deeds. Integration*. Berlin: Institut für Europäische Politik, Integration 1/2017, pp. 11–30.

2 A European pivot towards Asia? Inter-regionalism in a new era

Julie Gilson

Introduction

In 2009, the US Administration launched its new "pivot" towards Asia, based on the conviction that the "lion's share of the political and economic history of the 21st century will be written in the Asia-Pacific region" (Campbell and Andrews, 2013: 2; Etzioni, 2012). This idea of a return to Asia, or a rebalancing of key international relations, reflected the growing economic and strategic influence of this region, particularly in the light of the failure of Western markets and the continuing rise of Chinese power (Ling, 2013). Since that time, Europe too has begun to reconsider the state of its own relations with East Asia, and some observers witness the start of a pivot by the European Union (EU) towards East Asia (see, for example, Casarini, 2013; Ungharo, 2012). This view has enjoyed high-level support, not least from EU High Representative Federica Mogherini, who stated that: "I have always been convinced that we should together pivot to Asia, the US and the EU" (cited in Twining, 2015). Similarly, at a "Friends of Europe" conference in 2014, long-time Asia–Europe Meeting (ASEM) watcher Shada Islam commented that ASEM is "ready for an upgrade" (Friends of Europe, 2014: 2). For David O'Sullivan, Chief Operating Officer of the EU's External Action Service, ASEM provides a "framework to address challenges of global concern with all of Asia at once" (Friends of Europe, 2014: 14).

This is not the first time that Europe has (re)turned its attention to Asia. In the 1990s, the EU launched a "new strategy" towards the East Asian region, and participated in the establishment of ASEM in 1996. This summit-level inter-regional engagement seemed to herald the start of a new strategy for managing collective international relations, whilst its three pillars of economic, political and socio-cultural linkages sought to address many of the major concerns and opportunities presented by the demands of globalisation and shared by the two growing regions (Gilson, 2002). The present chapter interrogates this apparently renewed European approach to

Asia and the current state of inter-regional relations in the ASEM framework, particularly in light of the inauguration of the US President Donald Trump, and in the face of dramatic intra-regional changes in Asia and Europe themselves. In so doing, it assesses the relevance of inter-regionalism as a tool for understanding distinct structures within the changing architecture of global governance today.

The chapter contends that weak institutional structures combine with a rise in the number of bilateral agreements, a confused US posture towards both regions and contentious intra-regional dynamics within Asia and Europe, to dilute the relevance of inter-regionalism. It proposes that we should regard inter-regionalism as an issue-led and process-led form of managing foreign policy, rather than as an overarching narrative for understanding relations among regions today. In order to shape this line of argument, it makes the distinction between the differing values of implicit and explicit inter-regionalism.

Reassessing inter-regionalism

The very idea of inter-regionalism is still relatively new, introduced as a response to the changing behaviour of regions in a globalising world, especially from the 1990s. Whilst there existed precedent in engagements like dialogue between the European Union and the Association of Southeast Asian Nations (ASEAN), the 1990s saw the most significant developments of "regions" as global actors, in the face of the need to create economies of scale and respond to trans-border problems (Grugel, 2004; Katzenstein, 2000). Despite its "elusive" nature, Mansfield and Milner set out the parameters of regionalism as issuing from "a period marked by substantial economic interdependence, a desire by countries to mediate trade disputes, and a multilateral framework that facilitates such mediation and the organization of commercial relations" (1999: 591 and 621). And as the Europeans forged ahead with their project for economic and political integration, the North American free trade area and the rise of the so-called "Asian tigers" and subsequent economic dynamism of China suggested that large-scale endeavours represented the path to the future (see, for example, Beeson, 2005; Väyrynan, 2003).

As regions grew and proliferated in their various forms, so too did the need for them to engage economically and politically with one another, whilst at the same time, as argued elsewhere, the very form of engagement also shaped ongoing definitions of regions as actors (Gilson, 2002: 11). As with regions themselves, different forms of inter-regional behaviour began to be inscribed on the global landscape. Thus, alongside trans-regional institutions such as the Asia-Pacific Economic Co-operation (APEC) forum, which embraced a broader membership and wide remit of economic interests, explicitly region-to-region dialogues also began to form. These included ASEM, ASEAN–Latin America economic agreements, the EU–Community of Latin American and Caribbean States dialogue and the EU–South Asian Association for Regional Co-operation agreements (Gilson, 2005). Some of these were formalised through clearly defined institutional structures, whilst others were more loosely constituted and/or issue-specific (see Vleuten and Hoffmann, 2013). ASEM began – in narrative terms at least – as this explicit form of interaction. In their work on "new regionalism', Hettne, Inotai and Sunkel suggest that regions are "created and recreated in the process of global transformation" as "territorial based subsystems of the international system" (1999: xv). In this way, inter-regionalism can be seen as part of the process of growing regionalism, as levels of interdependence and institutionalised responses are adjusted to address collectively joint problems. In this formulation, the "region" becomes a reflexive agent that both constitutes and is constituted by its inter-regional interaction and its ongoing externalization (Scholte, 2000).

For the purposes of understanding different values of inter-regionalism, we find it instructive to focus on a distinction between formal and informal modes of inter-regionalism. On the one hand, *formal* inter-regionalism hinges on strongly articulated institutional frameworks, which codify formal relations between two pre-existing units. Regions can be identified independently of their inter-regional behaviour and have definable institutional structures. Thus, for example, ASEAN has a regularised set of meetings and a secretariat, whilst the EU is the most institutionalised form of regional arrangement and often sets the template for regional behaviour (Murray and Moxon-Browne, 2013). Indeed, the EU has utilised inter-regionalism as a means of strengthening its own external legitimacy and projecting its "normative power" (Manners, 2002), managing relations with multiple actors, and creating a dominant normative frame of reference for regional – and, by extension, inter-regional – behaviour (see, for example, Whitman, 2011). This is attributable not simply to some kind of normative European power but also to the fact that, as Aggarwal notes, policy-makers tend to modify rather than introduce new institutions, and usually base the formation of new institutional dimensions upon those which already exist. Thus, "bargaining over institutional modification is likely to be strongly influenced by existing institutions" (Aggarwal, 1998: 1). The EU now retains a portfolio of region-to-region dialogues, increasingly based upon a template for engagement that is formulated and sustained by the institutional mechanisms of the EU itself. In this way, mutual interaction and the practice of engagement may also result in the creation of new conceptions of regional affiliation and identity. Gilson has argued elsewhere, for example, that the enactment through ASEM of an explicitly region-to-region dialogue served to consolidate a particular (ASEAN Plus Three) identity for Asia as an increasingly recognised global collective

(Gilson, 2002). Some observers regard this form of inter-regionalism as a "double regionalist" project, whereby states maximise advantage in a world of increasingly larger power units by engaging in economies of scale (Hettne, Inotai and Sunkel, 1999: xxii).

On the other hand, *informal* inter-regionalism does not presuppose an *a priori* fixed regional identity for participating units. This form of inter-regionalism corresponds to what is sometimes labelled "trans-regionalism", a structural attempt to combine – rhetorically at least, if not always in practice – a range of states within a coherent unified framework. Examples include fora such as APEC, the Transatlantic Dialogue between the US and the EU, and the ASEAN Regional Forum, in which clearly delineated regional entities do not exist prior to the establishment of the pan-regional gathering. This version of inter-regionalism facilitates an inclusive approach to membership, which itself can be varied according to the issue being addressed, and, although there may be a loose notion of region-to-region involvement, it is not the defining narrative of interaction. At its heart, then, the concept of regional cohesion remains important, but the very constitution of the "regions" involved may be a slippery concept. Moreover, the reasons for the establishment or development of the inter-regional project may emanate from or offer a reflex to external forces.

These two forms of inter-regionalism can be distinguished on four levels. First, they depend on the level of regional integration of each "side". Arguably, significant achievements can be made within an inter-regional framework only where the regions involved are clearly demarcated, either from their own internal development or as a result of their inter-regional encounters. The EU is the most institutionalised and formalised regional structure, with the Commission, the Parliament, the Council and – following the most recent Treaty of Lisbon in 2009 – a far clearer external policy face, in the person of the EU's own High Representative and a clearer role for the EU's External Action Service. Indeed, when Catherine Ashton took up the appointment as the first High Representative, she stated publicly that the EU needed to "punch its weight" in the international arena (Ashton, 2009: 457). In the case of the "Asian" membership of ASEM, the ASEAN secretariat has provided some level of institutional core, but the idea of East Asia has never been formally defined and has – as will be shown below – been weakened by competing claims over regional definitions. Where there is no identifiable interlocutor, continuity of dialogue can be harder to achieve, and it is harder to measure whether or not inter-regional objectives have been met. Second, the difference between formal and informal inter-regionalism also resides in the level of institutionalisation of the inter-regional format itself. Where strong institutional structures are present, there is dense ongoing communication and an institutional memory on both sides of the region-to-region dialogue. This approach also enables agenda items – such as climate change or counter-terrorism

A European pivot towards Asia?

– to be addressed at a variety of levels of authority and for deadlines and goals to be set. Third, the intensity of bilateral negotiations can also lie in competition with attempts to achieve pan-regional agreements. Whilst some scholars argue that the proliferation of free trade agreements (FTAs) in recent years has in fact set a template for unified behaviour and therefore created a pattern of "lattice regionalism" (Dent, 2003) or pushed states towards particular regional identities (Corning, 2011), others contend that the proliferation of FTAs can damage any regionalising projects. For Terada, for example, in Asia the "bilateral approach to financial cooperation, together with a constellation of bilateral rather than regional free trade agreements, signified the lack of a regional approach to formal integration in East Asia" (2012: 365). Fourth, and linked to the third factor, external actors may have a significant impact on inter-regionalist behaviour, not only as a force for bringing regions together but also as a means of keeping them apart. These four dimensions will be examined in relation to ASEM, following a brief history of this particular inter-regional encounter.

Establishing inter-regional relations between Asia and Europe

By the early 1990s the EU had (somewhat belatedly) started to respond to the growing economic advances of East Asia. In the EU's *New Asia Strategy* of 1994, it stated that it "needs as a matter of urgency to strengthen its economic presence in Asia in order to maintain its leading role in the world economy", and that the "increase of the relative weight of Asia in the world economy will considerably reinforce the political weight of this region on the international political scene" (European Commission, 1994). Resulting from a subsequent proposal by Singapore, the first ASEM summit was held in Bangkok in 1996. This meeting was lauded as the first real attempt to consolidate and advance relations between two dynamic and increasingly significant regions of a globalising world (Gilson, 2002). This consolidation of relations sought to address a number of pressing concerns. First, the economic imperative of achieving and sustaining competitiveness led to a growing interest in region-to-region approaches. A Eurostat report for 2008 illustrated that ASEM partners were worth 32 per cent of EU imports and 18 per cent of exports, representing a growth of around 60 per cent in overall trade with the EU since 2000 (Eurostat, 2008). The overall EU trade deficit with its ASEM partners had grown in this period from €139 billion in 2000 to €231 billion in 2007 (Eurostat, 2008). That deficit would go on to peak at €300 billion in 2008, but return to €280 billion by 2011 (Eurostat, 2012). Much of this growth could be attributed to the rise of the Chinese economy, accounting for nearly half of EU imports and one-third of its exports, according to Eurostat (2008). By 2012, ASEM partners accounted for 43 per cent of imports from the EU and 31 per cent of exports (Eurostat, 2012).

Against the background of these unfolding figures, ASEM as an institution has contributed to fostering economic relations among the states of the two regions. For one thing, ASEM provides an important point of contact and sounding board for developing ideas and strategies within the World Trade Organisation framework, and offers a pre-negotiation forum for its member states. Most tangibly, ASEM developed the Trade Facilitation Action Plan, to remove non-tariff barriers to trade among the states of the two regions. This initiative has also been regarded as an important locus of up-to-date information for European and Asian businesses (Santiago, 2011: 59). Similarly, the Investment Promotion Action Plan aims to promote investment between the two regions. In addition, and among other agendas for economic enhancement at a range of levels, the Asia–Europe Business Forum ensures that the views of private industry are included in ASEM dialogue.

Second, ASEM promised to intensify political linkages among key players of the two regions. Although informal and largely non-binding, the ASEM process was designed to offer its participants a regular, institutionalised channel for communication and the exchange of information. The political pillar of ASEM has been used at a range of levels – from high-level summits to ministerial and working-group meetings – to address issues as diverse as counter-terrorism, environmental protection, human rights and cultural interests. In terms of outcomes, ASEM has provided a novel framework for the valuable exchange of information over issues as diverse as the Korean peninsula and climate change. However, differences over issues such as human rights approaches and the position of Burma have plagued attempts at agreement throughout its history (Japan Center for International Exchange, 2006). Despite the intentions set out in 1996 and in spite of the fact that it has grown in membership to 53 partners, there has been a stagnation in the delivery of initiatives by ASEM, and in the level of participation by key actors.

Following a start full of co-operative pledges, then, ASEM delivered a number of modest initiatives, not least providing a stable and regular forum for region-to-region dialogue. However, the second decade of its existence coincided with a stagnation in relations, as global recession, institutional weakness and the continued rise of China required global and national responses and did not correspond to particular regional – or inter-regional – agendas. The economic reality – that in 2012 ASEM states accounted for 57.2 per cent of total global economic output, based on GDP (Eurostat, 2014: 49) – was not matched by a commitment for binding and institutionalised relations. A number of papers were delivered by the European Commission to define the state of play between the two regions and, as Yeo notes, the "Asia-Europe Cooperation Framework" of 2000 represented an attempt to emphasise the value of ASEM's informality (2013: 3). The 2001 strategy paper *Europe and Asia* then identified the six broad objectives of co-operation covering everything from peace and security, improved mutual trade opportunities, to development co-operation, good governance and environmental protection.

Since that time, various reports and ASEM summits have sought – largely without success – to reinvigorate or relaunch the ASEM project. The EU even declared 2012 to be the "Year of Asia" in Europe.[1] Despite these and other initiatives, during its lifetime "ASEM has clocked up an impressive quota of diplomatic air miles but very little in the way of substantive and value-added cooperation" (Gilson, 2011: 394). We will assess the prospects for a new promised pivot at the end of this chapter, but first it is worth examining each of the three dimensions of inter-regionalism outlined above to demonstrate how that gap has arisen.

First, in terms of the regional identities of Asia and Europe, the original objective of ASEM was to establish an explicitly inter-regional dialogue based on an "equal partnership" of two regions.[2] Since that time, however, ASEM has increased its membership considerably and a region-to-region structure is hard to discern. Whilst ASEM was originally formed around the structure of the EU plus ASEAN plus three in which "Asian ASEM" was a recognisable interlocutor with the EU, it now accommodates members that include Australia, Russia, India and Kazakhstan. At the heart of the narrative of a strong inter-regional linkage was the notion that Europe and (East) Asia could be regarded as independent units and increasingly important global economic and political actors.

Whilst the region of Asia lacks an institutional core, as suggested above, the normative force of the EU model was for a long time held up as the gold standard for region-building. The states of the EU had in 1992 signed the Maastricht Treaty, which established the three-pillar structure of Europe, thereby ensuring that a significant amount of European business (under the "European Community" pillar) would henceforth be conducted at supranational level under the auspices of the Commission, Parliament and Court of Justice. It also led to the creation of the euro zone, a common currency for the majority of EU states. Since that time, additional treaties have further consolidated the legal character of the EU, and in 2009 the Lisbon Treaty increased the number of issue areas for which qualified majority voting could be applied, increased the power of the European Parliament and established the posts of long-term President of the European Council and a High Representative of the Union for Foreign Affairs and Security Policy (see Smith, 2004). In so doing, the treaty further strengthened the power of the Union to act on behalf of its constituent member states and to present its own unique foreign-policy credentials.

However, during the period of ASEM's existence, and especially since the global recession from 2008, there have been a number of internal problems in Europe, including the crisis of the Greek economy which threatened not only the Eurozone's future but the future of the EU itself in its current form. In 2016, the blow to the EU from the Brexit vote elicited a region-wide questioning of the European project. The reverberations around the continent, coupled with ongoing economic crises and a dramatically increasing problem of inflowing refugees, have ensured that European eyes are rarely turned on Asia at the moment. As will be shown later, US responses to Brexit have further emphasised the chasms within Europe, as President Trump pledged his support for a US–UK free trade deal.[3]

For its part, the region of East Asia began to develop its institutional parameters through the ASEAN Plus Three (APT) framework during the 1990s. Despite this positive attempt to bring the "plus three" states (of Japan, China and South Korea) to the negotiating table with ASEAN, institutionally the region remained at a low level of co-operation. And whilst Jones and Smith had long warned us of the "illusory" nature of the idea of East Asia (2007: 186), the changes in regional dynamics during the 2000s further confused any intra-regional coherence. In fact, during this period, a number of regional initiatives emerged, with the result that the conception of a future Asian region became more fractured rather than cohesive. By the 2010s, most notable were the opposing directions taken by China and Japan, making Southeast Asia a "site of contestation" (Chung, 2013: 819): on the one hand, China continued to favour the APT model, limiting the region to "Asian" participants and ensuring the primacy of Beijing at the heart of regional initiatives. According to Shekar, "China has extensively used its energy and resources in supporting the APT forum and in undermining the EAS [East Asian Summit] process, which it sees as an effort to restrict China's strategic engagement with the region" (2012: 258). In contrast, the Japanese government promoted participation within the broader EAS framework, involving eighteen states, including the US and Russia, and enabling it to participate alongside India in an forum to balance the growing power of China (Camroux, 2012). In fact, as Camroux states, these initiatives render terms like "community" problematic, as such concepts "may very well be discursive subterfuges for promoting multilateral relations within a porous Asia" (2012: 111).

Second, in terms of the level of institutionalisation enjoyed by ASEM, Rüland is not alone in witnessing only "diminished multilateralism" (2012). Despite the three pillars upon which ASEM was built, it was from the start, and remains, only a loosely organised set of regular meetings underpinned by no formal sanctions and based on consensus. The responsibility for managing ASEM's agenda falls to a rotation of Asian and EU partners, alongside the European Commission, and the lack of a formal bilateral secretariat means that agendas are often relatively diluted and based upon issues arising in global institutions like the United Nations and World Trade Organization.

A European pivot towards Asia?

Since the ASEM grouping expanded membership beyond its two original regions, it has brought a complex range of other relations into the group, including the challenging reality of the EU–Russia relationship. In many ways, ASEM has "grown too much too fast" (Friends of Europe, 2014: 18). ASEM, as Yeo notes, "remains essentially a forum for dialogue", whose breadth of membership and range of activities have rendered it weak and superficial and unable to match its initial rhetorical promises (2013). What is more, at the heart of the ASEM process lies the EU–ASEAN relationship. Beyond the scope of the present chapter, it is fair to suggest that the failure of the EU and ASEAN to negotiate a free trade agreement by 2009 was a significant sign that the institutional parameters of EU–ASEAN relations were insubstantial. Despite the fact that ASEAN is the third largest external trading partner for the EU (enjoying over €246 billion of trade in goods and services in 2014),[4] the deal was stalled as a result of ongoing EU concerns over Burma's human rights record.[5] As the ASEM structure is far broader and looser, it is no surprise that frequent recourse to the lowest common denominator becomes the usual order of play.

Third, for reasons similar to those cited above, it is also unsurprising to see the proliferation of bilateral free trade agreements in recent years. By way of example, some of the numerous FTAs with Asian states include: Japan's bilateral agreements with ASEAN, Indonesia, Malaysia, Thailand, Singapore and Vietnam; China's agreements with ASEAN, Hong Kong, Thailand, Singapore and Taiwan. For its part, the EU has concluded over thirty FTAs, including its FTA with South Korea. From one viewpoint, these FTAs collectively – in a similar vein to Dent's "lattice" effect – could combine to form "building blocks for regional agreements" (Friends of Europe, 2014: 18), as the nature of contemporary trading agreements becomes far more complex (see Dent, 2014). From another perspective, however, the proliferation of FTAs and preferential and specific agreements might in fact serve to weaken any attempts at region-wide agreement. Beyond economic agreements, the EU has also sought to develop its "strategic partnerships" with a range of key players, including in Asia, India, China, Japan and South Korea. Most prominently to date, the EU–Japan partnership was finally concluded in the summer of 2017.[6] From this perspective, multilateral engagements like the ASEM process need to be regarded as only one strand of foreign policy-making in the toolkits of European and Asian states, rather than as an overarching framework for "bilateral" region-to-region interaction.

External influences

The preceding section examined those three factors related to institutional opportunities and limitations presented by Asia–Europe relations. Within both forms of inter-regionalism outlined above, it is also necessary to consider the impact of a fourth factor, namely key external forces, which may shape the membership and agenda, and may bring together participating inter-regional partners, or may indeed split them apart. In the case of Europe–Asia relations the key external agents have historically been China and the United States, each of which is examined in turn here.

China

The challenges faced by the rest of the Asian region with regard to China are highlighted in the foregoing sections. China's inexorable "rise" – in economic and increasingly military, particularly naval, terms – has had the effect both of pushing regional (especially ASEAN) states together to seek common ground in order to work with China, and also of splitting the region into its bilateral engagements with Beijing. Attempts at integrating the "plus three" states into ASEAN's ambit have largely been silenced, and the gap between Chinese and Japanese visions of the region's future continues to grow. The US withdrawal from the Trans-Pacific Partnership (see below) struck a blow for Japan's regional plans, whilst unilateral initiatives like China's Asian Infrastructure Investment Bank continue to mark out its own region planning.

It should be noted that the rise of China, despite representing a common challenge to Europe and the rest of Asia, elicits bilateral national-interest-based responses. Vichitsorasatra goes as far as to say that "there is little evidence to suggest that the EU pursued a multilateral strategy with China" through the ASEM process, and every indication that it is addressed in most instances as a bilateral (EU–China) issue (2009: 65). Indeed, by 2003, China was already the number two trading partner for the EU (after the US), but the EU's biggest trade deficit was also with China (Vichitsorasatra, 2009: 73). The current efforts to develop a comprehensive EU–China Investment Agreement, launched in 2013 at the EU–China Summit, represent an attempt to remove ongoing restrictions to one another's markets. Concerns voiced by the EU include non-tariff barriers, a lack of protection for intellectual property rights in China and continued strong Chinese government intervention in its economy.[7] For Europeans, this agreement aims to increase access to the Chinese market, and will be the "first stand-alone investment agreement negotiated by the Union based on the competences gained under the Lisbon Treaty".[8] In 2013, they also agreed the EU–China Strategic 2020 Agenda, with the aim of increasing and formalising the scope and range of their mutual interests, from trade and investment and space and aerospace to public policy and educational exchanges. This approach to developing strategic bilateral relations with key partners has become increasingly significant for the EU, which has negotiated a range of "strategic partnerships" around the world. Indeed, at the EU–China Summit in June 2015, both sides reiterated the need to forge ahead further with these strategic plans.[9] With an EU focus on addressing this trade imbalance and the overall improvement of bilateral trading opportunities, the role of ASEM in contributing to EU–China relations is regarded by Vichitsorasatra as "passive" at best (2009: 78).

The US

The most difficult external actor to assess at the present time is the US under President Trump. After initial concerns about the rocky road Trump appeared to wish to travel in Asia, and in spite of Trump's warm overtures to Taiwan and its agreement to sell US$1.42 billion in arms to Taipei in the face of Chinese protestations,[10] the US Administration seems to wish to chart a more stable route in the region. In spite of his campaign rhetoric to make changes to relations with Asia, Trump has in fact showed a desire to date to keep relations on an even keel, emphasising his intention, for example, to retain the main military alliances with Japan, Australia, South Korea and the Philippines.[11] The reality for both the US and China is that their relationship remains economically important, accounting for 36 per cent of the global economy; they have ironed out some of their mutual concerns over economic issues; and the US has come to accept China's "One Belt, One Road" project to develop Asian infrastructure.[12]

The central tenets of Obama's original pivot rested on the Trans-Pacific Partnership and regional security. First, Trump pulled the US out of the Trans Pacific Partnership trade deal in his first week in office, a move met with dismay in Asia. Indeed, countries like Japan and Vietnam were seeking the benefits of having lower tariffs on their exports to the US, but Trump made it clear that his focus on US jobs first required only bilateral negotiating.[13] The withdrawal of the US split the region: Australia suggested that China might replace US leadership in the Partnership, whilst Japanese Prime Minister Abe stated that without the US any such Partnership would be "meaningless".[14] Despite the warnings by some observers that this gap would leave the field open for greater Chinese leadership, responses to the withdrawal suggest that there is no Asian regional appetite to replace US leadership there.

Second, since Trump's inauguration, military tensions in the Asia-Pacific have increased. The Obama Administration expressed its desire to strengthen US--Asia defence partnerships, especially with countries like the Philippines and Vietnam, but these have been challenged not only by the arrival of President Trump but also by the election of Philippine President Rodrigo Duterte, with his severe approach to leadership and his verbal attacks on the US for criticising his brutal and bloody war on drugs.[15]

The most pressing military issue in the region is the question mark over North Korea's next move. In April 2017, Trump's Administration sent naval ships towards Korea, and his rhetoric towards the North has become increasingly bellicose. And as the US and North Korean rhetoric becomes ever more tense, concerns and uncertainty in the region continue to rise. Although China has supported UN calls for greater sanctions against Pyongyang, the US remains frustrated at Beijing's reluctance to use its considerable power over the North to force Pyongyang's hand.[16] Meanwhile, South Korea, whose capital lies only forty miles south of the border with North Korea, is concerned that it could become the principal arena for a show of force by Pyongyang. As North Korea proves its ability to reach the US mainland with its nuclear warheads, the US president is increasingly likely to make a unilateral decision to meet the threat with "fire and fury" and not to work closely with his Asian allies.[17]

In addition to these concerns, Trump's controversial campaigning with regard to Islam has also heightened tensions with the majority Muslim countries of Indonesia and Malaysia. Similarly, President Obama's form of the pivot embraced the role of the ASEAN, whilst its slow and cumbersome mechanisms are unlikely to align with Trump's more direct methods of diplomacy.[18] For Carl Baker, director of programmes at the think tank Pacific Forum CSIS (Centre for Strategic and International Studies) in Honolulu, the "Trump administration has not given any serious thought to an overarching Asian strategy" so far,[19] whilst elsewhere it is noted that "it often takes time for Asia policy to take shape even under a conventional administration with dedicated Asia firsters".[20]

In Europe, leaders have been considering how to deal with President Trump. The US has expressed its strong support for the UK's Brexit decision, whilst German leader Angela Merkel continues to push for a common EU stance on trade and multilateralism, and has expressed her hostility to the new US president in public, especially with regard to climate change.[21] Indeed, Trump's July 2017 speech in Warsaw defended "Western civilisation" and echoed the sentiments of the populist right around the region.[22] Having softened his anti-NATO stance, during his somewhat awkward trip to Europe in May 2017 he nevertheless "failed to dispel persistent doubts about US commitment to North Atlantic Treaty Organization (NATO) by endorsing Article 5".[23] It is remarkable that Trump seeks to manage the threat of North Korea in Asia, but risks undermining the central alliance structure for managing the threat of Russia in Europe.[24]

Conclusion: Where does the "pivot" fit in?

Against this background of institutional weaknesses and changing external contexts, how credible is the claim that the EU has renewed its attention towards Asia and sought to pivot towards this loosely constituted region?

Of course, the demands for European co-operation with Asia are clear, and Parello-Plesner warns that the EU cannot afford to bury its head in the sand:

> Europeans retain a somewhat one-dimensional vision of Asia's rise and consider the region to be a place of economic opportunities. But the wave of disputes over islands and rocks between China and its neighbours is evidence of dangerous undercurrents in Asia. (2012)

Moreover, newly expressed European attention towards East Asia responds to calls that the "EU must wake up to the new reality in Asia". Parello-Plesner goes on to suggest that Europe "is no longer guaranteed a seat at the table and must work harder to remain relevant. ASEM is a good opportunity for it to do so" (2012). On the economic front, the need remains to reinvigorate economic relations, which would enable the EU to "buttress domestic reforms and boost growth" (Messerlin, 2012: 7) and would facilitate greater market opportunities for Asian economies. In terms of security, moreover, there are specific concerns of mutual interest to Asian and European partners, including the need to maintain strategic navigation in the South China Sea (Friends of Europe, 2014: 14), anxieties over the positioning of Russia and tensions over North Korea. Long-time ASEM watcher Michael Reiterer explains how inter-regionalism serves as a useful foreign policy tool for states within both regions, as it fits with the EU's "natural institutional bias in favour of inter-regionalism", enabling Europe to "project regional power more universally while East Asia, through its various forms of regionalism, strives to catch up politically and institutionally with the EU, both attempting to counter US unilateralism" (2009: 181). It was in this spirit that in 2015 the EU reignited talks with ASEAN about a possible FTA.[25]

However, today's reality is complex. Neither Asia nor Europe represents a unified or coherent vision of a "region". In Asia, vastly different regime types co-exist and contestations for regional power are being played out most notably in the East China Sea and among regional financial institutions. The challenging relationship between Japan and China, in particular, renders the possibility of greater regional coherence less and less likely, whilst the enduring institutional weakness of ASEAN means that the expanded "Plus Three" process has little role to play in fostering intra-regional bonds. In Europe, the impact of Brexit and the rise of right-wing forces echo the anti-immigration and anti-Muslim sentiment now emanating from Trump's America, leaving open questions about Europe's ability to take a lead in addressing its own region's problems, let alone co-operating with and influencing other parts of the world. All of these factors suggest both that the US's pivot towards Asia no longer has credence and that any European attempt to emulate that process is mired in internecine troubles.

Against this background, did the very concept of inter-regionalism ever have traction? The idea of formal inter-regionalism between Asia and Europe was always predicated on a grand narrative of a region-to-region framework for dialogue. In reality, however, not only were the inter-regional institutional ties loose, but the very constitution of each "side" was rarely coherent and often in crisis, particularly on the Asian side. The current membership of ASEM dismisses this region-to-region axis altogether, in favour of issue-led agendas. Seen as an overarching framework that encapsulates in its entirety the narrative of region-to-region engagement, then, it has been assessed largely as a failure, and any attempts to revive it are likely to end in tears. The Asia–Europe Meeting was only ever designed to be a loose institutional framework and accommodated only a generalised notion of the region of "East Asia", despite the fact that it showed some normative pressure for East Asian states to behave *as* a region for the purposes of interaction.

What remains indisputable is the fact that there is a greater need than ever before for Europe and Asia to work effectively together. The US's unilateral management of the North Korean crisis needs to be met with a unified approach from Europe and Asia to encourage negotiation and dialogue; and in Europe only support for the strengthening of existing alliances can act as a brake on potentially dangerous Russian behaviour. To this end, the ASEM process does not need to be formally institutionally strong, but needs to support informal inter-regionalism, giving those states involved a regular and reliable channel of dialogue among states that recognise that major issues like climate change and military tensions can be addressed only together.

Notes

1 See http://eeas.europa.eu/asia/docs/2012_eu_in_asia_year_facts_figures_en.pdf, accessed online 7 August 2017.
2 See /www.aseminfoboard.org/about, accessed online 7 August 2017.
3 See http://dailysignal.com/2017/07/10/president-trumps-europe-trip-success, accessed online 7 August 2017.
4 See http://ec.europa.eu/trade/policy/countries-and-regions/regions/asean, accessed online 7 August 2017.
5 See www.euractiv.com/sections/trade-society/eu-and-asean-kick-start-free-trade-agreement-talks-314100, accessed online 7 August 2017.
6 See www.bbc.co.uk/news/business-40520218, accessed online 7 August 2017.
7 See http://ec.europa.eu/trade/policy/countries-and-regions/countries/china, accessed online 7 August 2017.
8 See www.euractiv.com/sections/global-europe/xis-european-tour-and-china-eu-relations-301156, accessed online 7 August 2017.

9   See https://www.consilium.europa.eu/media/23732/150629-eu-china-summit-joint-statement-final.pdf, accessed online 7 August 2017.
10 See www.forbes.com/sites/ralphjennings/2017/07/17/they-say-trump-has-no-asia-policy-here-it-is/#6589d3827b01, accessed online 7 August 2017.
11 See www.cfr.org/expert-roundup/what-future-asia-pivot-under-trump, accessed online 7 August 2017.
12 See www.aljazeera.com/indepth/opinion/2017/05/trump-asia-policy-working-170522065641843.html, accessed online 7 August 2017.
13 See www.forbes.com/sites/ralphjennings/2017/07/17/they-say-trump-has-no-asia-policy-here-it-is/#6589d3827b01, accessed online 7 August 2017.
14 See www.aljazeera.com/indepth/opinion/2017/05/trump-asia-policy-working-170522065641843.html, accessed online 7 August 2017.
15 See www.cfr.org/expert-roundup/what-future-asia-pivot-under-trump, accessed online 7 August 2017.
16 See http://edition.cnn.com/2017/08/07/opinions/china-north-korea-opinion-lind/index.html, accessed online 7 August 2017.
17 See http://edition.cnn.com/2017/08/08/politics/north-korea-missile-ready-nuclear-weapons/index.html, accessed online 7 August 2017.
18 See www.cfr.org/expert-roundup/what-future-asia-pivot-under-trump, accessed online 7 August 2017.
19 See www.forbes.com/sites/ralphjennings/2017/07/17/they-say-trump-has-no-asia-policy-here-it-is/#6589d3827b01, accessed online 7 August 2017.
20 See http://thediplomat.com/2017/06/the-truth-about-trumps-asia-commitment-problem, accessed online 7 August 2017.
21 See www.theguardian.com/commentisfree/2017/jul/02/the-guardian-view-on-donald-trump-in-europe-an-edgy-welcome-awaits, accessed online 7 August 2017.
22 See http://dailysignal.com/2017/07/10/president-trumps-europe-trip-success, accessed online 7 August 2017.
23 See www.theguardian.com/us-news/2017/may/27/donald-trumps-europe-tour-leaves-leaders-shaken, accessed online 7 August 2017.
24 See www.washingtonpost.com/opinions/global-opinions/how-a-trump-presidency-could-destabilize-europe/2016/07/21/9ec38a20-4f75-11e6-a422-83ab49ed5e6a_story.html, accessed online 7 August 2017.
25 See www.euractiv.com/sections/trade-society/eu-and-asean-kick-start-free-trade-agreement-talks-314100, accessed online 7 August 2017.

References

Aggarwal, Vinod. (1998). *Institutional Designs for a Complex World./* Ithaca: Cornell University Press.
Ashton, Catherine. (2009). Remarks to the European Parliament, 2 December, http://europa.eu/rapid/press-release_SPEECH-09-567_en.htm?locale=en, accessed online 7 September 2018.
Beeson, Mark. (2005). "Rethinking Regionalism: Europe and East Asia in Comparative Historical Perspective", *Journal of European Public Policy* 12 (6): 969–85.

Campbell, Kurt, and Brian Andrews. (2013). *Explaining the US "Pivot" to Asia*. http://kritisches-netzwerk.de/sites/default/files/explaining_the_us_pivot_to_asia_-_kurt_campbell_and_brian_andrews_-_the_asia_group_-_august_2013_-_9_pages.pdf, accessed online 9 August 2017.

Camroux, David. (2006). "The Rise and Decline of the Asia-Europe Meeting (ASEM) Assymmetric Bilateralism and the Limitations of Interregionalism". Working paper 4. *Les Cahiers Européens de Sciences*. Paris: Centre d'études européennes at Sciences Po.

Camroux, David. (2012). "Regionalism in Asia as Disguised Multilateralism: A Critical Analysis of the East Asia Summit and the Trans-Pacific Partnership", *The International Spectator* 47 (1): 97–115.

Casarini, Nicola. (2013). *The European "Pivot"*. https://publications.europa.eu/en/publication-detail/-/publication/e7221c17–9338–4f91-bb14-c4dd1c9e7f04, accessed online 6 August 2017.

Chung, Chien-Peng. (2013). "China and Japan in 'ASEAN Plus' Multilateral Arrangements", *Asian Survey* 53 (5): 801–4.

Corning, Gregory P. (2011). "Trade Regionalism in a Realist East Asia: Rival Visions and Competitive Bilateralism", *Asian Perspective* 35 (2): 259–86.

Dent, Christopher M. (2003). "Networking the Region? The Emergence and Impact of Asia-Pacific Bilateral Free Trade Agreement Projects", *The Pacific Review* 16 (1): 1–28.

Dent, Christopher M. (2014). 'Principal Developments and Future Directions in Asia's Trade', in Saadia Pekkanen, John Ravenhill and Rosemary Foot (eds), *The Oxford Handbook of the International Relations of Asia*. Oxford: Oxford University Press, pp. 263–84.

Etzioni, Amitai (2012). "The United States' Premature Pivot to 'Asia'", *Society* 49 (5): 395–9.

EU Commission. (1994). "Towards a New Asia Strategy: Communication from the Commission to the Council". COM (94) 314 final, 13 July.

Eurostat. (2008). News release 145/2008, 20 October.

Eurostat. (2012). News release 151/2012, 29 October.

Eurostat. (2014). *Asia-Europe Meeting (ASEM): A Statistical Portrait*. Luxembourg: European Union Statistical Books.

Friends of Europe. (2014). *Asia-Europe Meeting (ASEM): A Partnership for the 21st Century*. Brussels: Friends of Europe.

Gilson, Julie. (2002). *Asia Meets Europe: Inter-Regionalism and the Asia–Europe Meeting*. Cheltenham: Edward Elgar Publishing.

Gilson, Julie. (2005). "New Interregionalism? The EU and East Asia", *Journal of European Integration* 27 (3): 307–26.

Gilson, Julie. (2011). "The Asia–Europe Meeting", in Mark Beeson and Richard Stubbs (eds), *Routledge Handbook of Asian Regionalism*. London: Routledge, pp. 394–405.

Grugel, Jean B. (2004). "New Regionalism and Modes of Governance – Comparing US and EU Strategies in Latin America", *European Journal of International Relations* 10 (4): 603–26.

Hettne, Björn, Andras Inotai and Osvaldo Sunkel (eds). (2001, 1999). *Studies in the New Regionalism*. London: Macmillan.

Japan Center for International Exchange and University of Helsinki Network for European Studies. (2006). *ASEM in its Tenth Year: Looking Back, Looking Forward*. Tokyo.

Jones, David Martin, and Michael L.R. Smith. (2007). "Constructing Communities: The Curious Case of East Asian Regionalism", *Review of International Studies* 33 (1): 165.

Katzenstein, Peter J. (2000). "Regionalism and Asia", *New Political Economy* 5 (3): 353–68.

Ling, Wei. (2013). "Rebalancing or De-Balancing: U.S. Pivot and East Asian Order", *American Foreign Policy Interests* 35 (3): 148–54.

Manners, Ian. (2002). "Normative Power Europe: A Contradiction in Terms?", *JCMS: Journal of Common Market Studies* 40 (2): 235–58.

Mansfield, Edward D. and Helen V. Milner. (1999). "The New Wave of Regionalism", *International Organization* 53 (3): 589–627.

Messerlin, Patrick. (2012). "The Much Needed EU Pivoting to East Asia", *Asia-Pacific Journal of EU Studies* 10 (2): 1–18.

Murray, Philomena, and Edward Moxon-Browne. (2013). "The European Union as a Template for Regional Integration? The Case of ASEAN and Its Committee of Permanent Representatives", *JCMS: Journal of Common Market Studies* 51 (3): 522–37.

Parello-Plesner, Jonas. (2012). "Europe's Mini-Pivot to Asia", online blog of China–US Focus, www.chinausfocus.com/foreign-policy/europes-mini-pivot-to-asia/, accessed online 7 September 2018.

Reiterer, Michael. (2009). "ASIA-EUROPE MEETING (ASEM): Fostering a Multipolar World Order Through Inter-Regional Cooperation", *Asia Europe Journal* 7 (1): 179–96.

Rüland, Jürgen. (2012). "The Rise of 'Diminished Multilateralism': East Asian and European Forum Shopping in Global Governance", *Asia Europe Journal* 9 (2–4): 255–70.

Santiago, Charles. (2011). "The European Union and ASEAN: Perspectives and Challenges Ahead", in Christoph Marcinkowski, Constance Chevallier-Govers and Ruhanas Harun (eds), *Malaysia and the European Union: Perspectives for the Twenty-First Century*. Berlin: Lit Verlag, pp. 45–78.

Scholte, Jan Aart. (2000). *Globalization*. London: Macmillan.

Shekar, Vibhanshu. (2012). "ASEAN's Response to the Rise of China: Deploying a Hedging Strategy", *China Report* 48 (3): 253–68.

Smith, Michael E. (2004). *Europe's Foreign and Security Policy*. New York: Cambridge University Press.

Terada, Takashi. (2012). "ASEAN Plus Three: Becoming More Like a Normal Regionalism?", in Mark Beeson and Richard Stubbs (eds), *Routledge Handbook of Asian Regionalism*. London: Routledge, pp. 364–74.

Twining, Daniel. (2015). "Europe's Incomplete Pivot to Asia", Asian Forum, 3 (3), www.theasanforum.org/europes-incomplete-pivot-to-asia/, accessed online 7 September 2018.

Ungharo, Alessandro Riccardo. (2012). "Developments in and Obstacles to the US Pivot to Asia: What Alternatives for Europe?", *SSRN Electronic Journal*.

Väyrynan, Raimo. (2003). "Regionalism: Old and New", *International Studies Review* 5 (1): 25–51.

Vichitsorasatra, Natee. (2009). "The EU and China in the Context of Inter- Regionalism", in Georg Wiessala, J.F. Wilson and Pradeep Taneja (eds), *The European Union and China: Interests and Dilemmas*. Amsterdam: Rodopi, pp. 65–82.

Vleuten, Anna van der, and Andrea Ribeiro Hoffmann. (2013). "The Politics of Inter-Regionalism", in: Bob Reinalda (ed.), *Routledge Handbook of International Organization*. London: Routledge, pp. 430–44.

Whitman, Richard G. (2011). *Normative Power Europe*. London: Palgrave.

Yeo, Lay Hwee. (2013). "Towards a Dynamic Asia–Europe Meeting (ASEM)?", *EUC Working Paper* 14.

PART II

Major issues and themes

3 European Union security policy and initiatives in the Asia-Pacific

Fulvio Attinà

The national security policies of the states and the collective and multilateral management of international security problems in regions like the European and the Asian region have gone through a remarkable process of transformation passing from the past to the contemporary world system. The traditional instruments for providing security to the state like hi-tech armaments and well-trained armies, and also the ways of building security in geographically limited international systems and regions like military pacts and alliances, have been joined by new forms of security management like multilateral peace operations, arms control arrangements and regional security partnerships. Differently from the traditional means and forms of international security, the new instruments of security include mechanisms of so-called co-operative and comprehensive security to manage the threats to the safety of the states. In the past two decades, the countries of Europe and Asia have experienced this process of security management. They engaged themselves in multilateral negotiations at the regional and interregional level and have been adapting their national security to such policy process. Analysing the EU security initiatives in Asia, one has to keep in mind also that the security practices of the world system develop in close relation with the existing structure of power and government at the world level. They are influenced by the competition for power that develops between the leading world states and between the coalitions of states that want to play the leading role in the world structure of government (Attinà, 2011). In harmony with this view of the world political system, in the present chapter the analysis of the EU security initiatives in Asia is put in the context of the involvement of the European and Asian states in the political competition on the world system power. The current state of the EU, which is characterised by the start of the negotiations on the exit of the United Kingdom and an atmosphere of multiples crises and fragmentation pressures, is also a condition that may affect the continuity of the EU policy towards the Asia security process.

The present chapter is organised as follows. Section one reviews the modes of security management in Europe and Asia since the end of the Second World War and their relationship with the world system structure and competition for global power. Section two deals with the vexed question of the international actorship of the EU and takes into consideration the state of the integration process, in particular the stress caused by the British decision to leave the Union. Following from these topics, section three examines and assesses the present EU's security initiatives in Asia and advises about next steps.

The collective management of security in Europe and Asia since the Second World War

This section reviews the management of security by the states of Europe and Asia in the contemporary world system from the end of the Second World War. During this period of time, the two regions have passed through different experiences and circumstances that were in tight relation with the domestic development of the local states and the world system conditions and process as well. However, not everything differed in the process of change of the two regions. In the last decades, for example, Asian and European governments have engaged themselves in developing their own regional security arrangements in a way that is well represented by the concept of "region security partnership". This concept refers to a set of mechanisms, practices, procedures and institutions that the countries of a region voluntarily share in order to co-manage the security threats and risks that affect the region (Attinà, 2016).

As Jetschke and Murray (2012: 175) remark, the analysts of the comparative study of the two security systems have advanced two perspectives. Some have argued that the European security partnership, which started and developed earlier in the 1970s with the process that is known as the Helsinki Process, has been the model that the Asian policy-makers selected to start building and organising regional security co-operation in the late 1980s and 1990s. In the opposite perspective, instead, security regionalism started and developed in Asia independently from the European regionalism. The present overview of the management of international security by the states of the two regions since the end of the Second World War shares the latter view, the autonomous and unique construction of the Asian security partnership. In fact, there are many and big differences between the two regions' security processes, institutions and mechanisms. They are highlighted also in the present chapter.

In the first phase of contemporary world politics, from the end of the Second World War to the very early 1970s, the United States-led coalition of the Western states, which was dominant in the world economic regimes and in the United Nations, created a network of military pacts and political alliances for the sake of defending the Western nations from the diffusion of the socialist party-led regimes that was pursued by the Soviet Union. The Cold War competition and the two blocs and alignments of countries heavily influenced the management of international security in Europe and Asia.

In Europe, the strengthening of the Western countries was achieved by fostering economic co-operation among the capitalist economies and by integrating the national economies in networks like the Organisation of European Economic Cooperation (today Organisation for Economic Co-operation and Development), and the European Coal and Steel Community (ECSC) and European Economic Community (EEC) that later merged into the European Union. In the defence sector, two opposite groups of countries pursued security co-operation in Europe by integrating the national armies of almost all the West European states in the North Atlantic Treaty Organisation, and the national armies of the East European countries in the Treaty of Friendship, Co-operation, and Mutual Assistance, known as the Warsaw Pact.

In Asia, the difficult process of constructing the nation and the state, and the weak capacity of the new-born states to perform as expected enabled the institutionalisation of authoritarian regimes which chose nationalist strategies of security and economic management. Co-operation on security, then, was negotiated and organised at the bilateral level. The few collective security arrangements and alliances, like the Southeast Asia Collective Defence Treaty, also known as the Manila Pact, were all but vital alliances as were also the organisations they gave place to like the Southeast Asia Treaty Organisation.

The diversity of the politics, economics and security practice that came into existence in the two regions kept going in the following phase of contemporary world politics, from the early 1970s to the end of the 1990s. The circumstances, however, were ripe for experimenting with multilateral arrangements also in security affairs as they were for developing and reshaping multilateralism in international trade. The governments of the two regions, separately and in different ways, decided to address security issues by building regional co-operation systems.

In Europe, the nations of the European Economic Community responded to the crises that in the early 1970s transformed global and regional politics – like the end of the Bretton Woods monetary regime, the oil shocks following the Six-Day War in the Middle East and the end of the Vietnam War with the consequent reshuffling of the US policy in Asia – by deepening the economic integration process and by starting the process of harmonisation of the national foreign policies. In the 1969 The Hague Summit of the Heads of Government and State of the European Economic Community, the member governments decided to enter the process for building the

European Political Co-operation, also known as EPC, that is, the process towards the common foreign, security, and later on defence policy. At the same time, the Conference on Security and Co-operation in Europe (CSCE), the so-called Helsinki Process, overturned the politics of the entire European region by transforming the relations between the two political and military blocs and *de-freezing* of the Cold War. Briefly, the EEC states relaunched the economic and monetary union strategy as the condition for *rescuing the state* from the heavy costs of the growing world economic interdependence that were curtailing the privileged position the European economies had enjoyed in the world market in the last two centuries. This economic and monetary union strategy was started to respond to the first oil crisis and was renewed in the late 1980s by the single market strategy launched by Jacques Delors, the President of the European Commission, to respond to the effects of the globalisation process in Europe. At the same time, the EEC states moved from the European Political Co-operation towards building the common foreign, security and defence policy through a long process of co-operation that is still going on. The process reached the institutional recognition status in the 1986 Single European Act. This was the first "reform treaty" and, in particular, the first treaty of the European integration process with norms about foreign and security policy.

As experts of Asian regionalism remark (see, for instance, Alagappa, 2011; Solingen, 2008), the beginning of the economic community-building process in Asia is also explained by the aspiration of the governments of a group of states, the six Southeast Asia nations that created the Association of Southeast Asian Nations (ASEAN), to strengthen the capacity of the state in the world system as this was evolving from economic interdependence to globalisation. The legitimacy of the ASEAN member nations increased thanks to the ability of the political leaders to drive social change and master the growth of the national economy in the globalising world economy. At the same time, the building of co-operation in the security field was directed towards minimising the role of force among the states and in preventing violent conflict without curtailing their sovereign rights. Together, the Asian leaders were able to consolidate peace and prevent war in conflict-ridden cases, like the China–Taiwan and the North–South Korea cases, also by resorting to deterrent capabilities and the technology of force.

In the current, third phase of the contemporary global politics that started in the 1990s, the overturning of the two regions in respect to the building of security partnership systems is apparent. Today, the security partnership of Europe is in a bare standstill condition. The mechanisms and means that the national governments and the international organisations like NATO and OSCE (the Organisation for Security and Co-operation that took the place of the CSCE) employed twenty years ago to contain the violent disintegration of the Yugoslav Federation and finally helped to bring peace to the Balkans have been employed very much marginally in the

EU security policy and initiatives 63

violent conflict that plagues Ukraine and has achieved no result so far. The backsliding process of the European security partnership is fully shown by the recourse to a very minor instrument of security co-management like the Special Monitoring Mission of the OSCE, which was mandated to report-making about developments on the ground throughout Ukraine. To this, the EU has added the Advisory Mission that assists the government of Kiev to reform the civilian security sector.

In addition to demonstrating the decline of the European security partnership, the contrast of the co-management of the Bosnia-Herzegovina crisis in the 1990s with the almost complete lack of collective management in the Ukraine crisis at the present time demonstrates also what has been argued earlier in this chapter, namely that the political competition between the major states of the global system influences the political process of the regional systems, including the collective security programmes that the states of the region would like to bring forward. Accordingly, the fortune of the European security partnership is strictly linked to, and dependent on, what is going on at the level of the global political competition.

The European security partnership was formed in a long period of time, from the 1970s to the 1990s, thanks to the direct dialogue between the US and the Soviet Union and to the pressure of the European states, especially the Western ones, which played the role of the proactive supporter, and succeeded in pushing the process forward. But they could not help to protect the region security partnership from the consequences on the existing security arrangement in Europe of the choice of the American President Obama for the so-called "pivot" on Asia. The European governments have been unable also to avoid the negative impact of the assertive foreign policy of the Russian president, Vladimir Putin. In particular, at the time of the reorientation of the foreign policy of the US and the relocation of the country's best energies and major resources in Asia, the European governments and the EU institutions have been unable to master the situation created by the clash between the tense Russia–Ukraine relations and the transition of Ukraine to democracy and the aspiration of the Kiev government to tighten relations with the EU. Consequently, they had to adapt their response to the crisis to the soft policy of the American government that refrained from pushing the Russian president towards negotiating the crisis in the frame of the regional management scheme. The circumstances has worsened up to 2018, in which the new American president, Donald Trump, has entrapped the relationships between the Western countries and Russia in a standstill that is hard to know how will be overcome.

Contrary to what happened in Europe in the past twenty years, the building of the regional security arrangement in Asia did not recede in the same period of time. One can say that the many intergovernmental arrangements and the important non-state dialogues that have been created in Asia to manage security and security-related issues did increase the fragmentation of security management rather than the advancement of co-management because the new arrangements have neither the same membership nor the same organisation format. However, the growing number of networks of states that oversee the transnational issues and problems that have an impact on the security of the states is impressive. Briefly, the process of organisation-building for co-managing security issues in Asia is an important one. It also demonstrates that the Asian model of regional co-operation in security affairs is, for the time being, a productive one inasmuch as it has taken a form that is very much distant from the European one.

The experts point to the preservation of state sovereignty as the condition that explains the ability of the Asian governments to produce effective results while organising their co-operation in an institutional framework which is much less formalised and ruled by norms than the European one (Acharya, 2014; Alagappa, 2011). Decision-making is always based on consensus. No state is stripped of veto power. These characteristics that have been put in place in the last decades of the past century by governments that were authoritarian and undemocratic are in place also in today's Asia where some democratic reforms have been made and, as Hameiri and Jones (2016) remark, the transformation of the state by the transnational apparatuses that promote international interdependence are promoting also a change of the past nationalist foreign policy.

EU actorship in global politics

Considering the EU as an international political actor capable *inter alia* of designing and running initiatives in distant geographical areas is a shared concept of the community of students of EU politics. At the same time, the concept has a conventional meaning. Accordingly, a political actor is the unit (person, group and organisation) that has the capability of choosing and accomplishing actions to foster its own interest by influencing the subjects, institutions and events of a political system. Particularly speaking, then, an international political actor is the unit capable of making decisions and actions aimed at influencing other international actors and the institutions and policies of the international political system. Consequently, a union of states is an international political actor on two conditions. First, the member states share the set of values and interests that guide their actions in world politics and interstate relations. Second, the member states mandate the union institutions and offices to act in the international system following the decisions that are made according to the institutionalised decision-making procedures they have agreed on in a legal document binding all of them. These conditions hold true for the EU. The EU member states agree to make joint decisions and do common actions in the world system because they consent to a cluster of international values, share important international interests and pursue common external goals. They have created policy-making offices and operational mechanisms in the areas of international politics and economic external relations and favour the expansion of the international action capabilities of the common institutions to achieve better results out of their common actions in world politics. They have created also institutions and organs mandated to prepare the decisions and to act in world affairs. This assignment is quite recent, especially in defence matters, and is carried out following the traditional intergovernmental methods.

The adhesion of the EU member states to an important set of international values and goals is stated in the Treaty of the European Union. This Treaty depicts the world of the EU international affairs as a pluralist and communitarian system, and the EU as an actor engaged in defending values related to this image of the world. In the pluralist world, individuals, peoples and non-governmental organisations and associations are legitimate primary actors as much as the states. In such a world, communitarian solidarity and the mutual respect of all the subjects must be promoted. States, in particular, are called to respect the communitarian principle of mutual recognition by all the subjects and therefore rigorously adhere and contribute to the development of international law and the principles of the United Nations Charter. In harmony with this pluralist and communitarian view, the European governments see the EU as a legitimate international actor that wants to defend values such as peace and security, sustainable development, free and just trade, elimination of poverty and the defence of all human rights.

The Treaty of the European Union states also that the promotion and defence of European identity, territorial integrity and Europe-specific values and interests are the goals of European international action. It also claims that all available means will be employed to achieve the international goals of the Union. In respect to this, it is worth remembering that the 2003 European Security Strategy[1] stated a preference for effective multilateralism as the fundamental instrument of any international action aimed at fostering the development of a stronger international society, the efficient operation of the international institutions and an international order based on international law.

However, the European governments have not dismantled the foreign policy-making organisation of the member states since they want to promote and defend their national interests also autonomously from the common interest that is defined by the EU institutions. Consequently, many analysts warn about the complexity of building the common foreign and security policy but concede that the EU has international capacity. The less enthusiastic analysts have doubts about the possibility of building the European, that is a single, foreign policy in the near future because the differences between existing national traditions and standards, which are recognised as legitimate by the Treaty, make it impossible to achieve such a goal. To other analysts, since the success of any international actor in the current times depends on the actor's economic strength, the EU's performance in international politics and security depends on the economic resources of the EU and the member states. Last, some analysts claim that Europe's attempt to be an actor in international politics has been linked to the EU's ability to perform as a civilian power in the diffusion of values such as environmentalism, cultural pluralism and human rights. These analysts warn the European leaders about exerting normative power as the best way to be an influential international actor.

With respect to security and defence affairs in particular, the process of integration that sustained the development of the EU over the past sixty years and the pan-European co-operation process known as the Helsinki Process, lasting for about thirty years, from 1971 to the end of the past century, are the seminal experience that created a European preference for the so-called global approach to the solution of problems at the regional and region-to-region levels. Over the past fifty years, the European countries have recognised that peaceful relations and co-operation among neighbouring countries can arise from the balanced and multidimensional management of political, economic, and social interactions. On this premise, the European governments constructed the principle that any co-operative programme must be comprehensive or global – that is, it must encompass the political and security dimension, the economic and financial dimension, and the social, cultural and human dimension.

The myth of the European civil and normative power – articulated by academics and encouraged by the EU institutions and officers – is also at the root of the vision of what European foreign policy values are and what drives the EU's role as an international actor. Indeed, the global approach lies at the core of the EU grand strategy as an international actor and has been restated by the European Global Strategy, the June 2016 document issued by the High Representative, Federica Mogherini, to update the 2003 European Security Strategy. The European Neighbourhood Policy and the region-to-region co-operation programmes, like the ASEM (Asia–Europe Meeting) and the EU–Gulf Co-operation Council relations, are examples of this type of international behaviour. Although, at present, the results of this strategy are meagre, Europe can show itself on the world stage as a new kind of actor with a strong preference for multilateral agreements and for the global approach as the best way to manage security co-operation programmes with other countries.

The EU's security initiatives in Asia

In the European Security Strategy, which was published on the initiative of the High Representative Xavier Solana, the EU declared that interest in the

Asia-Pacific region was focused only on the security challenges posed by nuclear proliferation and terrorism in the region. In the 2016 Global Security Strategy document, instead, the EU acknowledges the centrality of Asia in world affairs and the EU task to cut a fully fledged strategy in the region. The EU is ready to work together with the Asian countries to manage the political and security tensions of the region and avoid violence and the use of force. Aware of the existing tensions that could jeopardise the continued success of Asian economies, the document stresses that the EU can offer consistent and customised support to regional co-operation efforts in Asia. As Stumbaum remarks, "with the Asia-Pacific region not only the global economic powerhouse these days, but also the main trading area for the EU, the EU has a strong interest in stability in the region and in keeping its maritime routes – as 90% of EU trade is seaborne – open and free from sources of conflict, ranging from territorial disputes to piracy" (Stumbaum, 2014: 5).

Such approach towards security in Asia, however, follows the path the EU has gone in the last twenty years. The 1996 agreement to set up the biannual ASEM, the region-to-region dialogue on political, economic, social and cultural issues meeting every two years, is a reminder of the early milestone of the road of the co-operation strategy that the EU and Asian leaders want to foster in the current phase of global politics. Security co-operation is one of the objectives the European and Asian leaders included also in the 2001 solemn declaration on 'Europe and Asia strategy for enhanced co-operation'. It identified six objectives for EU–Asia co-operation, including strengthened peace and security, increasing mutual trade and investment flows, enhanced development co-operation, protection of human rights, spread of democracy and good governance, and actions raising mutual awareness. In 2012 the EU acceded to the Treaty of Amity and Co-operation in Southeast Asia (TAC) and expressed interest in participating in the East Asia Summit (EAS) as well as in the enlarged meeting of ASEAN Defence Ministers. In that year, the *East Asia Policy Guidelines* were published by the Council of the EU to provide a broad orientation for the EU and the member states on the maritime and territorial disputes in East Asia. The Council did not take sides on the sovereignty issues and advocated diplomatic and peaceful conflict resolution according to international law, without any threat or use of force. Further landmarks of the EU engagement in the security of Asia are the EU's strategic partnerships with four Asian countries (China, India, Japan and South Korea), and the longstanding dialogue with ASEAN that includes the EU's active participation in the ASEAN Regional Forum and the above-mentioned admission of the EU to the ASEAN TAC.

The EU encourages also regional integration process in the rest of the Asia-Pacific; notably it supports the South Asian Association for Regional Co-operation (SAARC). Security is not the priority objective of this co-operation between the EU and the eight SAARC member countries, which are Afghanistan, Bangladesh, Bhutan, India, the Maldives, Nepal, Pakistan and Sri Lanka. The EU observer status to SAARC is very important to foster co-operation in financial and technical issues that contribute to the stability of the area and the individual SAARC member countries. In such a perspective, it is worth remembering that in 2004 the EU upgraded to a strategic partnership its existing relationship with the most important SAARC member country, India.

Hard security change in Asia

Experts do not share a single view about the state of international security in Asia today. Many highlight *the volatile security situation* created by the ongoing redefinition of power relationships and the unresolved territorial disputes, especially in maritime areas (see, for example, Reiterer, 2014). Others draw attention to the change of the hard security policy of countries like India and China and remark that such change resembles the change that European states experimented with in the 1990s by fostering the principles of comprehensive and co-operative security. These analysts suggest that some policy diffusion has been going on from Europe to Asia in the field of security policy and co-management (see, in particular, Stumbaum, 2014: 8).

The existing multilateral platforms focused on regional security uphold such an argument about the rising Asian concern about strengthening the co-management of security problems in the region. The informal mechanisms of communication, dialogue and interaction that are organised by actors of different sectors, the so-called "track-two" diplomacy, contribute to the stability of the region by lowering the level of tension in international disputes. An example of these multilateral fora is the Council for Security Co-operation in the Asia-Pacific, which has been debating security issues and providing recommendations to the ASEAN Regional Forum for over twenty years. The track-two diplomacy mechanisms have become increasingly popular because their non-binding, consultative nature reflects the region's culture of informal negotiation that the security experts consider as key to the Asian model of regional security building.

The EU's support to the Asian regional security partnership

The building process of the Asia security partnership is vaguely comparable to the European one. Through a long process that culminated in the 1990 Charter of Paris for a New Europe, the European governments stated the existence of the pan-European security partnership by underwriting common values and ideas like good governance, rule of law, democracy and the social market economy, and by assembling the existing organisations – like the

EU, the Council of Europe, the OSCE and NATO – that had different and complementary tasks and also different and overlapping memberships. Asian recent history, as has been remarked in the first section of this chapter, lacks especially the latter feature in recent European history, that is the multilateral security organisations encompassing all the countries of the region, which in Europe formally managed the transition from the opposite military-alliances security system to the regional security partnership. In other words, the Asian security partnership is different from the European one mainly because the groups of countries that promote security co-operation in Asia do not co-ordinate their initiatives in a formal negotiating environment like that provided by existing security organisations in Europe.

The ASEAN Regional Forum (ARF) is acknowledged as the first multilateral initiative in Asia aimed at fostering security partnership co-operation. The EU, a dialogue partner of ARF, has strongly supported ASEAN and ARF in the view of enhancing their capacity of promoting a pan-Asian security structure. Under the 2013–17 Brunei Plan of Action, the EU and ASEAN are co-operating on a wide range of so-called non-traditional security issues like maritime security, border management, counter-terrorism, disaster management, mediation and crisis response.

Supporting ASEAN's efforts to enhance security through confidence building is an important EU contribution to Asian security. But, "'in the fast-moving developments of forums becoming central and obsolete in the overlapping security forums in East Asia, the ARF has lost a lot of centrality by losing momentum" (Stumbaum, 2014: 19). The meeting of the defence ministers of the states of the EAS, known today as the ASEAN Defence Ministers Meeting Plus (ADMM+) has superseded ARF as the most important Asian security forum. EAS, which has existed since 2005, and the ADMM+, which was inaugurated in 2010, include 16 Asia-Pacific countries and the US and Russia but not the European Union. This notwithstanding, the EU continues to engage in co-operative security in Asia and wants to expand its involvement from hard security to non-traditional security issues. Issues like climate change, environmental degradation, terrorism and pandemics may open up new opportunities for the EU to become more involved in the Asia security co-operation process, especially since the US has decided to leave the 2015 the Paris Agreement of the United Nations Framework Convention on Climate Change.

Conflict over maritime territory in the South China Sea and the East China Sea and also territorial border disputes may escalate into a military confrontation and blow down the security co-operation process. In such a case, the security process would be negatively affected. However, in the current circumstances the EU has few if at any means to play actively to defuse the tensions and avoid such traditional security threats exploding in these times "of testing expansion and limits of capabilities and spheres of influence of the emerging powers, underpinned by bold economic growth, flourishing nationalism and rapidly increasing arms expenditures" (Stumbaum, 2014: 11).

Criticism of the EU security policy in Asia

The lack of EU military capabilities that would back up European political and economic interests in Asia is reason for raising criticism against the EU aspiration to play a role in the security of Asia. As Stumbaum remarks, "Despite the increased efforts, European and EU activities in 'hard security' fields addressing traditional security challenges have so far exhibited only limited success, due to a lack of capabilities, for example in permanently deploying navy capabilities to the Far East, and lack of political will to assign adequate resources" (2014: 20). The EU High Representative has pointed to such weakness of the common defence policy in the Implementation Plan on Security and Defence that was published in November 2016 to forward the common defence policy in line with the Global Security Strategy.

Criticism targets also the focus on humanitarian issues and state failure that has driven the EU response to the domestic crisis of Asian countries involving the security dimension. Such response has been inspired by the objective of underpinning the normative reputation of the European security priorities. The norm promotion policy reflects the academic debate about the European identity and the conception of Europe as a civilian power. The concept has been increasingly contested and today it has lost momentum also because of the EU's negative response to the expectations of many refugees and migrants.

Criticism of the EU's policy towards Asia is overshadowed by the pessimistic view that EU actorship in global affairs is altogether in decline because of the financial crisis and the consequent failure of the European leaders to save the economy of the countries of the Eurozone. In such circumstances, the EU's leverage instruments are not military coercion and economic incentive instruments but the instruments of persuasion and communication.

Last, critics highlight that, beyond the EU's own limitations, the situation in Asia invites caution about furthering the European engagement in security problems. Alignments are rather volatile in Asia today. Neither China nor the US retains a strong influence position in the region. Evolving competition creates new uncertainties.

Concluding remarks

It is in the EU's interest to keep playing the role of the broker of the diplomatic institutions and mechanisms of the region security partnership.

Should the EU choose to become a hard-security actor in Asia, stepping up its military leverage in the region would be counter-productive. As the first section of this chapter contends, the global system dynamics impact on the processes at the regional system level. In clear words, in the political competition of the current phase of global politics, with the three major powers – China, Russia and the US – engaged in a strategic dialogue that mixes co-operation and confrontation, there is no reward for those who want to make groundbreaking strategic moves in the most vibrant region of the world today. Engagement on strengthening regional security mechanisms, on supporting preventive diplomacy and codes of conduct to manage territorial conflicts, and on co-operating on non-traditional security issues remains the most suitable contribution the EU should give to the security of the Asia-Pacific region.

Note

1 The title was 'A Secure Europe in a Better World. European Security Strategy'. In 2008, the High Representative Catherine Ashton released a brief review of the state of execution of European Security Strategy, titled 'Providing Security in a Changing World'.

References

Acharya, Amitav. (2010). "Asia-Pacific Security: Community, Concert or What?", in *Pacific Forum CSIS, Honolulu. PacNet*, 11, http://csis.org/publication/pacnet-11-asia-pacific-security-community-concert-or-what, accessed online 27 March 2016.
Acharya, Amitav. (2014). "Power Shift or Paradigm Shift? China's Rise and Asia's Emerging Security Order", *International Studies Quarterly* 58: 158–73.
Alagappa, Mutiah. (2011). "A Changing Asia: Prospects for War, Peace, Cooperation and Order", *Political Science* 63 (2): 155–85.
Attinà, Fulvio. (2011). *The Global Political System*. Basingstoke: Palgrave.
Attinà, Fulvio. (2016). "Traditional Security Issues", in Wang Janwei and Song Weiqing (eds), *China, The European Union, and the International Politics of Global Governance*. Houndmills: Palgrave Macmillan, pp. 175–94.
EEAS. (2015). *European Union Global Strategic, The EU in a Changing Global Environment*. Brussels, https://europa.eu/globalstrategy/en/european-union-changing-global-environment, accessed online 27 March 2016.
Hameiri, Shahar and Lee Jones. (2016). "Rising Powers and State Transformation: The Case of China", *European Journal of International Relations* 22 (1): 72–98.
Jetschke, Anja, and Philomena Murray. (2012). "Diffusing Regional Integration: The EU and Southeast Asia", *West European Politics* 35 (1): 174–91.
Rees, Nicholas. (2010). "EU and ASEAN: Issues of Regional Security", *International Politics* 47 (3/4): 402–18.

Reiterer, Michael. (2014). "The EU's Comprehensive Approach to Security in Asia", *European Foreign Affairs Review* 19 (1): 1–22.

Solingen, Ethel. (2008). "The Genesis, Design and Effects of Regional Institutions: Lessons from East Asia and the Middle East", *International Studies Quarterly* 52 (2): 261–94.

Stumbaum, May-Britt U. (2014). "How Europe Matters in Asian Security. Addressing Non-Traditional Security Threats under Climate Change Conditions: Towards a New Research Agenda on Norm Diffusion in EU–Asia Security Relations", *NFG Working Paper Series* 9, June, NFG Research Group "Asian Perceptions of the EU", Freie Universität Berlin.

4 Assessing the European Union's economic relations with the Asia-Pacific

Miguel Otero-Iglesias

Introduction

Over the past decade a number of factors have increased the interest of the European Union (EU) and its member states in the Asia-Pacific region: the global financial crisis initiated in the US in 2007–8, which showed the weaknesses of US-led financial capitalism; the Eurozone crisis in 2010–12, which demonstrated the structural flaws of the single currency and the sclerotic state of the Old Continent; Obama's 2011 "pivot" to Asia, which confirmed that the centre of gravity of the world economy is rapidly moving from the Atlantic toward East Asia (Quah, 2011); the signing in 2016 of the Trans-Pacific Partnership (TPP) agreement among 12 Pacific Rim countries,[1] which was supposed to be the biggest trade deal ever, representing close to 40 per cent of the world's GDP; and subsequently, in early 2017, the withdrawal from the agreement by the new American President, Donald Trump, which has left a vacuum in West–East economic relations, which the EU is now eager to fill.

Against this rapidly changing backdrop, with the Asia-Pacific region acquiring ever more importance, the EU has eventually reacted and in its latest trade strategy called *Trade for All* it has declared that strengthening its presence in Asia and the Pacific is one of the key priorities for the future (European Commission, 2015). Concretely the aims established in the document are, first, setting ambitious objectives with China; second, requesting a mandate for Free Trade Agreement (FTA) negotiations with Australia and New Zealand; and third, starting new Association of Southeast Asian Nations (ASEAN) FTA negotiations with the Philippines and Indonesia.

As can be seen, the EU's focus prioritises China, but it covers the whole region, with renewed economic interest in ASEAN and Oceania, and also greater emphasis, from a geostrategic point of view, in strengthening relations with the other Asian powers: South Korea, Japan and India. Two at first sight contradictory factors explain this new European approach to diversify away from the Middle Kingdom in Asia: first, China's rise, which scares most of its neighbours and therefore pushes them to seek more European presence in the region to counterbalance China's presence (especially now that President Trump seems ambivalent about the region); and second, the slowing down of the Chinese economy, which means that a lot of European businesses are starting to look for opportunities in other countries within the region.

Certain authors have stated that the EU and its member states are missing out in the Asia-Pacific (Khandekar, 2013). A few years ago, the dominant view was that Europeans lack a strategy for the region and that, if the EU did not sign the Transatlantic Trade and Investment Partnership agreement with the US, the Old Continent would be excluded from the emerging global trade framework. Pundits used to highlight that since the start of the global financial crisis the EU had signed an FTA only with South Korea and that the European population was (and is) increasingly hostile to free trade and the liberal globalising order so prevalent since the 1990s. Brexit was just the most explicit reflection of this trend. In 2017, however, the context has slightly changed. With a more protectionist President in the White House, the East Asian powers and the EU have come closer together. China knows that it needs the EU to uphold the liberal world order that is so beneficial for its interests and Japan has shown great eagerness to finalise the FTA with the EU to compensate for the rejection of the TPP by the US. Thus, the EU appears to be declining, but it maintains its charm.

Under these circumstances, the following questions arise. Is Europe increasingly retreating in itself and stagnating, as many commentators argue, or does it have the capacity to shape the new phase of globalisation? More specifically, are the EU and its member states losing presence in Asia-Pacific, the most dynamic region in the world? If so, what are the implications for Europe and the world in general? Can this trend, if it is confirmed, be reversed or is it structurally bound to happen? This chapter will try to answer these questions. It aims to assess the EU's economic relations with Asia-Pacific from a holistic point of view, not only from a strict economic angle but also from a geostrategic perspective. Overall, its central message is that the EU's (geo-)economic presence is decreasing relative to China but augmenting in absolute numbers and has upside potential in the future. The chapter is divided in three parts. The first provides a mapping of European economic presence in Asia-Pacific, the second analyses the factors that hinder this presence and the third investigates how the given obstacles could be overcome in the future. The chapter ends with some concluding remarks.

Economic presence of the EU in Asia-Pacific: facts and figures++

The Asia-Pacific region – which has 4.4 billion inhabitants, thus more than half of the world's population – is the most dynamic in the world from an economic point of view. The staggering growth numbers over the past two decades confirm this. The region accounts for roughly two-fifths of global economic growth, according to the World Bank (2016), and in its 2017 regional outlook the IMF (2017a) states that the region continues to be the world leader in growth, although the Fund also warns that medium-term growth faces structural problems, including those arising from population ageing and sluggish productivity.

Hence, Asia-Pacific is full of contrasts. It is home to some of the world's fastest-growing economies such as Cambodia and the Philippines, which are growing at around 7 per cent (IMF, 2017b), and some of the key (re-)emerging global powers such as China and India, but it also hosts two-thirds of the world's poor. This fact proves one of the many challenges that Asia still needs to overcome: poverty and inequality. But it also indicates the enormous potential in the region.

The role of the Asia-Pacific as a prominent player in the world has led to the "pivot to Asia" trend, as President Obama named it: a political and diplomatic effort to tighten relations with this set of countries in order to seek advantage from their relatively new economic and political power. While the US has been able to change its strategy in a more forceful and cohesive way due to its role as the only global superpower (at least until the arrival of President Trump), traditionally the EU's approach toward the Asia-Pacific has been much less co-ordinated and generally based on its soft-power approach: including seeking economic alliances such as FTAs, increasing the number of mid- and high-level official meetings and consolidating the Asia–Europe Meeting (ASEM), established in 1996, as the primary platform for diplomatic exchanges between the EU and the Asia-Pacific countries. It is well known that the EU is mostly seen as an economic actor in the region, although more recently it is trying to develop a more geostrategic presence, covering security and defence, traditionally fields delegated solely to the US (Reiterer, 2016).

Asia counts with four of the EU's strategic trade partners (China, India, Japan and the Republic of Korea), China being by far the most important. Nonetheless, the ASEAN grouping is EU's fifth biggest trading partner, while the EU is the second biggest partner for ASEAN (after China), and before Japan and the US. The economic and political relations have intensified enormously over the past ten years. The numbers speak for themselves. Trade between the EU and ASEAN has almost doubled to over €200 billion a year (see Figure 4.5), with a persistent trade deficit for the Europeans. The EU is the biggest provider of foreign direct investment (FDI) to ASEAN, representing 22 per cent of the total. The EU "is in fact the number one foreign investor with an investment stock of €153 billion. ASEAN's investment into Europe is also growing and reached a total stock of over €57 billion at the end of 2013" (Yeo, 2016).

On the political front, the past years "have seen the largest number of high level visits to Southeast Asia", and "in October 2014, the EU and

ASEAN leaders met in Milan, the first of such meetings since 2007" (EU External Action Service, 2015). In 2017 there was also an EU–ASEAN Senior Officials' Meeting in Bangkok commemorating the fortieth anniversary of EU–ASEAN dialogue relations, the

fiftieth anniversary of ASEAN and the sixtieth anniversary of the Treaties of Rome. However, the attempt started in 2007 to negotiate an FTA with this region has not succeeded, hence the EU is now trying to boost the process with some of its members individually.

Negotiations with ASEAN countries

Negotiations of an FTA concluded in 2014 with Singapore, and the text "needs now to be formally approved by the European Commission and then agreed upon by the Council of Ministers and ratified by the European Parliament" (European Commission, 2017a). In addition, the European Court of Justice decided in 2017 that this treaty is of mixed competences, especially when it comes to investor–state dispute arrangements, therefore the text will also need to be approved by the national parliaments. This agreement is certainly important for the EU given that "Singapore is by far the EU's largest commercial partner in ASEAN, accounting for slightly under one-third of EU–ASEAN trade in goods and services, and roughly two-thirds of investments between the two regions" (European Commission, 2017a).

The text of the Vietnam–EU FTA was published on 1 February 2016, following the announcement that the negotiations had been concluded. It has now been translated into all the EU languages and Vietnamese, and the legal services are checking that everything is sound. Once this has been concluded, the Commission will present it to the Council of Ministers and finally the ratification and signature by the European Parliament will be needed. The Commission believes the treaty will enter into force in 2018, although this might be delayed because certain EU member states are concerned about the human rights record in Vietnam.

As for the FTAs with Malaysia and Thailand, "both are not progressing well because of domestic political problems, and, for Thailand, this includes concerns over use of trafficked labour in its seafood industry" (Yeo, 2016: 9). In March 2017 there appeared to be a breakthrough in the negotiations with Malaysia as the EU decided to resume the negotiations, but a few months later the Malaysian government again poured cold water over the agreement when the EU declared that it would establish tariffs and technical barriers on Malayan palm oil, one of the key exporting commodities of the country.

Following the *Trade for All* strategy, the EU has also started FTA negotiations with the Philippines. The first meeting took place in May 2016 and the second in February 2017. The Commission is optimistic about the final

Assessing the EU's economic relations 77

outcome, but the talks are in an early stage and the next round of negotiations had not been agreed by the time of writing (December 2017).

Indonesia, for its part, is the largest economy within ASEAN and a key partner of the EU. The total trade between them in 2015 amounted to €25.3 billion. Investment by EU businesses in Indonesia currently exceeds €30 billion, making the EU Indonesia's third largest trading partner and one of its main foreign direct investors (European Commission, 2017b). However, FTA talks started only in 2016 and, as in the case of the Philippines, have had only two rounds of negotiations. Thus, the current signed documents between the EU and Indonesia are limited to a Partnership Co-operation Agreement (PCA)[2] that entered into force in 2014, the first one of this kind between the EU and its Southeast Asian partners. When it comes to PCAs, negotiations with the Philippines, Singapore, Thailand and Vietnam have been completed. However, the PCA with Thailand will not be ratified until a democratic government is in place; and negotiations are ongoing with Malaysia and Brunei (European Parliament, 2016).

Negotiations with Japan and China

Thus, as mentioned above, the only completed and fully operational FTA between the EU and an Asia-Pacific country is the one signed in 2011 with South Korea. Negotiations are also ongoing with the two major economies of the region: Japan, and China. Progress has been slow with Japan but has accelerated since the arrival of Trump to the White House, while substantial disagreements, both in the political sense and in the content of the possible compromises, are blocking the process with China.

Japan and the EU have been embarked on FTA negotiations since March 2013 and they reached a political agreement in July 2017 (just a few days before the G20 summit in Germany) and a final accord in December 2017. From the start both the European Commission and the European Parliament supported close relations with Japan and endorsed the launch of an FTA. However, they insisted on conditions designed to ensure that both partners benefit equally from the deal and that negotiations will be stopped if Japan does not deliver on its commitments to reduce technical trade barriers (European Parliament, 2017). With the withdrawal from the TPP agreement by US President Donald Trump, Japan appears to have softened its stand and facilitated progress in the negotiations towards achieving both an Economic and a Strategic Partnership Agreement. The EU, for its part, has always been eager to conclude negotiations with Japan and bring new momentum to its trade agenda in the Asia-Pacific after concluding its FTA with Canada in 2016. Furthermore, the European business community has always wanted a comprehensive FTA with Japan in order to achieve "ambitious results in terms of market access, procurement, the removal of non-tariff measures, geographic indications, services and investment" (Beyrer,

2016). This seems to be included in the final text (with Japan allowing penetration in the traditionally protected car and financial sectors), but there are still disagreements in regards to the investment dispute mechanisms (with the EU promoting its Multilateral Investment Court idea), regulation and standards in various sectors and information sharing.

China and the EU are key trading partners and their economies are strongly interlinked, with the EU being China's top trading partner (€429 billion, 13.4 per cent of total share), closely followed by the US (€396 billion, 12.4 per cent). For the EU, the US is the top-trading partner (€484 billion, 14.2 per cent), and China comes second (€428 billion, 12.5 per cent) (Business Europe 2015: 3). Their economic and political interdependence is reflected in the strategic partnership that the EU established in 2003, the role that China has played in helping to stabilise the Eurozone during its 2010–12 existential crisis (Otero-Iglesias, 2014), and the launching of negotiations for a Bilateral Investment Agreement (BIA) in 2012 (Godement and Stanzel, 2015). Traditionally, the EU has always been one of the biggest FDI providers to China, but slowly China is also becoming a big investor in Europe. In 2016 Chinese foreign direct investment in the EU reached €35 billion, an increase of 77 per cent compared to 2015, and overall Chinese investment stock accumulated since 2000 has now surpassed €100 billion, with the UK, Germany, Italy and France the largest beneficiaries (Hanemann and Huotari, 2017). This shows that, despite its apparent decline, the Old Continent remains a very attractive place to do business.

The aim of the BIA is to provide legal certainty for investors about the general rules of fair treatment in both China and the EU, which may lead to longer-term investments (Godement and Stanzel, 2015). There are, however, significant disagreements that prevent progress on the BIA and then the start of negotiations on an FTA. China is very cautious when it comes to opening up its public procurement and services markets to European competition while the Europeans fear unfair Chinese competition in trade, to the point that they have decided to join the US in not granting China "market economy" status at the end of 2016 as was envisioned in the World Trade Organisation (WTO) agreement, prompting immediately a legal challenge by China to the WTO (Donnan et al., 2016). During the past years, major trade disputes brought both parties in front of the WTO (especially in the raw materials, iron, steel, footwear and solar panel sectors), which shows that, although economic and political relations have intensified between China and EU member states, tensions and disputes have also risen. This is especially the case because both sides have very different normative stands on what role the state should play in the market and the development of society.

China's new Silk Road, called the "Belt and Road Initiative" (BRI) or the "One Belt, One Road" project is another big, and ambitious, jump in bringing China and Europe closer together, but it has also generated certain tensions (Van der Putten et al., 2016). China's increased economic presence in the southern and eastern flanks of the EU, and the establishment of the 16 + 1 format in the latter, and attempts to establish something similar in the former, are regarded with huge suspicion in Brussels. Furthermore, the purchases of high-tech companies such as Italy's Pirelli (tyres) and Germany's Kuka (robots) by Chinese buyers have set off the alarm bells in a number of countries, encouraging the ministers of the economy of Germany, France and Italy to ask the Commission to study the possibility of establishing a European foreign-investment screening mechanism similar to the Committee on Foreign Investment in the US. Increasingly, the mood among European policy-makers towards China, even in Germany, is hardening. The feeling is that China has benefited from European economic openness, but that reciprocity, although long promised, has never happened. To the contrary, as the EU Chamber of Commerce indicates in its annual position papers, the business environment in China is getting increasingly tougher for European companies.[3]

Nonetheless, despite the tensions and obstacles, the EU–China strategic partnership is progressing. The entry of numerous EU member states as founding members in the Asian Infrastructure and Investment Bank (AIIB) and the active support of the Europeans in favour of the internationalisation of the RMB are the latest examples of this long-brewing trend (Casarini and Otero-Iglesias, 2016). Whether this is enough to sign a free trade and/or a bilateral investment agreement is a different matter.

Less progress with India

Finally, perhaps the least developed EU strategic partnership in the Asia-Pacific is the one with India, despite the EU being India's largest trading partner before China and the US. In 2016 annual trade did not even reach €80 billion, and the latest 2015 investment figures show that the overall FDI stock of the EU in India was only €51 billion (European Commission, 2017c). India and the EU started negotiations for an FTA in 2007 but progress has been very slow. As a matter of fact, there was no EU–India summit from 2012 until 2016 (Panda, 2016), which shows two things: first, that for many years the EU has been inward-looking due to its crisis, and, second, that 2016 was the year of reaching out again under the new *Trade for All* strategy.

Obstacles and barriers to the EU's Presence in the Asia-Pacific

Domestic divisions

The relative absence of the EU in partnership with the Asia-Pacific when compared to China and the US is due to the political divisions in Europe.

These differences have increased over the past years. The EU is not only disunited in its foreign relations; the Eurozone crisis, the Grexit and Brexit debates and the West versus East chasm in tackling the migrant crisis have also shown the internal tensions within the club. The truth is that over the past two decades, first with the negotiations of the Lisbon Treaty and then with the aftermath of the global, Eurozone and refugee crises, the EU has been too occupied with sorting out its own house to be able to have a major impact overseas. As long as the EU remains more united than an international organisation but less so than a federal union, it will always be in a disadvantage against continental-sized and more cohesive economies such as the US and China. The fact is that the EU member states compete; they do not work together in the Asia-Pacific.

When analysing the economic relations between the EU and the Asia-Pacific one is obliged to look at the national level. There one can see major success stories, especially when it comes to German, French and Dutch businesses. As a matter of fact, this competition is not necessarily bad per se. It encourages the other European countries to follow the lead. Italy has in recent years increased its efforts to penetrate Asia. The same goes for Spain, although from a lower level. Business associations in these countries are starting to put more efforts and resources into finding business opportunities not only in China but also in Japan, Korea and ASEAN. However, as mentioned, in many ways these European divisions are also a hindrance to project power and influence and to utilising limited resources in the most efficient manner.

It is difficult to know to what extent European divisions are a positive or negative feature. Perhaps if the Europeans were more united, there would be less competition between them and less market penetration. Historians have always highlighted that one of the features that made the Old Continent dominate the world was its internal competition which had lasted since as long ago as the Middle Ages, first between the Italian city states, and afterwards between the major European nation states: England, France and Spain (Ferguson, 2012). It could also be that, despite more unity among Europeans in political and diplomatic terms, with the EU emerging as a more cohesive geopolitical actor, on the economic front competition would continue, making the Europeans an even more powerful force both economically and politically. Counterfactuals are always difficult to construct. What is true is that, when one looks at the figures, the Europeans have not performed that badly over the past decade, despite the numerous internal crises.

If we take South Korea and ASEAN as case studies, we can see that China (including Hong Kong and Macao) has been without doubt the big winner in increasing market share (see Figures 4.1 and 4.2). We can see that China's share of imports to South Korean and ASEAN imports, has gone from less than 10 per cent in 1996 to around 25 per cent in 2016.

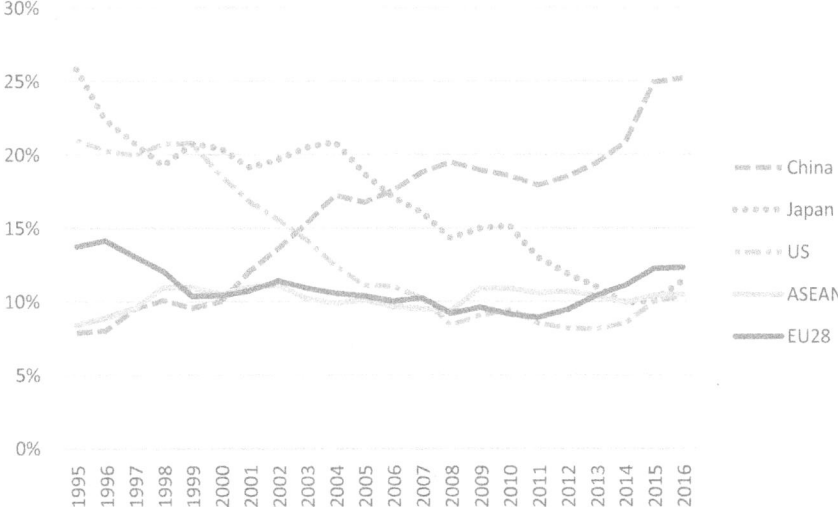

Figure 4.1 Percentage share of South Korean imports by origin, 1995–2016.
Source: UNCTAD

This is a clear reflection of China's rise. However, when it comes to the second biggest loser after the obvious case of Japan, in contrast to the general perception, it is not necessarily the EU but the US. Its market share of South Korean imports has decreased from over 20 per cent to a little more than 10 per cent, while that of the EU has hovered between 15 per cent and 10 per cent, performing better since the global financial crisis. A similar story can be observed in ASEAN. Also there, while both have gone from 15 per cent to around 10 per cent of market share, the EU seems to perform slightly better than the US.[4] This proves that the EU is not in as sharp a decline as it is widely portrayed as being.

Interestingly, when one looks at the figures of the largest EU member states, as predicted it becomes immediately obvious that Germany has benefited enormously from the development of this part of the world (Figures 4.3 and 4.4). Its annual export figuress to South Korea and ASEAN have gone from around US$10 billion in the 1990s to a peak of over $30 billion in recent years. But in these two cases exports have increased for all major European economies, including Italy and Spain. It is also true, however, that while their overall volumes have increased their relative market shares have decreased. This is a good illustration of the general geo-economic and, one could say, geopolitical trend that we are witnessing. The Asia-Pacific economic cake is increasing. This provides a situation of win–win, as Chinese policy-makers like to highlight. But in relative terms

Figure 4.2 Percentage share of ASEAN imports by origin, 1995–2016. Source: UNCTAD

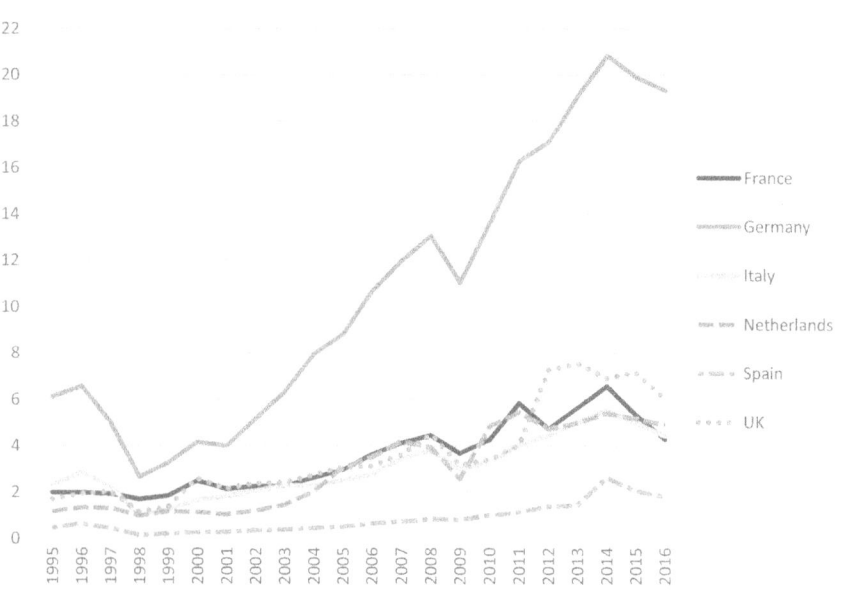

Figure 4.3 Main EU countries' exports to South Korea in absolute figures, 1995–2016 (US$ billion). Source: UNCTAD

Assessing the EU's economic relations

Figure 4.4 Main EU countries' exports to ASEAN in absolute figures, 1995–2016 (US$ billion). Source: UNCTAD

China is considerably augmenting its market share, while the US and Europe, and especially Japan, are seeing theirs decline.

Would the EU be able to reverse this trend by being more united? It is difficult to say for the reasons given above, but, as long as current demographic trends do not change, the most likely scenario is that the EU's relative economic presence in the Asia-Pacific region might continue to increase in absolute numbers as long as the region maintains its economic dynamism, but in relative terms the big winner will be China, and in the future some of the ASEAN economies, and even India, which have much younger and still increasing populations.

Asian regionalism

When trying to become a relevant actor in the region, the EU is facing a new reality: Asian regionalism. There is an intention in this region of becoming progressively united institutionally and economically in order to enlarge its presence and strengthen its performance as a whole in the ever-more competitive world of international business and relations. This is a trend that will only increase if the US finally decides to disengage from its international duties as world leader, as feared by the new secretary general of the United Nations and many others (Sengupta, 2017). China, for instance, is certainly keen to take up the baton and deepen regional integration the Asian way

– in other words, respecting national sovereignty, with loose and flexible institutionalisation and bottom-up, with economic rather than political actors driving the regionalisation process further.

For the EU this is a new reality. ASEAN does not function as a bloc. Therefore a bi-regional trade agreement is almost impossible. Furthermore, the emerging ASEAN common market, labelled the ASEAN Economic Community (AEC), will be very different from the EU one. The political, economic, cultural and even religious differences among its member states are huge and the "blind adherence to the overarching principles of consensus and non-interference, combined with the lack of a robust and sound institutional architecture, have left intact the problem of ensuring compliance and effective implementation of targets by national governments and agencies". In fact, "although 95% of tariff lines are at zero, non-tariff barriers on goods and services render cross-border trade particularly painful" (Seller, 2016). But this institutional weakness does not mean that East Asian economic interdependence is not progressing at considerable speed. If we look at the figures, one can see that intra-ASEAN trade has increased enormously over the past years, and its relative share has kept up despite economic growth, more consumption and the increased presence of a heavyweight such as China (see Figures 4.5 and 4.6).

Asian intra-regional trade as a whole has been growing enormously (14 per cent per year as opposed to 11 per cent with the rest of the world),

Figure 4.5 ASEAN trade with main trading partners in absolute figures, 1995–2016 (US$ billion). Source: UNCTAD

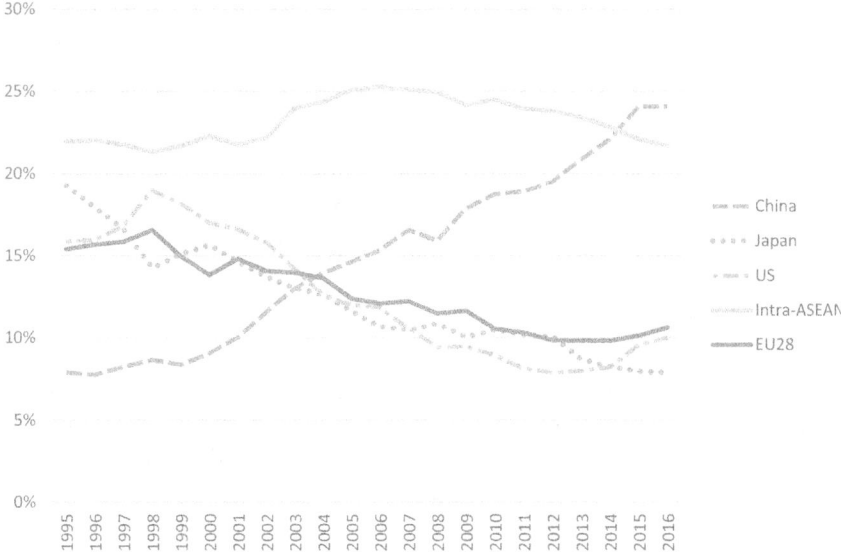

Figure 4.6 Percentage share of ASEAN commerce with main trading partners, 1995–2016. Source: UNCTAD

with plenty of initiatives aiming towards a Free Trade Area of the Asia-Pacific: the now defunct TPP which may revive at some point; the China-led Regional Comprehensive Economic Partnership; the China–Japan–South Korea Trilateral; and the AEC (Khandekar, 2013). All of them are organised by the Asia-Pacific Co-operation (APEC) and serve as examples of regional trade associations where the EU remains excluded while the US is present. Furthermore, the proliferation of bilateral FTAs within the region contributes to the so-called "noodle bowl": a net of overlapping agreements that may cause the problem of having a product being subject to different tariffs, but a good example of how Asian regionalism advances bottom-up with multiple arrangements which should not be underestimated either at the economic or at the geostrategic level.[5]

It is precisely because of this complex network of deals, and the fact that the difficulties of negotiating FTAs with multilateral actors are greater, that the EU has been focusing on a bilateral approach, as we have seen, negotiating FTAs with different Asian countries individually.

According to Gauri Khandekar, Asia's noodle bowl phenomenon essentially responds to geographical proximity, some Asian countries' unilateral liberalisation via bilateral FTAs and the recession following the global financial crisis in the EU and the US (Khandekar, 2013). Also, China is shifting its export-oriented economy to a consumption-based model, in which countries like Vietnam, Indonesia and Malaysia, with their inexpensive and abundant labour supplies, are meant to become Asia's next production bases. All this means that in the future it will be much harder for Europeans to penetrate Asia, because competition will be harder and because the local-regional consumption tastes, trends and desires might be more difficult to grasp from Europe or from a Western mindset.

US dominance and Chinese power in Asia

Another big obstacle to the EU's aim of achieving the status of relevant economic and strategic actor in Asia-Pacific is the presence of the two major global powers in the region – the US and China – which are increasingly seen to be in competition for supremacy not only in the Asia-Pacific but also in the world (Mearsheimer, 2014).

On the one hand, China appears as the Asian leader that everyone fears because of its military power and authoritarianism, but it is at the same time the main economic engine of the region. The US, on the other hand, intends to compensate for China's pre-eminence by promoting its role as a commercial and security partner, through the conclusion of commercial and investment agreements that exclude the Asian giant, as was the case of TPP promoted by the Obama Administration; and by developing a more active role in regional institutional fora such as APEC, and having a much harder diplomatic rhetoric towards Beijing, which is the case now with the Trump Administration. There is no doubt that the US takes advantage of its military potential in order to come across as a security and peace defender by actively denouncing China's more aggressive stand in its border disputes such as those in the South China Sea and its softer approach towards North Korea.

Both powers are doing their best to attract the rest of the Asia-Pacific countries as their allies, with the main intention of containing each other's influence. It is also clear that many ASEAN countries are keen to have the US as their security guarantor in order to reduce China's influence and North Korea's threat. In a situation like this, the role of the EU, especially in political and security terms, remains minor. This has naturally also consequences for the economic dimension. Europe lags behind the US in defence- and security-related businesses and this is starting to be acknowledged by the Europeans who have started to insist that they have a key interest in participating in securing the trade routes from Asia to Europe (Hébrard, 2017).

Ultimately trade and investment agreements have also a geopolitical dimension and in this regard the Europeans until the arrival of Trump were falling behind. The EU was far from reaching a major comprehensive trade agreement like the American-driven TPP. As mentioned above, the EU's approach in terms of commercial partnerships is more bilateral and was seen as relatively weak compared to the one coming from the US. However, with a more inward-looking and protectionist US led by Trump, even the EU's small advances seem to be giant's steps in improving economic, and even political, co-operation with the Asia-Pacific region and keeping the global order as free and liberal as possible.

The untapped potential in EU–Asia-Pacific economic relations

While Asia's new regionalism, international and internal political differences and the slowdown of the EU's economy during the past years are admittedly great obstacles to the EU's becoming Asia-Pacific's substantial business and strategic partner, there is considerable potential in the relationship. The latest breakthrough with Japan, the third biggest economy in the world, towards a comprehensive economic and political partnership agreement is a clear example.

A new approach to the FTAs

Given that bilateral FTAs have become the EU's main tool for strengthening its relations with the Asia-Pacific, it is likely that Brussels will focus its efforts on some strategic countries. In this sense: Japan now, and later Taiwan, China, and Indonesia, are likely to take a predominant role. Interestingly, in order to be closer to the region, the European Commission also announced in September 2017 that it was seeking a mandate to start FTA negotiations with Australia and New Zealand (Stone, 2017).

Being Asia's most developed economy, a Free Trade and Investment Agreement (FTIA) with Japan would provide "at least the same market expansion opportunities (scale and scope) to EU firms and consumers than the combined three (possible) FTAs with Brazil, India and Russia" (Messerlin, 2012: 5). Plus, Japan's market is sometimes better regulated than some of the Europeans' and it can be a door to reinforce EU's relations with the ASEAN, owing to the close ties between them and Japan. Last but not least, Japan's participation in the possible revival of the TPP makes it even a more attractive partner.

As for Taiwan, the justifications are very similar and have been laid out in the EU's "Trade for all" strategy: attractive economic activity, good networking with other Asian countries and a pro-trade regulation. Taiwan is a key hub in Asian value chains and the EU has developed over the years a strong regulatory co-operation with the island (EU External Action Service, 2016). Also, like the EU and China, it has remained excluded from the TPP negotiations, so an alliance between them as a response to this could be beneficial for both. Logically, China can become an insurmountable obstacle to achieving an investment agreement with Taiwan, but from a European perspective it could be seen as a first step towards reaching an agreement with China because European businesses based in Taiwan could penetrate the Chinese market more easily.

China's regulatory trade norms in regards to market access are not so advantageous, rather on the contrary. The EU's biggest worries when trading with China are its lack of transparency, discriminatory tariffs against foreign companies, a strong intervention by the government, which favours state-owned enterprises; and a poor protection of intellectual property rights (European Commission, 2017d). Nonetheless, it would be – together with Japan – the most interesting FTIA to achieve for the EU due to the economic size and potential of the country. With the arrival of Trump, a more protectionist and China-bashing US president, there might be a window of opportunity to conclude the Bilateral Investment Agreement and start negotiations for an FTA. In the 2017 World Economic Forum in Davos, the Chinese President, Xi Jinping, declared China was ready to step into the gap left by the US in the promotion of the next phase of globalisation. European officials should use these words to convince their Chinese counterparts to open further their internal market, especially in the service sectors. Reciprocity is here the key word. China, as it develops, is starting to invest considerable sums in the European market. If it wants to have easier and more secure access to the more mature markets of the Old Continent, it will have to reciprocate at home (García-Herrero et al., 2017). Likewise, the EU will have to resist its internal protectionist tendencies if it wants to continue to benefit from the development of China (Seaman et al., 2017).

After South Korea, China and Japan, Indonesia is certainly the most important player in the Asia-Pacific region. It is the largest economy of ASEAN, representing over one-third of the region's GDP. It has 250 million inhabitants and it is a member of the G20. It is no surprise therefore that the EU has in recent years intensified its desires to sign a trade and investment agreement with this country. From the Indonesian side the attitude is also very positive. If Singapore and Vietnam can sign an FTA with the EU, Indonesia should explore the possibility too. Both sides have set ambitious goals since the beginning of the negotiations, declaring that the final aim should be to reach an agreement "that facilitates trade and investments and covers a broad range of issues, including customs duties and other barriers to trade, services and investment, access to public procurement markets, as well as competition rules and protection of property rights" (European Commission, 2016). The agreement will also include a comprehensive chapter aiming to include environmental protection and social development.

Political commitment and defence of human rights

For critics, the EU is thought to be basing its economic alliances in an "old development and technical assistance model" (Gippner, 2016), ignoring the real economic significance of the region as an emerging global power and its changing political environment. In this sense, the EU has still enormous potential to leverage its role as a policy leader in order to serve as an example for Asian countries on values such as freedom, democracy, rule of law, environmental protection and human rights. Fortunately, European leaders are starting to understand that economic interest cannot by itself drive the whole of the EU–Asia-Pacific partnership: Asians attach strong importance to inter-personal relations, so a deeper political involvement beyond the ASEM framework would be necessary if the EU wants to play a more active role in the region.

Nevertheless, this position would need to be held carefully and coherently: it is not feasible to pursue the conclusion of trade and investment alliances and to turn a blind eye to human rights violations or corrupt political regimes. Furthermore, Europe also needs to drop its Eurocentric lens. It cannot give lectures on regional institutionalisation and development models. This will not be accepted any more by Asian leaders. A more multipolar economic world order means also the acceptance of different models of development and international relations. The EU should continue to support a liberal, rules- and norms-based multilateral global economic governance, but it should also draw on the experiences of its own member states in regards to understanding that moving from a *dirigiste*-state interventionist capitalist model to a market-oriented one is never easy and needs to be nurtured by compensatory measures. In this regard, the Commission's latest reflection on harnessing globalisation (European Commission, 2017e) is a welcome step but it is still too much focused on "lowering barriers" and "preserving the EU's high social, labour and environmental standards" without sufficient reflection on how this can be achieved in partnership with the other trading partners, especially in Asia.

Security matters for trade

Recent events around the world such as the South China Sea conflict, the tensions in the Korean peninsula, the refugee crises in Europe and international conflicts such as the ones in Syria, Libya and Afghanistan, or the rise of Islamic-extremist terrorism, have shown the importance of the issue of security in all its dimensions, from the hard to the soft.

Therefore, the EU is starting to combine its *soft power* model with a stronger foreign policy that can make it regionally more relevant as a *hard power* actor by focusing more on security-related matters (Berkofsky, 2014).

The role of the advocate of the rule of law and moral values needs to be backed by a firmer attitude when needed to apply coercive measures or even the use of military power. Given the competitive environment in Asia, with actors in play such as China and the US, this is the only way for the EU to be able to achieve credibility and international respect (Gippner, 2016).

To make this possible, the determination to reinforce the military and security dimensions must be supported by a unified political will. The EU is certainly known for basing its foreign relations in economic interests first: even within its own territory, economic integration is far more advanced than political integration, not to speak about the military sphere. As a result, when the EU wants to act as a unified actor, its response to certain events such as the refugee crisis and the South China Sea dispute has been rather weak, giving an impression to the rest of the world that does not benefit Europe for the purpose of becoming an influential player.

However, the internal weaknesses in Europe can be overcome in the medium to long term. The increased threat of Russia, the refugee crisis, Brexit and the election of Trump in the US have accelerated the ambitions to create a defence union in Europe. These moves are still in an embryonic state, but the more the Europeans are faced with external threats and the more the US makes clear that it is not willing to be Europe's security guarantor *in perpetuum*, the more the Europeans will have to come closer together in order to be better protected. Nonetheless, until this sort of unity is achieved (if it happens at all) some of the most important strategic countries in Europe such as France and the UK should certainly have a more active military presence in the Asia-Pacific to secure trade routes, while at the same time the EU can present itself, like ASEAN, as this neutral player in the emerging rivalry between the US and China.

Participation in the Belt and Road Initiative

Europe's centrality and neutrality are visible when analysing China's BRI. It is clear that this is a strategy designed in Beijing that starts with domestic considerations: to improve the connectivity of the western, and less developed, part of the country; to export the over-capacity; to internationalise Chinese expertise and competitive advantage in sectors such as transport and infrastructure; to increase access to brands and technology abroad; and to gather more political influence in Southeast Asia, Central Asia, Russia and even eastern and southern Europe. But tthe reality is that the BRI has Europe as its end destination, which automatically makes the Old Continent the western pillar of the whole project. This means that European actors should be well placed to shape the initiative and increase their presence and influence eastwards along the new Silk Road all the way to Beijing and Shanghai.

Here the geostrategic and geo-economic balancing act will be to find the complementarities between the mature and developed markets of Europe and the dynamic and fast-growing economies of Asia. The willingness to co-operate between China and the EU member states is certainly there. The inclusion of Europeans in the AIIB and the participation of China in the European Bank for Reconstruction and Development are good examples. Overall, as Garcia-Herrero et al. (2017: viii–ix) point out:

> [BRI] related Chinese investment, alongside the EU's "Juncker Plan", can help address some EU infrastructure bottle-necks, especially in port and rail facilities in Central and Eastern Europe, and through new rail freight routes between China and Europe ... For their part, EU financial institutions can bring expertise in the long-term financial management of complex infrastructure investment projects, while European investment could help BRI projects meet the necessary global standards for environmental and other forms of sustainability.

Here both Europeans and Chinese need to be smart. They need to understand that the BRI project will not progress if the former try to derail it and the latter try to implement it the "Chinese way" without the participation and input of the other partners, be they Asian or European.

Conclusions

Economic relations between the EU and the Asia-Pacific are one-sided. The economic side is very strong but the political and strategic side is underdeveloped. This unbalanced relationship is problematic because usually the economic dimension cannot progress without the political one. China's new BRI, which aims to bring China and Europe closer together, is the latest example. Thus, EU–Asia-Pacific economic relations must be understood in the context of the interaction of multiple actors and interests. The economic but also political, diplomatic and security spheres should be analysed when studying the interactions between these two regions. This chapter has been an attempt to do so.

The EU appears to be in the process of moving beyond the mere economic and commercial focus that drives its relations with the Asia-Pacific. This trend is likely to continue now that the US has in Trump an illiberal president and now that the benefits of unfettered globalisation are openly questioned inside the EU. In the next years the EU will be faced with a paradox. While it wants to benefit from Asia-Pacific strengths, which are based on its economic growth and dynamism, it is precisely in its flaws (political conflicts, human rights violations, institutional and law-enforcement weakness) that the EU has the possibility of emphasising its importance as an ally by offering its collaboration in these areas. Strengthening the relations in this sense (without falling into the old-fashioned patronising mode), will make it much easier to be seen as a reliable and profitable trade and investment partner by the Asians.

A coherent European foreign policy that englobes all of the above-mentioned aspects, and therefore combines the economic with the political, could increase the EU's strategic presence not only in the Asia-Pacific but also in the rest of the world. In a time when the liberal order is under considerable stress from protectionist and populist forces the EU will need to move in parallel on the two fronts. Domestically, by deciding how it reorganises itself in order to confront in a more robust manner the many challenges that come with globalisation. And internationally, by ensuring that globalisation does not evolve into deglobalisation driven by geopolitical and social conflicts (European Commission, 2017e). In many ways, the US apparent (although certainly not conclusive) withdrawal from its leadership role serves as an opportunity for the EU. If it is able to overcome Brexit successfully and complete the governance architecture of the Eurozone, as the core group of the remaining EU, it can certainly become one of the forces, or perhaps the leading force, in shaping the new phase of globalisation marked by the fourth industrial revolution and a more multipolar world order. As of now it is well positioned to do so. Economically the figures show that China has gained a lot of market share in the Asia-Pacific, as it could not be otherwise, but the European economies are keeping up well, in certain cases even better than the US, thanks to their competitiveness and innovation. Finally, on the governance side, the EU is also at the vanguard in proposing new multilateral mechanisms, whether in state-investor disputes, public procurement, funds to mitigate the effects of globalisation, tackling tax avoidance or protecting the environment. However, in order to keep its economic and political standing the EU will need to have strong partners. The US, of course. But increasingly also the major economies of the Asia-Pacific, the fastest-growing and most dynamic region on earth.

Notes

1 These are the countries that have signed the TPP: Australia, Brunei, Canada, Chile, Japan, Malaysia, Mexico, New Zealand, Peru, Singapore, United States and Vietnam.
2 With a more general scope than FTAs, Partnership and Co-operation Agreements seek to provide a suitable framework for political dialogue; to support the efforts made by the countries to strengthen their democracies and develop their economies; to accompany their transition to a market economy and to encourage trade and investment.
3 The European Union Chamber of Commerce in China Position papers can be found here: www.europeanchamber.com.cn/en/publications-position-paper.

4 The reader might be thinking that this comparison is unfair given that the EU has increased the number of member states over the years, but the ten newcomer states do not export much to this region so their contribution has been very small.
5 More information about the intra-Asian trade agreements and the 'noodle bowl' phenomenon can be found in M. Okano-Heijmans, 'Trade Diplomacy in EU–Asia Relations: Time for a Rethink', Clingendael Institute, The Hague, September 2014.

References

Berkofsky, Axel. (2014). "The European Union (EU) in Asian Security: Actor with a Punch or Distant Bystander", *Asia Pacific Review* 21 (2): 61–85.
Beyrer, Markus J. (2016). "The EU–Japan FTA/EPA and Regulatory Cooperation: Where We Stand, What We Want, and the Role of Business", EU–Japan Business Round Table, Tokyo, 20 April, www.eu-japan-brt.eu/system/files/presentations/2016-TD1-BusinessEurope.pdf, accessed online 27 March 2018.
Business Europe. (2015). "EU–China Relations, 2015 and Beyond", Brussels, March, www.businesseurope.eu/sites/buseur/files/media/imported/2015-00194-E.pdf, accessed online 29 March 2016.
Casarini, Nicola, and Miguel Otero-Iglesias. (2016). "Europe's Renminbi Romance", *Project Syndicate*, 4 April.
Donnan, Shawn, Hornby, Lucy, and Arthur Beesley. (2016). "China Challenges EU and US over Market Economy Status", *Financial Times*, 12 December.
EU External Action Service (EEAS). (2015). "The EU-ASEAN Relationship in 20 Facts and Figures", http://eeas.europa.eu/delegations/asean/asean_eu/fact_figures/index_en.htm, accessed online 20 April 2018.
EU External Action Service (EEAS). (2016). "Taiwan and the EU", https://eeas.europa.eu/headquarters/headquartershomepage_en/2000/Taiwan%20and%20the%20EU, accessed online 22 April 2018.
European Commission (EC). (2015). "Trade for All", http://trade.ec.europa.eu/doclib/docs/2015/october/tradoc_153846.pdf, accessed online 2 May 2018.
European Commission (EC). (2016). "EU and Indonesia Launch Bilateral Trade Talks", 8 July, http://trade.ec.europa.eu/doclib/press/index.cfm?id=1528, accessed online 5 May 2018.
European Commission (EC). (2017a). "Trade with Singapore", http://ec.europa.eu/trade/policy/countries-and-regions/countries/singapore/, accessed online 12 May 2018.
European Commission (EC). (2017b). "Trade with Indonesia", http://ec.europa.eu/trade/policy/countries-and-regions/countries/indonesia/, accessed online 12 May 2018.
European Commission (EC). (2017c). "Trade with India", http://ec.europa.eu/trade/policy/countries-and-regions/countries/india/, accessed online 12 May 2018.
European Commission. (2017d). "Trade with China", http://ec.europa.eu/trade/policy/countries-and-regions/countries/china/, accessed online 12 May 2018.

European Commission. (2017e). "Reflection Paper on Harnessing Globalisation", 10 May, https://ec.europa.eu/commission/sites/beta-political/files/reflection-paper-globalisation_en.pdf, accessed online 12 May 2018.

European Parliament (EP). (2016). "Driving Trade in the ASEAN Region: Progress of FTA Negotiations, Briefing, December", www.europarl.europa.eu/RegData/etudes/BRIE/2016/595850/EPRS_BRI(2016)595850_EN.pdf, accessed online 12 May 2018.

European Parliament (EP). (2017). "EU–Japan Trade Deal Finalised", At a glance, December, www.europarl.europa.eu/RegData/etudes/ATAG/2017/614637/EPRS_ATA(2017)614637_EN.pdf, accessed online 12 May 2018.

Ferguson, Niall. (2012). *Civilization*, London: Penguin.

García-Herrero, Alicia, Kwok, K.C., Liu, Xiangdong, Summers, Tim, and Yansheng Zhang. (2017). *EU–China Economic Relations to 2025: Building a Common Future*. London: Chatham House Report, September.

Gippner, Olivia. (2016). "Changing Waters. Towards a New EU–Asia Strategy", *LSE IDEAS* – Dahrendorf Forum Special Report, London.

Godement, François, Angela Stanzel. (2015). "The European Interest in an Investment Treaty with China", Policy Brief, ECFR, London, February.

Hanemann Thilo, and Mikko Huotari. (2017). "Record Flows and Growing Imbalances: Chinese Investment in Europe in 2016", *Merics Paper on China* 3, January.

Hébrard, Patrick. (2017). "Challenges to Freedom of the Seas and Maritime Rivalry in Asia", European Parliament, Directorate-General for External Policies, Policy Department, March, www.europarl.europa.eu/RegData/etudes/IDAN/2017/578014/EXPO_IDA(2017)578014_EN.pdf, accessed online 22 May 2018.

IMF. (2017a). "Regional Economic Outlook: Asia and Pacific, May 2017: Preparing for Choppy Seas", www.imf.org/en/Publications/REO/APAC/Issues/2017/04/28/areo0517, accessed online 22 May 2018.

IMF. (2017b). World Economic Outlook, April, www.imf.org/en/Countries/Infographics/APD-REO-2017/Growth-Table-Outlook, accessed online 22 May 2018.

Khandekar, Gauri. (2013). "EU–Asia Trade: In Need of a Strategy", Policy Brief 13, Fride, Madrid, January.

Mearsheimer, John J. (2014). "Can China Rise Peacefully?", *The National Interest*, 25 October.

Messerlin, Patrick A. (2012). "The Much Needed EU Pivoting to East Asia", *Asia-Pacific Journal of EU Studies*, 10 (2): 1–18, http://keusa.or.kr/korean/kor_publication/APJournal/2012_No10_2/Eu-10–2-01%20Patick%20A.%20Messerlin.pdf, accessed online 2 June 2018.

Okano-Heijmans, Maaike. (2014). "Trade Diplomacy in EU–Asia Relations: Time for a Rethink", Clingendael Institute, The Hague, September.

Otero-Iglesias, Miguel. (2014). "The Euro for China: Too Important to Fail and Too Difficult to Rescue", *The Pacific Review* 27 (5): 703–28.

Panda, Ankit. (2016). "Where Do European Union–India Relations Stand", *The Diplomat*, 31 March.

Quah, Danny. (2011). "The Global Economy's Shifting Centre of Gravity", *Global Policy* 2 (3): 3–9.

Reiterer, Michael. (2016). "Asia as Part of the EU's Global Security Strategy: Reflections on a More Strategic Approach", in O. Gippner (ed.), *Changing Waters: Towards a New EU Asia Strategy*, Report LSE Ideas.

Seaman, John, Huotari, Mikko, and Miguel Otero-Iglesias. (2017). "Chinese Investment in Europe: A Country-Level Approach", *ETNC Report*, December, www.ifri.org/sites/default/files/atoms/files/etnc_reports_2017_final_20dec2017.pdf, accessed online 2 June 2018.

Seller, Elodie. (2016). "The ASEAN Economic Community: The Force Awakens?", *The Diplomat*, 12 January.

Sengupta, Somini. (2017). "UN Chief Warns US of Risks of Rejecting Leadership Role", *New York Times*, 20 June.

Stone, Jon. (2017). "EU Moves Ahead of Britain on Opening Trade Talks with Australia and New Zealand", *The Independent*, 13 September.

Van der Putten, Frans Paul, Seaman, John, Huotari, Mikko, Ekman, Alice, and Miguel Otero-Iglesias. (2016). "Europe and China's New Silk Roads", *ETNC Report*, December, www.merics.org/en/merics-analysis/merics-reports/europe-and-chinas-new-silk-roads/, accessed online 2 June 2018.

World Bank. (2016). "East Asia Pacific Overview", 13 June, www.worldbank.org/en/region/eap/brief/global-economic-prospects-east-asia-and-pacific?cq_ck=1465835257739, accessed online 2 June 2018.

Yeo, Lay Hwee (2016). "EU Strategy towards Southeast Asia and ASEAN", in O. Gippner (ed.), *Changing Waters; Towards a New EU Asia Strategy*, Report LSE Ideas, April.

5 Public diplomacy of the European Union in East Asia

Suetyi Lai and Li Zhang

Introduction

When public diplomacy broadly refers to attempts by one government to influence foreign publics, governments from Europe have been among the first to practise it, for example with the establishment of the Alliance Française in 1883 and of the British Council in 1934. Yet the public diplomacy of the EU as a collective institution appeared much later, while studies of public diplomacy itself focus mostly on the country level. This chapter is devoted to understanding the public diplomacy programme on the EU level.

The EU started gaining competence in external relations, the so-called Common Foreign and Security Policy, in 1993 after the implementation of the Maastricht Treaty. Since then, the EU has been struggling to increase its international presence, whilst public diplomacy has been one option in the toolbox. While, in traditional diplomacy terms, the role and weight of the EU in Asia have been less prominent compared to unitary actors like the US and Russia; the Union's public visibility and awareness among Asian publics have also lagged behind. This chapter examines the public diplomacy programme of the EU in Asia.

Since the European Commission's (1994) Communication *Towards a New Asia Strategy* was published in 1994, the Union has determined to strengthen connection and co-operation with Asia, especially countries in East Asia which became the growth engine of the world's economy. In order to boost its presence in the region, public diplomacy has been one of the many efforts in the toolbox. While this book examines the EU's various policies towards the Asia-Pacific, this chapter addresses the Union's public diplomacy towards East Asia, as part of the Union's external strategy. Acknowledging that the Union's public visibility and awareness among Asian publics have ample room to improve, this chapter is devoted to examining the public diplomacy programme of the EU in Asia in order to determine how it has (or has not) contributed to the EU's engagement with Asia.

This chapter acknowledges that the EU's definition of Asia is indeed subjected to adjustment. The 1994 New Asia Strategy (NAS) divided "Asia" into three sub-regional groups: East Asia, South Asia and Southeast Asia. The three groups together covered 26 countries and economies, including China, Japan, North Korea, South Korea, Mongolia, Taiwan, Hong Kong and Macao in East Asia; India, Pakistan, Bangladesh, Sri Lanka, Nepal, Bhutan, the Maldives and Afghanistan in South Asia; and ten countries of Association of Southeast Asian Nations (ASEAN) in Southeast Asia. It is noteworthy that the East Asia group was renamed Northeast Asia in the 2001 European Commission (2001b) Communication, which added also a fourth group, Australasia, including Australia and New Zealand. While East Timor is located also in Southeast Asia, it has been assigned a member of the African Caribbean Pacific grouping since 2005 by the EU. Mongolia, which is located in Northeast Asia, has not been listed in any of the EU's policy papers on Asia thus far.

This chapter cannot cover all of the afore-mentioned Asian countries. It focuses on the EU's public diplomacy in the countries of the ASEAN+3 group in East Asia. They are subdivided into Northeast Asia (China, Japan and South Korea) and Southeast Asia (the ten member states of the ASEAN).[1] It is noted that the public diplomacy efforts of individual EU member states, namely France, the UK and the Netherlands, which had had a previous colonial presence in the region, started much earlier than those of the EU as a communal organisation. As the public diplomacy of the EU as an institution on its own is the focus of this volume, this study excludes the public diplomacy of the individual member states.

As already stated, the EU published its *New Asia Strategy*, which marked the beginning of the Union's rediscovery of Asia, in 1994. Therefore, this chapter covers the period between 1994 and the present. The analysis begins with a quick overview of the concept of public diplomacy, followed by a more detailed analysis of the understanding of public diplomacy by the EU. This chapter reviews existing research on the EU's public diplomacy, including research related to Asia. The actual efforts of the EU's promotion of public diplomacy in the ASEAN+3 countries are then analysed. The final part of this chapter lists the results of existing research projects which assessed the external image of the EU in Asia.

Defining public diplomacy and EU's public diplomacy

In today's age of globalisation and information, public diplomacy has been the fastest growing sub-set of diplomatic studies. Public diplomacy aims at informing and shaping more positive perceptions of a government or its policy among domestic and foreign audiences. As a result, good public diplomacy promotes the essential values, norms and interests of one government. Therefore, it is regarded by many scholars (Anholt, 2005; Melissen, 2005; van Ham, 2005, 2008) as part of a government's strategy to brand a nation and to wield the nation's soft power. Joseph Nye (2008) also believed public diplomacy to be conveying information, selling a positive image of a government, and building long-term relationships with foreign governments and publics to facilitate the policies of one government.

As a concept, public diplomacy can mean a wide range of things according to the understanding or need of a government, researcher or individual. There is a plethora of definitions of public diplomacy, some more referred to and used than others. The term "public diplomacy" emerged in the middle years of the Cold War in the United States. It was first officially used when Edmund Gullion, a retired US diplomat, launched the Edward R. Murrow Centre for Public Diplomacy at Tufts University in 1965. Gullion was concerned with the conduct of foreign policy through engagement with international publics, but did not like the old word "propaganda", partly because of its negative connotations. Different from propaganda, which communicates one way, public diplomacy is a two-way communication. The purpose of public diplomacy is to inform foreign publics and governments in order to gain trust and support, rather than controlling information for the purpose of propagandist deception.

A widely recognised definition of public diplomacy was developed by Cull (2009): public diplomacy

> deals with the influence of public attitudes on the formation and execution of foreign policies. It encompasses dimensions of international relations beyond traditional diplomacy; the cultivation by governments of public opinion in other countries; the interaction of private groups and interests in one country with another; the reporting of foreign affairs and its impact on policy; communication between those whose job is communication, as diplomats and foreign correspondents; and the process of intercultural communications.

Cull also listed five principal areas in the practice of public diplomacy: listening, advocacy, cultural diplomacy, people-to-people exchange and international broadcasting.

In those definitions, public diplomacy is conducted by national governments, and closely linked to a government's foreign-policy objectives and its national interests. However, the EU is not a nation-state. As a supranational organisation, it is often hard for the EU to reach a consensus on its foreign policies, objectives and interests, even though a general aim has been agreed among EU officials that the EU wants the rest of world to know what it is and how it acts.[2]

In the Commission's understanding, the EU's public diplomacy deals with the influence of public attitudes. Its central objective is to build trust and understanding between the EU and non-EU countries (European Commission, 2016). This is subdivided into three aims, which are to increase

Public diplomacy of the EU in East Asia   99

understanding of EU views, policies and priorities; to promote values and interests of the EU; and to improve perceptions of the EU. In addition, four groups are listed as targets of this public diplomacy policy: academics and students; policy-makers, policy influencers and multipliers; civil society organisations; and cultural operators and artists.

The EU's public diplomacy at a glance

Shaping images and defining the limits, outreach, and soft power of governments, public diplomacy finds itself at the heart of today's diplomatic activities. It dominates not only governments' foreign affairs agendas but also the attention of studies on diplomacy and international relations. There has been a plethora of existing research and studies on public diplomacy as well as the establishment of a field of study. Apart from work on public diplomacy in general, there are also plenty of studies of public diplomacy of various national governments, particularly the US (e.g., Rugh, 2014; Brooks, 2015) and many other countries, such as the UK(e.g. Leonard et al., 2005), China (e.g. Wang, 2011; Hartig, 2016), France (e.g. McKenzie, 2005) and so on.

As a multinational organisation and united power, research on EU public diplomacy has not been less. However, these studies have focused mainly on the institutional structure of how the EU's public diplomacy is conducted as well as its outcome and limitations. Many of them end up with practical policy recommendations for the EU. This chapter takes a more academic approach and reviews the conduct of the EU's public diplomacy from 1994 to the present, including its conduct in the Asia region, with a focus on the message and the institutional delivery of the EU's public diplomacy. The following text discusses these two aspects in turn.

In terms of the messages sent by the EU's public diplomacy activities, comparing with the EU's public diplomacy to its closer audiences, such as the European Neighbourhood Policy, which focuses on promoting EU's prosperity, stability and security, EU's public diplomacy in the Asia region has fallen behind. For a long time, the aim of the EU's public diplomacy in the region has been focusing on increasing its visibility and profile. For instance, the 1994 NAS stated that "[t]he Union needs to conduct a coordinated programme of public relations in order to raise its profile in Asia", and one section of "EU Strategy toward China" published in 2001 (European Commission, 2001a) focused on "[r]aising the EU's profile in China by strengthening all aspects of EU information policy vis-à-vis China". As time goes by, a normative power EU has become one key message that the EU uses to promote its image, together with its norms on democracy, human rights and the rule of law (Manners, 2002). The message that the EU wants its foreign audiences to understand about the EU became clearer at the EU's fiftieth anniversary celebration in 2007. That is to deliver the EU as an internally diverse political entity, a peace protector and a model to be followed by other states and regions (European Commission, 2007). In its most recent global strategy document *Shared Vision, Common Action: A Stronger Europe* (European Commission and European External Action Service, 2016), the main objective of public diplomacy was to connect EU foreign policy with citizens and better communicate it to its partners.

In terms of institutional delivery of EU's public diplomacy, there has not been a clear structure on this, nor a cohesive organisation of the relevant activities. Trying to conduct public diplomacy as good as the national government of EU member states, which have their own agencies for public diplomacy – for instance, the BBC World Service and the British Council of the UK, the Deutsche Welle and the Goethe Institute of Germany, and France 24 as well as the Radio France International of France – the EU has been working hard to build up its own.

On the side of international broadcasting, the Commission established a website on YouTube known as EUTube. On the side of engaging foreign publics, the Erasmus Mundus, Jean Monnet Programme and the EU Centre of Excellence, which are currently all grouped together as the Erasmus+ Programme, encourage people-to-people exchange between foreign and European higher education institutions and provide funding for education, research and training all over the world on EU-related issues. Moreover, the European Union Visitors Programme, launched in 1974, invites approximately 160 government officials, journalists and leaders from NGOs and trade unions on a five-to-eight day visit to the EU involving meetings with EU officials every year (Rasmussen, 2009).

No EU document clearly states which EU institutions should take the public diplomacy role, as the Council, the Parliament and the Commission can all act for public diplomacy. In practice, the European Commission has been a chief actor, particularly its external directorate-general (DG RELEX). After the implementation of the Lisbon Treaty, it is the European External Action Service (EEAS) which takes over the greater part of such duty. In Brussels, it was said that the head of DG RELEX's Information and Communication Unit normally chairs a monthly meeting to co-ordinate the information and communication of other directorates-general (DGs) which also do external communication, such as DG trade, DG enlargement and DG development. Outside the EU, it is now the some 140 EU delegations that play the dominant role, whose work involves the management of local websites, organisation of events, delegation visits around the host country, contact events with local schools and universities, the publication of brochures and newsletters, local media monitoring, management of journalist training programmes, the running of small EU information centres and activities to promote "civil society dialogue" (Rasmussen, 2009).

Nevertheless, the actual conduct of EU public diplomacy is sporadic and fragmented, with different delegations having their own agendas. These have been changed slightly for the better since the adoption of the Lisbon Treaty in 2009. After Lisbon, EU public diplomacy has also been extended to the newly established EEAS, which came to be in charge of the Union's diplomacy service (Duke, 2013). The strategic understanding of the public diplomacy activity has been better understood by high-level EU politicians. And the EEAS has started to play a better, though limited, role in EU co-ordinating public diplomacy. In 2013, a *Handbook for EU Delegations in Third Countries and to International Organisations* was issued by the European Commission, which listed the areas of focus in the EU's public diplomacy as guidance for the EU delegations. This, so far, has not significantly improved EU public diplomacy practice: the EU still lacks cohesion, consistency and strategy in communicating EU policy and action to foreign audiences. It is as part of this institutional practice that the EU's public diplomacy in Asia has been conducted. The next section specifically analyses the EU's attempt at public diplomacy in the ASEAN+3 countries.

Instruments of EU public diplomacy in Asia

When conducting public diplomacy in Asia, the EU delegations and the EU centres funded by the Commission are the two major instruments. The following text examines the role and efforts of them in turn.

The EU maintains a network of currently 143 diplomatic missions around the world. The EU delegations are the *de facto* diplomatic presence of the EU. The first such delegation was opened in 1954 in London by the then European Coal and Steel Community (ECSC) with the aim only to serve as an information and communications office of the ECSC. But nowadays, these delegations have developed a role as embassies of the EU in third countries. To maintain diplomatic relations and development cooperation with African, Caribbean and Pacific states (ACP), the then European Community established forty-one delegations of the Commission in the ACP in 1960s and 1970s. It was not until 1976, when a new Asia and Latin America development budget came into force and the European Commission gained bigger responsibility in external trade policy, that the Commission opened more delegation offices in Asia (European Commission, 2004). These offices differed from those in the ACP countries and adopted "a more classically diplomatic approach" (European Commission, 2004).

According to Bruter (1999), the delegations have the responsibility of representing the EU in certain areas of external policy in a broad sense, though these are more technical or economic than political, and far more strictly defined than the regular foreign domain of nation-states; in the meantime, as the EU member states have also transferred large parts of their trade policy, development-related aid, humanitarian help, technical and scientific co-operation, and economic development to EU institutions, the delegations play a role in those areas as well. So far, the EU has set up 143 delegations or offices around the world, which are the main actors in conducting its public diplomacy (EEAS's "EU in the World").

In the Asia region, the EU opened its delegation office to Tokyo in 1974 to manage relations with Japan. Notably, this was the first European Commission Delegation Office to Asia. The then Delegation office of the European Commission for South and Southeast Asia was opened in 1979 in Bangkok. It was responsible for managing relations with eleven countries: Bangladesh, Bhutan, India, Indonesia, Malaysia, Nepal, Pakistan, the Philippines, Singapore, Sri Lanka and Thailand. Today, it covers Cambodia, Laos and Thailand.

After Tokyo and Bangkok, the European Commission opened other delegation offices in Asia only in the 1980s. In 1982, a delegation office was established in Dhaka to cover the European Community's relations with Bangladesh. Similarly, in 1983, management of relations with India, Bhutan and Nepal was taken over by a new delegation office set up in Delhi. In 1985, the Commission opened an office in Islamabad to foster ties with Pakistan. This office was upgraded to delegation office in 1988. Also in 1988, two delegation offices were established in Beijing and Jakarta respectively to cover the European Community's relations with China and Mongolia as well as with Indonesia, Brunei and the ASEAN Secretariat. A delegation office was opened in Seoul in 1989 to manage ties with both South and North Koreas.

More Commission delegations were opened in the 1990s and the early 2000s to manage bilateral relations between the EU and individual countries in South and Southeast Asia. The delegation to the Philippines opened in 1991, to Vietnam in 1996, to Malaysia in 2003, and in Singapore in 2004. The Office of the European Union in Myanmar is the most recent, inaugurated in April 2012 in Yangon. Today, there are a total of ten EU offices among the thirteen ASEAN Plus Three (APT) countries. In addition, there is an EU Office in Hong Kong and Macao, established in 1993, as well as a European Economic and Trade Office established in Taiwan in 2003 to act as the EU's office in Taiwan.

Apart from their role as an embassy, one of the key responsibilities of the EU delegations in third countries is to increase EU visibility and improve the EU image abroad. The EU has attached great importance to these delegations, believing that it is imperative to strengthen and expand the network of EU delegations in the region, as they can help to raise the profile of Europe in Asia, to strengthen inter-regional educational and cultural exchanges, to broaden and intensify the range of seminars and conferences bringing together think tanks and policy-makers from both regions, and to strengthen information and communications activities (European

Commission, 1994). To do so, the EU delegations have made much effort, including managing individual websites, engaging with the media, running various activities with the publics in the hosting countries and so on. In the bigger delegations, there is also a section responsible for engaging with foreign publics. For instance, the delegation in Tokyo has a Press, Public and Cultural Affairs section; the delegation in Beijing has a Press and Information Section.

Another institutionalised physical presence of the EU in third countries is the EU Centres. The EU Centre was initiated in the middle of 1990s to strengthen transatlantic relations under the "New Transatlantic Agenda" (European Council, 1995) between the EU and the US, as "bridges across the Atlantic". In order to enhance neutrality and credibility, the EU Centre initiative is incorporated into existing universities. As a result, twelve EU centres were established in American universities and three in Canadian universities in 1998. The establishment of EU centres is not only as a kind of promotion in education, but also as a complement to the work of EU Delegations. As stated by the EEAS on the programme's webpage (EEAS website), the objectives of EU Centres are to promote greater understanding of the EU, its institutions and its policies, to disseminate information and EU views on issues of interest within regional communities, and to increase awareness about the political, economic and cultural importance of the relationship between the EU and the specific country. The EU Centre initiative has been expanded to other industrialised countries. The first EU Centre in Asia was opened in Tokyo. By 2013, there were fifteen EU centres in the APT countries: three in mainland China, four in Japan, four in South Korea and one each in Singapore, Taiwan, Hong Kong and Macao.

The mandate of these EU centres in non-EU countries is to raise public awareness and understanding of the Union, especially through teaching, research, outreach and networking. Apart from launching their own courses, research and activities, the EU centres work also with local schools, international organisations, chambers of commerce, local government, local media and the EU delegation office. Their official websites, social media platform and publication (both electronic and physical) serve as credible sources of information about the EU in a third country.

Apart from physical presence via the EU's own delegation or via local scholars in the EU centres, other regular public diplomacy tools of the EU include direct people-to-people exchange and internet presence managed directly by the institutions in Brussels, namely the EU Visitors Programme. For instance, each year dozens of Asian elites from researchers to scientists, from artists to journalists, travel to the EU with the support of EU funds. Meanwhile, the Union also gives support to equivalent elites from EU countries to travel abroad. Direct people-to-people exchange, including student exchange, plays an important part in improving external awareness and understanding of the EU outside its border. When they return home, some of these non-EU visitors turn into "EU ambassadors" to share their knowledge and interest in the EU and its countries. According to the statistics given by the EEAS, every year the EU gives around fifteen thousand scholarships to students and academics in Asia (Reiterer, 2013). In addition, the EU also occasionally launched projects to foster mutual understanding with Asia: for example, the three-year EU–Asia Dialogue Project on "Shaping a Common Future for Europe and Asia"[3] lasted between January 2012 and March 2015. Another example was the EU Public Diplomacy in Japan programme which started in July 2015 and cost €750,000.

In sum, these public diplomacy instruments of the EU in Asia are not different from the ones used in other regions. Resources invested in different countries do vary. The Delegation Office in the larger Asian countries, China and Japan, are the biggest in Asia, and there are many more EU centres in Northeast Asia than in Southeast Asia. Another noteworthy point is the co-existence of efforts made by the individual EU member states. The smaller EU countries co-operate with or depend on the EU to promote their external visibility, while their bigger counterparts still actively practise public diplomacy on their own. The next section examines the external image of the EU in Northeast Asia and Southeast Asia.

Assessment of the EU's public diplomacy in Asia

This section gauges the effectiveness of the Union's public diplomacy in raising its profile and communicating messages of the EU. These findings help the EU to understand how it is perceived in the news media, by decision-makers and by the wider public in East Asia. Understanding external perceptions can help the EU to identify any misconceptions, misunderstandings and misperceptions, and to adjust its policies accordingly.

Data used in this chapter are from four extensive studies[4] on external perceptions of the EU (Table 5.1): *The EU in the Eyes of Asia* (2006–10), *The Visibility of the EU as a Development Actor in the South and East Africa, South East Asia and the Pacific* (2006–8), *After Lisbon: The EU as an Exporter of Values and Norms through ASEM* (2010–12, hereafter called *After Lisbon*) and *EU Perceptions in 10 Strategic Partners: Analysis of the Perception of the EU and EU's Politics Abroad* (2015, hereafter called *EU Perceptions in 10 Strategic Partners*). These research projects are initiated and led by the National Centre for Research on Europe (NCRE) of the University of Canterbury, New Zealand. All projects employed identical data collection and analysis methods – news media analysis, in-depth face-to-face interviews with national decision-makers and public opinion survey.

As researchers in these projects, the authors of this chapter have access to the substantial and informative first-hand empirical dataset. The availability of such a rich dataset allows comparative analysis from various

Public diplomacy of the EU in East Asia   105

Table 5.1 The EU's public diplomacy in Asia, sources of empirical data

Projects	Timeframe	Northeast Asian countries covered	Southeast Asian countries covered
EU in the Eyes of Asia I	2006–2007	China (mainland and Hong Kong SAR), Japan, South Korea	Singapore, Thailand
EU in the Eyes of Asia II	2009–2010	China (Macau SAR)	Malaysia
Visibility of the EU as a Development Actor	2006–2008	–	Indonesia, the Philippines, Vietnam
After Lisbon	2010–2012	China, Japan, South Korea	Malaysia, Singapore, Thailand
EU Perceptions in 10 Strategic Partners	2015	China, Japan, South Korea	–

perspectives: across different geographic locations, longitudinally across time and across different sectors of society. Among the APT countries, nine countries (eleven locations including the Special Administrative Regions (SARs) of Hong Kong and Macao) were covered, as listed in Table 5.1.

Apart from media attention on the EU, this chapter also examines the public opinion about the EU by using the primary data from *After Lisbon* and *EU Perceptions in 10 Strategic Partners*. The public survey of *After Lisbon* was conducted in March 2012, that of *EU Perceptions in 10 Strategic Partners* in August 2015. Only data of these two newer projects are included as they were more up-to-date. In both projects, the sample size of each country was set at 1000, providing a margin of error of ±3 per cent at a confidence level of 95 per cent. A professional surveying company was hired, choosing samples from its online pool to complete the internet-based interview. A total of 9684 respondents are used in this chapter. Unfortunately, the questionnaires used in the two rounds were different, and hence most of the answers are not directly comparable.

Assessment of the promotion of awareness of the EU in East Asia

The first aspect to be analysed is the media attention which the EU received. In each research project on the EU's external perception led by the NCRE, the media analysis part always monitored three representative news dailies from each location. The prime-time television news bulletin was also monitored, except in the project conducted in 2015. All studied news outlets are listed in Table 5.2. In each project, the monitoring period of news reportage lasted from six to twelve months. Owing to time limitation of the project

Table 5.2 News outlets monitored in the research projects

2006–2011

	Popular daily	Business daily	English-language daily	TV news
China	People's Daily	International Finance	China Daily	CCTV
Hong Kong SAR	Oriental Daily	Hong Kong Economic Journal	South China Morning Post	TVB Jude
Macao SAR	Macau Daily News		Macau Daily Times	TDM
Indonesia	Kompas	Bisnis Indonesia	Jakarta Post	TVRI
Japan	Yomiuri	Nikkei Shimbun	Japan Times	NHK
Malaysia	Utusan Malaysia	The Edge Financial Daily	The Star	TV3
The Philippines	Philippine Daily Inquirer	Business World	Manila Bulletin	GMA7
Singapore	Lianhe Zaobao	Straits Times	Business Times	Channel 8
South Korea	Chosun Daily	Maeil Business	Korea Herald	KBS
Thailand	Thai Rath	The Manager	Bangkok Post	ITV
Vietnam	Youth	VNET	Vietnam News	VTV1

2015

	Popular daily 1	Business daily	Popular daily 2	
China	People's Daily	21st Century Business Herald	Global Times	
Japan	Yomiuri Shimbun	Nikkei Shimbun	Asahi Shimbun	n/a
South Korea	Chosun Ilbo	Maeil Business	Joong Ang Ilbo	

conducted in 2015, the media analysis part was set for three months –April, May and June 2015. Items of EU-related news (news items mentioning keywords "European Union/EU", "European Commission/EC" and "European Central Bank/ECB")[5] were put into the dataset, analysed and codedsystematically. In total, 19,120 news items from the EU external perception projects are used in this chapter.

As Figure 5.1 shows, visibility of the EU in the Asian press varied greatly in different locations. Among the nine countries (eleven locations)

Public diplomacy of the EU in East Asia

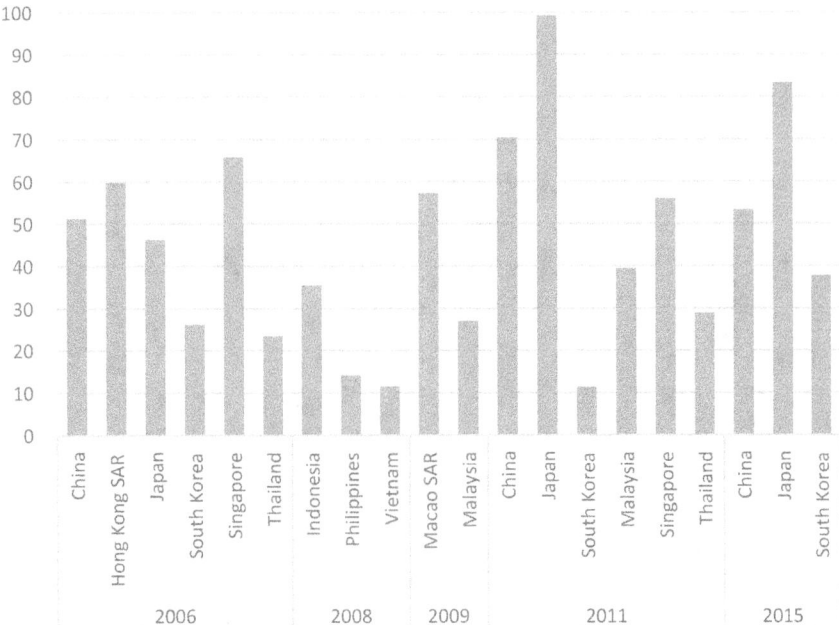

Figure 5.1 Monthly average of EU-related news items in each location per newspaper

monitored, Japan, Singapore and China (including mainland, Hong Kong and Macao) have been most interested in reporting the EU. In these locations, the monitored dailies published on average 64 EU-related news items every month, that is two news articles every day. It was found that media visibility of the EU was higher in Northeast Asian than in Southeast Asia. It is especially low in the Philippines and Vietnam in the 2008 sample, the monthly average of EU appearances were 14 and 12 news articles respectively.

It is noteworthy that, even in the Japanese and Chinese newspapers which reported the EU relatively more frequently, an average of two news articles in each edition was still not high. As a control study, the 2011 *After Lisbon* project recoded the number of news items which mentioned the US, China and India. All of them appeared more frequently in the monitored media outlets than the EU, especially the US and China. For instance, in the Japanese case, the visibility of the US and China is four times that of the EU. Strikingly, in the Thai case, the numbers of appearance of the US and of China were 67 and 75 times that of the EU in the Thai popular daily *Thai Rath*.

The results were even more negative in the most watched prime-time television news bulletin (Figure 5.2). Visibility of the EU was very low in

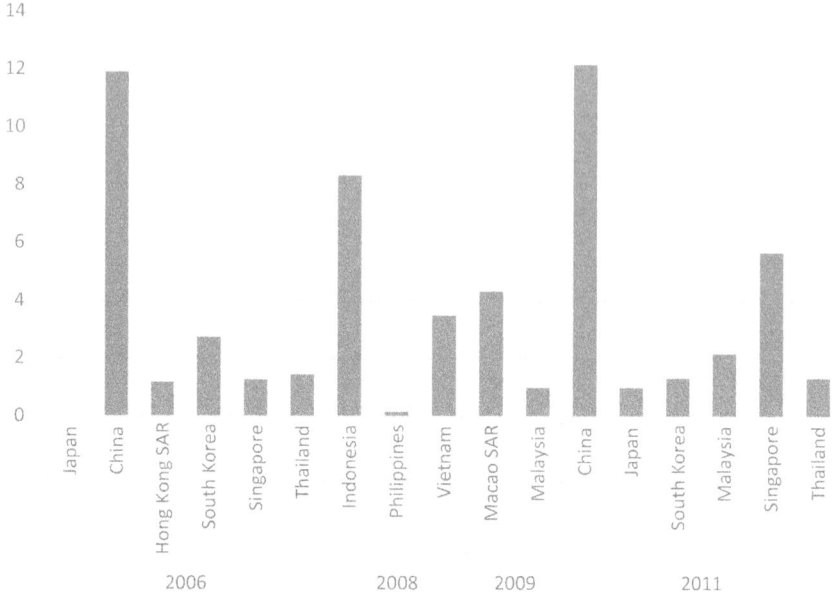

Figure 5.2 Monthly average of EU-related news items in prime-time TV news bulletins

all studied locations. *CCTV Xinwen Lianbo* in mainland China and *TVRI* in Indonesia were found the most interested in reporting the EU on television news. Yet the monthly average of EU appearances were only 12 and 8 news items respectively, which meant less than one report every three or four days.

When looking in more detail, it was found that, in the collected news items which mentioned one or more EU-related keywords, the majority featured the EU only as a minor actor. As shown in Figure 5.3, the numbers of news stories devoted exclusively to the EU in the monitored Asian media outlets were low. Most of the studied news outlets did not pay major attention on the EU.

As Figures 5.4 and 5.5 demonstrate, in the collected EU-related news items, the individual member states had had more visible representation of the EU in action than the communal institutions. Among the member states, the "big three"– France, Germany and the UK – had been consistently the most visible from the dataset collected in 2006 to the most recent one in 2015. Similarly, national leaders of the EU big three had appeared more frequently than EU officials. In the dataset collected after the outbreak of the Eurozone debt crisis, attention given at the time to the "problematic" countries, the so-called "PIIGS" countries (Portugal, Ireland, Italy, Greece and Spain), rose significantly. Another noteworthy point is that the EC/EU

Public diplomacy of the EU in East Asia 109

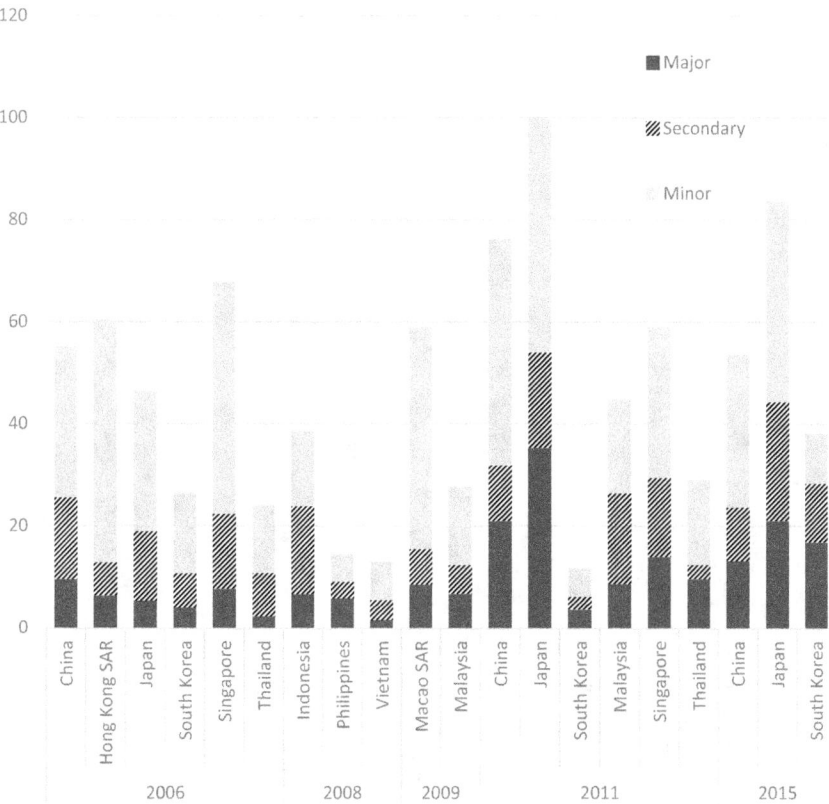

Figure 5.3 Centrality of the EU's actions in the collected EU-related news items (monthly average)

delegations were hardly visible in the news coverage in East Asia despite the fact that they serve as the on-the-ground diplomacy service.

From the elite interview dataset, responses from the editors and lead journalists in the studied Asian countries provided explanations of the lack of interest in covering the EU. One comment was that the EU had not been regarded as important as other Asian countries (especially the immediate neighbours) or as important as big power like the US and China. The limited amount of space (in press) and of air time (on TV) would be devoted to news stories which were either closer or had higher relevance to "home". As an editor of *Korea Herald*, a popular English-language daily in South Korea, remarked in an interview in December 2011 in Seoul:

> If we were to choose what to publish between the US-Korea FTA and the EU-Korea FTA, we will definitely select the US-Korea FTA. The US has stronger

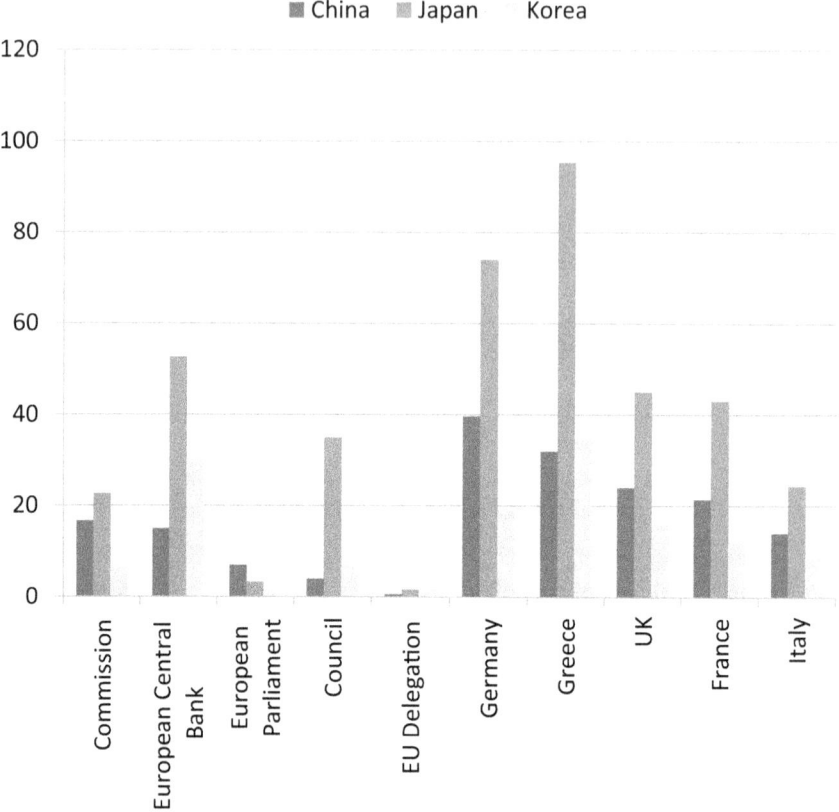

Figure 5.4 Comparison of visibility of EU communal institutions and EU member states in the 2015 media analysis dataset (number of news items, three dailies per month)

image to the public. The public tends to consider the US far more important to Korea than the EU despite the high trade volume with the EU. Next to the US, China is recognised as the crucial country to Korea.

Another explanation was from the news-making perspective, in which news media prefer stories with conflicts and controversies. Meanwhile, countries in the EU had been relatively stable in the studied period – the oldest project, "EU in the Eyes of Asia I", covered the whole year 2006, while the most recent project, "EU Perceptions in 10 Strategic Partners", covered April, May and June 2015.[6] An editor from *Kyodo*, a Japanese news agency, said in interview in October 2011 in Tokyo:

> News is wars, tsunamis, earthquakes, turmoil and riots. Europe is the most stable area in the world. But of course, now we are covering its financial crisis,

Public diplomacy of the EU in East Asia

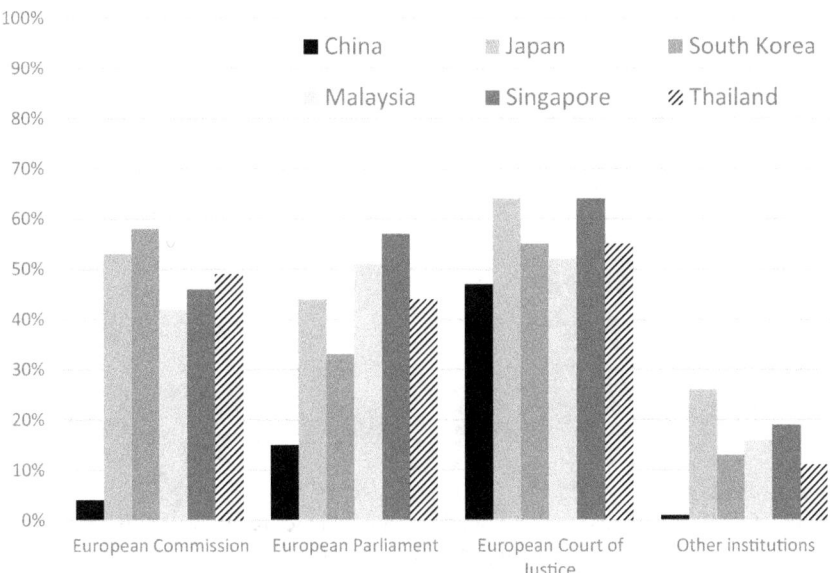

Figure 5.5 Respondents' awareness of EU institutions, surveyed in March 2012 (n = 6012)

and we place a very heavy weight on it. But if you then ask me is Europe at the centre of the news, I don't know.

The third most frequently given reason was the complexity of the EU. Named source of complication includes internal diversity among the EU member states, the institutionalisation which had still been evolving and the EU's differences from most of the Asian countries in culture, economic development and political system. On the news-production side, some interviewed news-makers found it difficult to understand the Union themselves. On the news-consumption side, some interviewees saw news about the EU as "hard to sell" to the audience, who found it difficult to understand or got bored easily.

In the public opinion survey, one set of questions helpful to indicate the public awareness of the EU asked respondents whether they had heard of the EU institutions, in the *After Lisbon* project. In all studied countries except China, around half of the respondents had not heard of the crucial communal institutions of the EU (Figure 5.4). In Japan and South Korea, 26 per cent and 13 per cent of respondents respectively admitted that they had never heard of any of the EU institutions. In Malaysia, Singapore and Thailand, this was true of 16 per cent, 19 per cent and 11 per cent of the interviewees respectively. The Chinese result was the most encouraging for

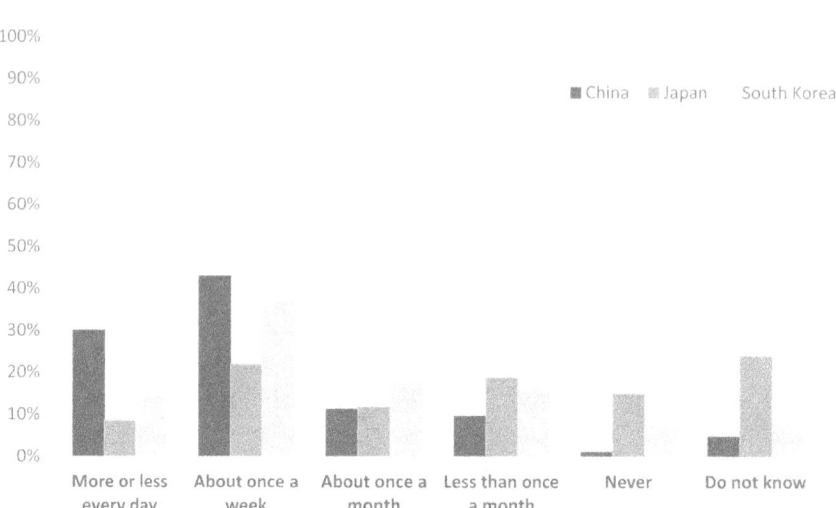

Figure 5.6 Respondents' frequency of hearing or reading about the EU, surveyed in August 2015 (n = 3672)

the EU: only 4 per cent of respondents had not heard of the Commission and 1 per cent had not heard of any communal institution of the EU.

In the most recent round of surveys (in August 2015) which included China, Japan and South Korea, the question that helped to indicate the public awareness of the EU was one which asked the respondents "How often do you hear/read about the EU?" Among the general public, 73 per cent in China, 30 per cent in Japan and 51 per cent in South Korea said that they had heard or read about the EU at least once a week (Figure 5.5). In combination with the findings of the questions presented in Figure 5.4, it is found that, among the examined East Asian countries, public awareness of the EU in China was the highest, whereas that in Japan was the lowest.

The next assessment is of the EU's perceived importance in East Asia. In the 2012 round, in none of the survey countries was the EU seen as the most important partner by the public. Interestingly, sub-regional difference was clear. While the Northeast Asian countries all listed the US as the number one important partner, the Southeast Asian countries named China. Whilst the public in Northeast Asia ranked the EU as the third most important partner, the public in Southeast Asia ranked the EU lower, only in fifth place.

EU Perceptions in 10 Strategic Partners asked if interviewees agreed on the EU's importance as their country's "trade partner", "partner in international relations", "partner in education exchanges" and "partner in science, research and technology". As shown in Figure 5.7, the general public in the three Northeast Asia countries recognised the EU's importance

Public diplomacy of the EU in East Asia

Table 5.3 Respondents' ranking of their country's most important partner, March 2012 (n = 6012)

Respondents in	First	Second	Third	Rank of EU
China	US	Russia	EU	3
Japan	US	Asia	EU	3
South Korea	US	China	EU	3
Malaysia	China	Asia/Japan (=)	Asia/Japan (=)	5
Singapore	China	US	Asia	5
Thailand	China	Japan	US	5

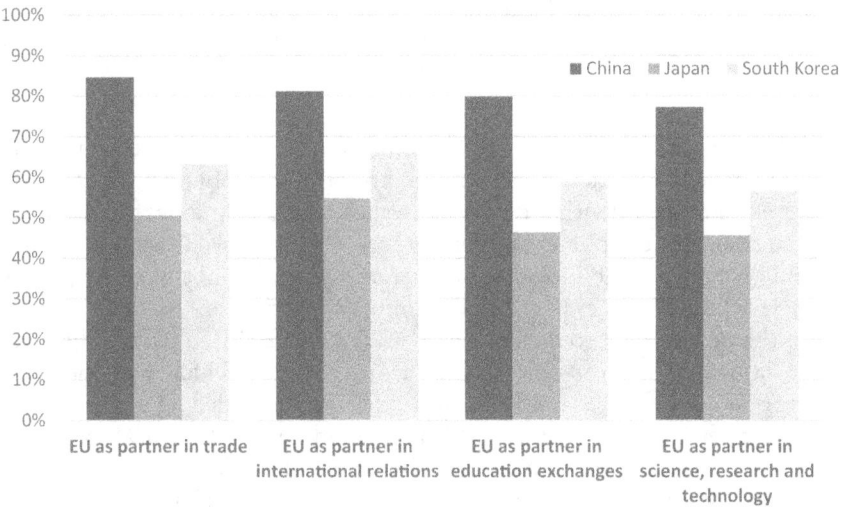

Figure 5.7 Respondents' conception of the EU as a partner to their country, surveyed in August 2015 (n = 3672)

in trade and in international relations the most. In the three analysed countries, the Chinese public, again, demonstrated stronger positivity towards the EU as a partner.

Assessment of the promotion of better understanding of the EU

Another aspect analysed is the understanding of the EU in the studied Asian locations. In terms of action, it is found that the media reports on the EU most frequently featured it as either political actor or economic actor. The role of the EU as the world's biggest trading bloc and an active global actor in international politics has been recognised by the monitored Asian media.

Table 5.4 Respondents' choice of adjective to describe the EU, 2012 and 2015

	First	Second	Third
2012			
China	Modern	Efficient	Arrogant
Japan	Modern	Peaceful	Likeable
South Korea	Modern	Peaceful	Likeable
Malaysia	Modern	Efficient	Peaceful
Singapore	Modern	Peaceful	Fair
Thailand	Modern	Efficient	Likeable
2015			
China	Multicultural	Modern	Strong
Japan	Multicultural	Modern	United
South Korea	Modern	Peaceful	Multicultural

Yet the continuous efforts of the EU to promote international co-operation in climate change, development and promotion of human rights have received minimal attention in the Asian media. These findings were echoed by the results of the public opinion survey. In the surveyed Asian locations, both in Northeast and in Southeast Asia, the general public most frequently associated the EU as either with economy or politics.

In the more recent rounds of survey (2012 and 2015), a list of adjectives was shown to the respondents for them to choose which was the most appropriate to describe the EU. These adjectives included aggressive, arrogant, efficient, fair, hypocritical, likeable, modern, multicultural, peaceful, strong, trustworthy and united. As shown in Table 5.4, the most chosen adjective associated with the EU was modern in the 2012 survey and multicultural in 2015. Peaceful was also very frequently chosen to describe the EU. These indeed match the images which the EU has been promoting about itself. Yet, with the EU facing various crises recently, namely the refugee crisis and the terrorism threat, there is doubt whether it's perception in Asia as multicultural and peaceful could persist.

Results from the three Northeast Asian countries enable longitudinal comparison. In general, the public in all studied countries had a rather positive perception of the EU. A cultural norm, namely that the Japanese are believed to be more reserved in expressing their negative feelings, has to be noted. Yet, when comparing across time, a decrease in positivity of the EU's image in the eyes of the Japanese and Korean publics is recorded. The Chinese case was opposite, recording a slight increase in positive attitudes towards the EU as well as an obvious drop in negative attitude. Combining this result with that about the public awareness of the EU in the three Northeast Asian countries, it is found that the Chinese public was

Public diplomacy of the EU in East Asia 115

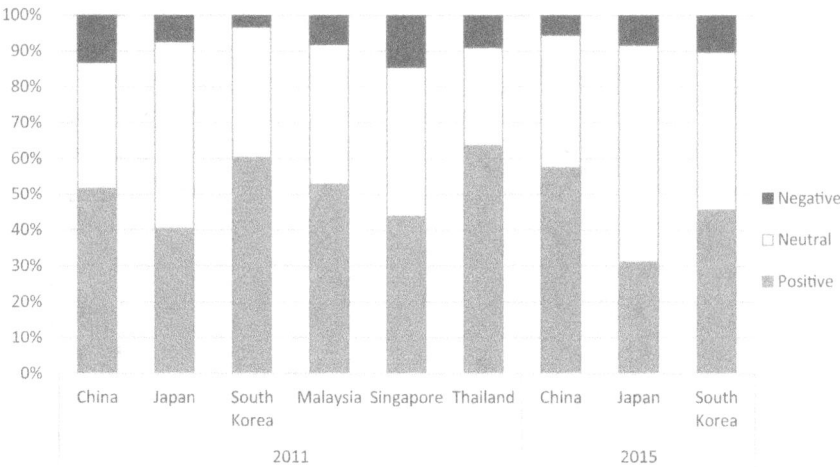

Figure 5.8 Evaluation of the EU by the general public, 2011 and 2015

both the most familiar with and most positive towards the EU. It is noteworthy that the Japanese were the least familiar with and most negative towards the EU, despite Japan hosting the Union's first delegation office and EU Centre in Asia.

In a difference from the Asian public's generally positive image of the EU, a neutral image was found in the Asian media. This can easily be understood as in the nature of professional journalism, which produces news as a neutral report of facts. When comparing across countries (Figure 5.9), EU coverage was much more polarised (high in both positive and negative evaluation) in Southeast Asian media than their Northeast Asian counterparts. When comparing across time, there was a clear rise in negative-tone reportage of the EU in both Asian sub-regions from 2006 to 2011. The lingering Eurozone debt crisis in the PIIGS countries was the major reason. In the 2015 datatset, the reportage in the Chinese and Korean media on the Greek sovereign debt crisis still contributed hugely to negativity of the EU's media image.

While the EU's public diplomacy intends to promote a positive profile, these results indicate that more effort is needed. Some policy recommendations are provided in the concluding section below.

Conclusions and discussions

Since the mid-1990s, the Union has determined to strengthen its connection and co-operation with Asia, especially countries in East Asia, which has

Figure 5.9 Evaluation of media reportage of the EU, 2006–15

been the growth engine of the world's economy and a huge market for the EU. In order to promote the EU's interests, the EU has sought to influence public attitudes toward itself outside its border, including the public in East Asia. When conducting public diplomacy in the studied Asian countries, the delegations of the European Commission/Union and the European Union Centres funded by the Commission are the two major instruments.

It is noteworthy that, although Japan was the first Asian country to host a European Commission Delegation Office and an EU Centre, its media and public awareness and understanding of the EU have not been the most positive. Indeed, the general visibility of the EU in the APT countries in this study was found to be low, especially compared to other global actors like the US and China. This appearance was weaker in Southeast Asia than in Northeast Asia, with the exception of Singapore. Besides, it is found that the individual member states have been more visible to the Asian media and public than the EU institutions. Given such a situation, a few policy recommendations are offered to the EU.

It should not be forgotten that public diplomacy is like a marketing tool: its results depend largely on quality of the "product". Public diplomacy is not the magic to make the Asian public perceive the EU as the most important partner in the region while the EU itself has not possessed any key stake or role in key regional issues, such as in the territorial conflict in the South China Sea or instability in the Korean peninsula. It is true that the EU has been among the top three trade partners of the APT countries, a role which has been recognised by the Asian media and public. Yet, as the EU itself has not transformed its economic power into a larger political role in the international arena, no public diplomacy can sell the Union as a political giant to third countries.

Media and social media act as a major source of information on foreign news for the general public in a society, as members of the general public normally do not have first-hand information. There is no doubt that they become key targets of any public diplomacy. Yet the EU should not blindly seek high visibility. The nature of media and social media to maximise readership makes them prone to bad news, news of crisis and conflicts. The EU should not look for this kind of visibility.

If the EU is to improve its profile in third countries, one key aspect to focus is to make itself easier to understand. The above media analysis and public survey showed that in Asia people found the EU difficult to report and comprehend. The fact that the Union is not a conventional international player like a nation-state, together with the fact that it is still an ongoing project where various reforms keep taking place, makes it hard to understand. Future public diplomacy can provide timely updates, especially to writers of media and social media, on its changes and new development. It can also use its own social media platform to clarify any misunderstanding.

Through the Delegation Offices and EU Centres, the EU has attempted to develop appropriate public diplomacy towards different Asian countries. Acknowledging the heterogeneity of Asia is good. It will be even better to further identify internal heterogeneity inside each Asian country, between different ethnic groups, regions and ages.

Good public diplomacy should have a clear sense of achievable goals and a strategy to attain these by realising its actual perception helps the EU to formulate such practical aims, and hence workable strategy. This chapter could not examine and compare the EU's public diplomacy in each of the APT countries. It would be worthwhile to further develop research in this direction.

Notes

1 They are Brunei, Cambodia, Indonesia, Laos, Malaysia, Myanmar, the Philippines, Singapore, Thailand and Vietnam.
2 Personal interview by author, July 2006, Brussels.
3 For more information, see www.eu-asia.eu/welcome/.
4 For more information, see www.canterbury.ac.nz/ncre/research/euperceptions/.
5 Full list of keywords includes also Council of European Union, European Council, European Court of Justice / ECJ and European Parliament / EP.
6 The migration crisis started getting serious only later in June 2015.

References

Anholt, Simon. (2005). *Brand New Justice: How Branding Places and Products Can Help the Developing World*. Oxford: Elsevier Butterworth-Heinemann Press.

Brooks, Stephen. (2015). *Anti-Americanism and the Limits of Public Diplomacy: Winning Hearts and Minds?* London: Routledge Press.

Bruter, Michael. (1999). "Diplomacy without a State: The External Delegations of the European Commission", *Journal of European Public Policy* 6 (2): 183–205.

Cull, Nicholas. (2009). *Public Diplomacy: Lessons from the Past, in CPD Perspectives on Public Diplomacy*. Los Angeles: USC Center on Public Diplomacy.

Duke, Simon. (2013). "The European External Action Service and Public Diplomacy", *Discussion Papers in Diplomacy* 127. The Hague: Netherlands Institute of International Relations Clingendael.

EEAS website, EU Centres, http://eeas.europa.eu/eu-centres/index_en.htm, accessed online 29 August 2016.

European Commission. (1994). *Towards a New Asia Strategy*. Brussels, COM (94) 314, 13 July.

European Commission. (2001a). *EU Strategy towards China: Implementation of the 1998 Communication and Future Steps for a More Effective EU Policy*. Brussels, COM (2001) 265, 15 May.

European Commission. (2001b). *Europe and Asia: A Strategic Framework for Enhanced Partnerships*. Brussels, COM (2001) 469 final, 4 September.

European Commission. (2004). *Taking Europe to the World: 50 Years of the European Commission's External Service*. Luxembourg: Office for Official Publications of the European Communities.

European Commission. (2007). *A Glance at EU Public Diplomacy at Work: The EU's 50th Anniversary Celebrations around the World*. Luxembourg: Office for Official Publications of the European Communities.

European Commission. (2013). *Information and Communication: Handbook for EU Delegations in Third Countries and to International Organizations*. Brussels, Ref: Ares (2013) 32604–11/01/2013.

European Commission. (2016). *Public Diplomacy through the Partnership Instrument*, http://ec.europa.eu/dgs/fpi/showcases/the_partnership_instrument_infographi_en.htm, accessed online 1 June 2017.

European Commission and European External Action Service. (2016). *Shared Vision, Common Action: A Stronger Europe, a Global Strategy for the European Union's Foreign and Security Policy*. Brussels, June.
European Council. (1995). *The New Transatlantic Agenda*. Brussels, 3 December.
European External Action Service, "EU in the World", https://eeas.europa.eu/headquarters/headquarters-homepage/area/geo_en, accessed online 8 September 2017).
Hartig, Falk (2016). *Chinese Public Diplomacy: The Rise of the Confucius Institute*. London: Routledge Press.
Leonard, Mark, Andrew Small and Martin Rose. (2005). *British Public Diplomacy in the Age of Schisms*. London: Foreign Policy Centre.
Manners, Ian. (2002). "Normative Power Europe: A Contradiction in Terms", *Journal of Common Market Studies* 40 (2): 235–58.
McKenzie, Brian. A. (2005). *Remaking France: Americanization, Public Diplomacy, and the Marshall Plan*. New York: Berghahn Books.
Melissen, Jan (ed.). (2005). *The New Public Diplomacy: Soft Power in International Relations*. New York: Palgrave Macmillan.
Nye, Joseph. (2008). "Public Diplomacy and Soft Power", *The ANNALS of the American Academy of Political and Social Science* 616 (1): 94–109.
Rasmussen, Steffen Bay. (2009). "Discourse Analysis of EU Public Diplomacy: Massages and Practices", *Discussion Papers in Diplomacy*. The Hague: Clingendael.
Reiterer, Michael. (2013). "The EU in Asia: Facts and Figures Concerning the EU's engagement in the Asia-Pacific", www.eeas.europa.eu/archives/docs/asem/docs/eu_in_asia_facts_and_figures_en.pdf, accessed online 4 March 2016.
Rugh, William. (2014). *Front Line Public Diplomacy: How US Embassies Communicate with Foreign Publics*. New York: Palgrave Macmillan.
Van Ham, Peter. (2005). "Brand European Power", *Place Branding* 1 (2): 122–6.
Van Ham, Peter. (2008). "Place Branding: The State of the Art", *The Annals of the American Academy of Political and Social Science* 616: 126–49.
Wang, Jian (ed.). (2011). *Soft Power in China: Public Diplomacy through Communication*. New York: Palgrave Macmillan.

6 The European Union's approach to human security: lessons from the Asia-Pacific

Evangelos Fanoulis

> This is a world of new dangers but also of new opportunities. The European Union has the potential to make a major contribution, both in dealing with the threats and in helping realise the opportunities. An active and capable European Union would make an impact on a global scale. (Council of the EU, 2003)

Introduction

The EU, representing its member-states and in co-operation with them, has pursued a foreign policy agenda that extends well beyond the European basin, with an aspiration – as noted in the chapter's opening quotation – to "make an impact on a global scale". One of the most remote places that the EU can possibly engage is the Asia-Pacific, the locus of this book. This chapter examines the following broad research question: to what extent does the EU qualify as a human security provider in the Asia-Pacific? To answer, I discuss the various means that the EU employs in pursuing human security in the region: development, trade, humanitarian aid, global health, environmental and foreign policy instruments. The narrative evaluates whether the member-states en bloc and under the aegis of the EU institutions offer human security, focusing on the most recent EU instruments, particularly on deployed funding schemes.

The chapter is divided into four sections. The first introduces the concept of human security and its role in EU foreign policy. Drawing on interregionalism, the second section briefly presents the institutional architecture of the EU–Asia-Pacific relations in an endeavour to justify the EU's pursuit of human security in the Asia-Pacific. The third section empirically concentrates on one specific dimension of the interregional EU–Asia-Pacific relations, looking at whether the Union delivers human security to the insular states in the Pacific. The concluding section draws reflections on whether questions of human security force a strategic revision of the EU's foreign policy agenda.

Human security in EU foreign policy

As an idea, concept and political objective, human security made its post-Cold War debut with the 1994 Human Development Report of the United Nations Development Programme. The report registered seven aspects of human security (economic security, food security, health security, environmental security, personal security, community security, political security), implying a very broad understanding of the concept (Acharya, 2001). Countries with a significant say in UN peacebuilding and peacekeeping activities came forward with their own definitions. Canada pushed human security as "freedom from pervasive threats to people's rights, safety or lives" (Global Development Research Center, undated). Japan insisted on a more holistic uptake of human security as "a life free of fear and free of want" (Global Development Research Center, undated). The UN Trust Fund for Human Security stretched the concept even further, adding "freedom to live in dignity" to freedom from fear and freedom from want (UN Trust Fund for Human Security, undated). In such a variegated context, Kaunert and Léonard (2011) have rightly argued that there is great variation amidst practitioners, national administrators and academics on what human security is and how it can be pursued.

The concept started appearing in the EU discourse in early 2000s and mostly after the adoption of the European Security Strategy (ESS) in 2003. It was strongly promoted by the EU Commission through the official statements of the Commissioner for external relations Benita Ferrero-Waldner. The EU High Representative (HR) Javier Solana commissioned a group of academics to report on the applicability of human security in the EU context (Kotsopoulos, 2006). The group, presided by Mary Kaldor, authored in 2004 the Barcelona report known as a Human Security Doctrine for Europe. The report embraces the (narrow) definition of human security as protection of human beings and societies from fear (Study Group on Europe's Security Capabilities, 2004). With an explicit focus on the implementation of ESS, the Barcelona report recommended that the EU should deliver security according to international humanitarian law, serving the security needs of people and societies without imposing on them, acting in a multilateral diplomatic framework (read the UN here) yet with a regional focus. To achieve such ambitious goals, the Barcelona report recommended the establishment of a fifteen-thousand Human Security Response Force (HSRF) for implementing the EU's human security doctrine (Study Group on Europe's Security Capabilities, 2004), a suggestion which has yet to be implemented.

The Barcelona report was welcomed by the EU institutions. However, the ambitious pursuit of a human security doctrine has lain dormant due to the decelerating pace of European integration. The failure of the Constitutional Treaty put the implementation of human security suggestions on ice (Kotsopoulos, 2006). Despite the temporary stagnation, the centrality of human security for EU foreign policy revived in 2006 when the Finnish presidency of the Council of the EU reassembled Kaldor's group for authoring the 2007 Madrid report known as a European Way of Security.

The Madrid report shifted definitional attention from human rights violations (emphasised by the Barcelona report) towards crisis management, no matter what the type of the latter is. The revised definition of human security is still closer to freedom from fear than freedom from want:

> Human Security is about the European Union helping to meet human need at moments of crisis, when people suffer not only because of wars but from natural and human-made disasters – famines, Tsunamis, hurricanes. ... ensuring Human Security under circumstances of extreme vulnerability means a concern for both physical and material wellbeing. (Human Security Study Group, 2007: 8)

Answering critiques that human security is not adequately precise, hence undermining implementation, the Madrid report presented it as a potential strategic "narrative" for the EU's foreign, security and defence policies (Human Security Study Group, 2007: 8), and an "ongoing and dynamic organising frame for security action" (Kaldor et al., 2008: 1).

Little does such definitional rearrangement add to the conceptual and functional clarity of the EU's approach to human security. It is this continuous ambiguity that Martin and Owen (2010: 218) criticise when they write "despite attempts to define human security and embed it within EU practice, a gap has persisted between the doctrinal and the institutional development of the ESDP [European Security and Defence Policy]". In the 2008 Implementation Report of ESS, human security is mentioned both as a desired political goal (p. 2) and as a conceptual tool that alters security attention from the nation-state to the human being (p. 10) (Council of the EU, 2008). Yet such generic mentions are no sign of crystal-clear political intention to render human security the cardinal strategic narrative of the EU.

The question that emerges is whether there is a role after all for human security in EU foreign policy apart from being a mere conceptual reference. The applicability of the notion is threatened by its all-encompassing, norm- and value-centred nature (Matlary, 2008). As transposed in the EU context by Kaldor and followers, human security resembles more of a politico-philosophical idea than an applicable political concept. Clarity is to date needed. Is human security an end or a means for EU foreign policy? Martin and Owen (2010: 222) contend that it can be both as long as it gets further specified. To that, we should note that the added value of using human security as the driving force of EU foreign policy should itself be specified. How is human security a better way for determining EU foreign policy in comparison to non-conventional security, civil security, non-traditional security – if human security is seen as end of EU foreign policy – and in comparison to EU as civilian power or defender of responsibility to protect – if human security is seen as the means of EU foreign policy? Moreover, is human security intended to confirm the global reach of the EU as an international security actor (Brattberg and Rhinard, 2012)? Proponents of the concept would claim that the real added value of the notion is the bestowal of a normative dimension to EU foreign policy, reinforced by policy suggestions such as the creation of the HSRF. Is this sufficient, though, for the fully-fledged operationalisation of a human security doctrine for the EU? Without describing the exact process for achieving human security in the world through a legally binding action plan, route map or implementation guidelines, the notion can be devalued into declaratory notes used by national and supranational policy-makers at their behest and for their own political interests.

Thus, without further functional specifications the strongly normative nature of human security seems to attack its own rationale. For example, the emphasis on action within the UN framework jeopardises the contingency of independently undertaking human security projects for the sake of protecting human beings. If the UN fails to reach a decision (e.g., in Syria), this obliges the EU to abandon initiatives of delivering human security, hence contrasting the normative core of the concept. To a certain extent, this innate contradiction is due to the way that the EU's official perception of human security has been much closer to freedom from fear, linked with Common Foreign and Security Policy (CFSP), Common Security and Defence Policy (CSDP) and ESS, rather than to freedom from want, which can associate with development, energy, health and environmental EU instruments.

Christou (2014) highlights that mentions of human security in the formal EU discourse have died down with the withdrawal of its key EU proponents, Commissioner Ferrero-Waldner and the HR Solana. This does not mean that the EU refrains from action translatable into human security (Christou, 2014). The post-Lisbon emphasis on the EU's comprehensive approach to security confirms such an insight; human security is mentioned as an end of the EU's comprehensive approach towards security in the 2016 Global Strategy for Foreign and Security Policy (EUGS), even though without further clarifications (European External Action Service, 2016: 28).

Comprehensive security implies a holistic reading of security, whose ends little differ from the combination of both freedom from fear and freedom from want. Such a broad understanding of security necessitates a great gamut of instruments for its implementation and not just military tools. For instance, to apply its comprehensive approach to security in the Horn of Africa, the EU has applied different policy instruments, from CSDP civilian missions and military operations to developmental and humanitarian aid, emphasising their complementarity and the need for co-ordinated action in the region (Gebhard and Norheim-Martinsen, 2011; Ehrhart and Petretto,

2014). The use of these different instruments in order to protect societies from conflict and secure their stability in the long run coincides with the normative premises of human security. Hence, one should not discard it too quickly as the driving force and underlying normative idea behind the design and execution of EU foreign policy. Besides, the frequent references in the 2016 EUGS on building resilience around the world – in particular in the countries receiving EU development aid – could also be seen as an implicit linkage to human security.

EU–Asia-Pacific relations: thriving interregionalism?

The interaction of the EU with the Asia-Pacific can be approached at interregional and trans-regional levels. Looking at the level of institutionalisation of these interactions can allow us to better grasp the rationale and actions behind the EU's pursuit of human security in the Asia-Pacific as presented in the section that follows.

The EU maintains strategic partnerships with five Asian countries, which are deemed important for the interests of the EU and its memberstates, China, India, Japan, Russia and South Korea (ESPO, undated); it has finalised Partnership and Co-operation Agreements (PCAs) with Indonesia, Japan, Pakistan, South Korea, Mongolia, Philippines, Singapore and Vietnam; and is discussing PCAs with Australia, Afghanistan, Brunei, China, Malaysia, New Zealand and Thailand; last but not least the EU participates in Asia-focused regional organisations and regimes of intergovernmental co-operation – bestowing upon them an inter-regional aspect – such as the South Asian Association for Regional Cooperation, the Pacific Island Forum, the Asia Europe Meeting (ASEM), the Regional Forum (ARF) and the Shangri-La Dialogue of the Association of Southeast Asian Nations (ASEAN) (ASEM factsheet, 2014). This complicated institutional framework implies both a strong EU interest in the Asia-Pacific and a multi-level engagement with the region, which extends from diplomatic dialogue with small nation-states (e.g., Thailand) to powerful powers of the international system (Russia, China) to regional organisations that see EU as an important partner (e.g., ASEAN). To be clear, high levels of institutionalisation of inter-regional ties do not automatically translate into increased bilateral collaboration between the EU and Asia-Pacific. As I will be showing below, there are substantial differences among the various interregional schemes; some of them do not surpass the level of political dialogue whereas others have moved to joint projects and synergies between the EU and the Asia-Pacific countries.

The nexus of EU–Asia-Pacific partnerships, agreements and contacts commences with the strategic partners of the EU in the region. A way to

Table 6.1 The EU's strategic partnerships in Asia

Dialogues (on annual basis)	China	Russia	Japan	South Korea
Summits	1	1	1	1
Ministerial dialogues	8	2	1	Missing data
Sectoral dialogues	51	35	34	Missing data
Other platforms	3	2	3	1
Total	63	40	39	2

Source: ESPO and EEAS

assess the scope and degree of importance of the partnerships is by looking at the dialogues occurring within their context. As shown in Table 6.1, China is the most frequent diplomatic interlocutor of the EU in Asia, followed by Russia and Japan.[1] The strategic partnership with Korea was formalised only in 2010, which explains the rather limited number of meetings between the two partners so far. Sectoral dialogues consist of a diplomatic platform allowing partners to discuss issues related to human security. This is mostly evident in the case of the EU–China strategic partnership acting as the broad institutional framework for a dialogue on security and defence policy, a dialogue on development, a political dialogue on non-proliferation and disarmament, a human rights dialogue, a high-level dialogue on migration and mobility, the sustainable development task force, a dialogue on energy and the climate change partnership (ESPO, undated). All these sectoral dialogues associate with freedom from fear and freedom from want. The institutional framework may show political willingness to co-operate without always translating into joint actions and projects. As Fanoulis and Kirchner (2015) note, the EU and China hold different interpretations of non-traditional security – the term is preferred in EU–China collaboration since the Chinese government seems hesitant to employ the norm-laden term human security – which has limited actual collaboration by means of joint actions in the fight against organised crime, cybersecurity, securitised migration and terrorism. Dorussen et al. (2016) have reached similar conclusions by looking at EU–China co-operation on civil protection and humanitarian aid.

What is more, the EU's engagement with the Asia-Pacific materialises through the Union's participation in Asian regional organisations. The EU has the opportunity to meet the Asia-Pacific every two years and at the level of heads of state or government in the context of the ASEM. The two continents have pledged to further their joint efforts on peace, security, poverty eradication, human rights protection, democracy and good governance, international collaboration and environmental protection. Even if not explicitly referenced in the proceedings of the ASEM summits, these grand thematiques link to the encompassing human security. With regard to human security as freedom from want, for example, the 2015 ministerial ASEM meeting in Luxembourg renewed its support to the "ASEM Sustainable Development Dialogue", considering the latter "an important platform to exchange best practices and to consolidate proposals for transforming global challenges *inter alia* related to water, food and energy security into opportunities for inclusive growth and sustainable development" (ASEM 2015: 2, original emphasis). Regarding human security as freedom from fear, ASEM affirmed inter-regional co-operation in the fields of crisis management and disaster reduction:

> Ministers underlined the importance of strengthening resilience through sharing knowledge and promoting cooperation on a broad and people-centred approach to disaster prevention, mitigation, preparedness and response to disasters, recovery, rehabilitation, including through awareness programmes, early warning systems, search, rescue and relief operation, capacity building, and promotion of innovation and technology. (ASEM 2015: 3)

What draws our attention in the above quotation is the highly declaratory note. The high-level works of ASEM nurture an ambiance of common political and diplomatic commitment rather than translating joint political willingness into concrete synergies and projects. This should not come as a surprise since above all ASEM remains a forum of political dialogue between European and Asian countries, with restricted executive and implementing powers and with decisions of no binding nature. According to Zhu (2015), the effectiveness of ASEM falls prey to the great diversity of interests and strategies of its participant members, rendering it often difficult to find common ground to deepen collaboration by means of concrete actions.

Unlike ASEM, EU–ASEAN co-operation has shown promising samples of practised inter-regional co-operation between the EU and countries of the Asia-Pacific. This can well be due to the long-lasting co-operation between the two organisations that dates from 1972. The EU maintains a strong presence in the organisation's different fora on security questions such as the ARF and the Shangri-La dialogue.[2] The former brings together ASEAN countries, the EU and nation-states active in the Pacific such as China, Japan, the US and Australia, in an effort to build inter-regional trust, whereas the latter is an annual high-level conference organised by the EU, taking place in Singapore, so as to discuss regional security questions (Asia-EU security factsheet, 2012).

The security agenda of EU–ASEAN co-operation is multifaceted.[3] However, and unlike ASEM, the EU–ASEAN joint focus on preventive diplomacy, maritime safety and security, counter-terrorism, border management and fight against transnational crime does not limit itself to declarations. The political willingness to proceed with concrete joint actions is

Table 6.2 EU–ASEAN collaboration on security questions

Security areas	EU–ASEAN actions
Preventive diplomacy	• Committing to multilateral, UN-led proposals for disarmament and non-proliferation • Setting in force the Preventive Diplomacy Work Plan and the Hanoi Plan of Action • Organising workshops, seminars and exchanges of best practices on preventive diplomacy
Maritime safety and security	• Sharing knowledge and experiences on maritime safety • Exchanging "information, technological co-operation and visits of relevant ASEAN and EU officials" in maritime search and rescue activity
Transnational crime	• ASEAN Senior Officials' Meetings on Transnational Crime – EU Consultations • Supporting the UN Convention against Corruption
Counter-terrorism	• Regular policy dialogues for exchanging information, experiences and capacity-building between responsible governmental authorities in both ASEAN and EU
Border management	• Setting in force the ASEAN Leaders' Joint Statement in Enhancing Cooperation against Trafficking in Southeast Asia • Implementing the ASEAN–EU Comprehensive Border Management Programme

Source: ASEAN, 2012

higher than in the case of ASEM. For instance, the EU regularly participates in the design and execution of ASEAN's disaster relief exercises (DiREX), which simulate scenarios of fighting maritime pollution and of safe and rescue actions after maritime disasters (Dorussen et al., 2016). Table 6.2 summarises EU–ASEAN concise collaboration in the aforementioned areas.

In sum, it appears that the EU and Asia-Pacific have ample venues to conduct inter-regional political dialogue with regard to security questions. The necessary institutionalisation that enables the EU to provide human security in the Asia-Pacific is already in place. Nevertheless, the existence of different inter-regional institutional frameworks has not always translated into concrete (security) co-operation via joint interregional actions, EU–ASEAN collaborative schemes being the exception rather than the rule.

EU activity in the Pacific:[4] signs of human security provision?

Owing to space limitations it is practically impossible to empirically examine all EU activities in the Asia-Pacific which relate and can broadly

Table 6.3 EU delegations in the Pacific

EU delegation	Yes	No	Developing	Least developed
Cook Islands		•	•	
East Timor	•			•
Fiji	•		•	
Kiribati		•		•
Marshall Islands		•	•	
Micronesia		•	•	
Nauru		•	•	
Niue		•	•	
Palau		•	•	
Papua New Guinea	•		•	
Samoa		•	•	
Solomon Islands		•		•
Tonga		•	•	
Tuvalu		•		•
Vanuatu		•		•

Source: EEAS, undated; UNCTAD
(The EU delegation in the Solomon Islands also covers Vanuatu.)

link to human security. The narrative concentrates on the Pacific islands as a representative sample of what the EU does in the region. Being the most remote from Europe, one would expect the EU's engagement to be limited in this sub-region. The empirical reality presented below shows instead a systematic support of the EU towards the Pacific, seen in the EU's foreign policy, development, trade, humanitarian aid, health and environmental instruments.

Foreign policy instruments (FPIs)

The establishment of permanent EU delegations, which can monitor the implementation of instruments and provide technical assistance to recipient countries when necessary, can be deemed a first sign of the EU's active presence in a region. Table 6.3 presents the distribution of EU delegations in the Pacific and categorises the region into developing and least-developed countries according to UN data. EU delegations have been established only in a few countries in the Pacific; the delegation in Fiji is generally responsible for the region.

FPIs under the title of CFSP include CSDP missions and operations, the Instrument contributing to Stability and Peace (replacing the Instrument for

Stability, IfS), the Partnership Instrument, election observation missions (EOM), restrictive and anti-torture measures (EU Commission, Service for FPIs, undated). Most of these instruments link to human security through freedom from fear. EOM and anti-torture measures target in particular political fear.

East Timor, Fiji and Papua New Guinea have been recipients of FPIs due to having experienced political instability and internal conflict in the 2000s, and they have been since in a phase of democratisation and political consolidation. The EU offered its support to UN mediation experts in Fiji in 2012 through the IfS and assisted the development of an early warning and early response system in East Timor in 2013 (EU Commission, Service for FPIs, undated).[5] Further, the EU launched an EOM for the parliamentary elections in East Timor in 2012 (EU Commission, Service for FPIs, 2012); and it followed closely the national elections in Papua New Guinea during the same year (Council of the EU, 2013). In addition, the HR and other EU spokespersons notify progress or stagnation of different indicators that can be associated with human security. For example, the EU saluted the "peaceful conduct ... and high turnout" in the 2014 parliamentary elections in Fiji (European External Action Service, 2014) whereas the HR Catherine Ashton deplored the reintroduction of the death penalty in Papua New Guinea in 2013 (European External Action Service, 2013).

Development

Developmental aid targets freedom from want even though it also associates with freedom from fear since lack of prosperity and growth can lead to conflicts. The Pacific countries are part of the ACP group (Africa, Caribbean Sea, Pacific), which has traditionally received official development assistance (ODA) from the EU. The corresponding institutional framework dates from the creation of the European Communities: from the Yaounde and Lome Agreements to the most recent ACP–EU Partnership known as the Cotonou Agreement. Different instruments and budgetary means emanate from these agreements in order to channel ODA to ACP countries. The Directorate-General International Co-operation and Development (DG DEVCO) of the EU Commission manages:

- the implementation of the thematic and regional versions of the Development Co-operation Instrument
- part of the European Initiative for Democracy and Human Rights
- funding for external relations issues overlapping with development (e.g., migration, asylum)
- part of the crisis and emergency response funds
- the biggest part of aid for the European neighbourhood, Asia and Latin America

- funds related to food security, environmental protection, human capital, and co-operation and co-ordination with countries receiving European ODA.

All the above fall under the EU budget. DG DEVCO also administers the European Development Fund (EDF), constituted by direct contributions of the member states. The Pacific countries have benefited more from the latter rather than from EU-budgetised, development-related instruments as depicted in Table 6.4. Table 6.5 shows the socio-economic sectors that have primarily benefited from the development funds (data from the tenth EDF, 2007–14) and Table 6.6 presents the allocation of commitments in the region for the eleventh EDF (2014–20).

Unlike foreign policy instruments, development assistance is of continuous and regular nature, becoming a reliable source for the economies of the Pacific countries. All 15 are recipients albeit in different capacities. Combining Tables 6.4 and 6.6 indicates that Papua New Guinea, Samoa, the Solomon Islands and East Timor tend to get larger amounts of European ODA than other countries in the region. The disbursements of the tenth EDF to the Pacific countries were mostly dedicated to projects on water, energy and sustainable development (education, good governance, strengthening institutions), all of which are cardinal for achieving freedom from want. Suffice it to say ODA is accompanied by political conditionality, most of the times related to good governance, building institutional capacity, rule of law and protection of human rights (Mold, ed., 2007). EU institutions and member states in principle agree that they will not sponsor non-democratic governments. This is conspicuous in the case of Fiji, where the EU ceased to wire EDF sources directly to the government of Fiji in 2007 because of the 2006 military coup (EU Commission, DG DEVCO, undated 1).

Along with the EU-budgetised ODA and the EDF country-based allocations, the EU Commission established within the EDF framework the Investment Facility for the Pacific (IFP) to boost investments in the region. Sums of €10 million were earmarked for the IFP from the tenth EDF for the years 2012–15 and €20 million from the forthcoming eleventh EDF (EU Commission, DG DEVCO, undated 2). Grouped together, EU development funds seem to be a financial source that the Pacific countries can use to build up their economies, reduce poverty and achieve sustainable and societal growth.

Trade

The Pacific countries benefit from the ACP–EU economic partnership, which treats in a privileged manner imports coming from ACP countries. Country-specific partnership agreements were concluded with Fiji and

Table 6.4 Disbursements of ODA managed by DG DEVCO to the Pacific countries, 2010–15 (€ million)

ODA	2010		2011		2012		2013		2014		2015	
	EUBUDG	EDF	EUBUDG	EDF	EUBUDG	EDF	EUBUDG	EDF	EUBUDG	EDF	EUBUDG	EDF
Cook Islands	0.00	0.08	0.00	1.12	0.00	0.56	0.00	0.26	0.00	1.00	0.00	3.00
East Timor	4.52	4.58	4.10	8.20	3.84	20.40	2.43	12.39	1.42	15.70	2.00	9.00
Fiji	1.07	3.63	3.38	1.78	4.92	0.80	5.96	3.14	4.95	1.94	11.00	5.00
Kiribati	0.00	0.60	0.00	2.58	0.00	1.97	0.00	2.76	0.00	5.19	0.00	3.00
Marshall Islands	0.00	0.42	0.00	0.02	0.00	0.09	0.00	0.09	0.00	0.55	MD	MD
Micronesia	0.00	0.38	0.00	1.11	0.00	0.05	0.00	0.61	0.00	0.39	0.00	0.00
Nauru	0.00	0.82	0.00	0.03	0.00	1.08	0.00	0.84	0.00	0.85	0.00	0.00
Niue	0.00	0.85	0.00	0.66	0.00	0.48	0.00	0.40	0.00	0.59	0.00	0.00
Palau	0.00	0.52	0.00	0.01	0.00	0.00	0.00	0.00	0.00	0.01	MD	MD
Papua New Guinea	1.92	35.63	1.04	12.97	1.56	10.33	0.95	3.99	1.27	8.12	3.00	17.00
Samoa	0.30	8.32	0.07	15.61	0.76	6.27	1.50	0.78	0.00	6.24	1.00	11.00
Solomon Islands	0.82	17.66	0.00	3.03	1.56	8.14	0.69	4.77	0.77	3.78	2.00	3.00
Tonga	0.00	1.22	0.00	6.43	0.00	0.55	0.00	0.41	0.08	3.81	0.00	4.00
Tuvalu	0.00	0.18	0.00	3.38	0.00	0.64	0.00	1.89	0.00	1.21	0.00	0.00
Vanuatu	0.12	1.10	0.36	1.00	1.67	2.10	0.23	2.72	0.22	0.58	1.00	6.00

Source: EU Commission, DG DEVCO, undated c.
EUBUDG = EU Budgetised Funds; EDF = European Development Fund; MD = missing data

Table 6.5 Societal sectors benefiting from the tenth EDF, target areas for development

Cook Islands	Water, sanitation, energy, regional integration, trade-related issues
East Timor	Sustainable development, health, strengthening institutions
Fiji	Sustainable development (focusing on sugar sector), democratisation
Kiribati	Water, energy
Marshall Islands	Water, energy
Micronesia	Renewable energy
Nauru	Water, renewable energy
Niue	Renewable energy, energy efficiency
Palau	Water, renewable energy
Papua New Guinea	Human resource development (education, vocational training), initiative of non-state actors, good governance, trade-related growth
Samoa	Water, sanitation, public health, initiatives of non-state actors
Solomon Islands	Sustainable rural development (capacity building), good governance
Tonga	Renewable energy, energy efficiency, initiatives of non-state actors, strengthening institutions
Tuvalu	Water, waste management, renewable energy, initiatives of non-state actors, trade-related issues
Vanuatu	Education, job growth and human resources development (vocational training), initiatives of non-state actors, capacity building

Source: EU Commission, DG DEVCO, undated c

Papua New Guinea in 2007, predicting "duty and quota-free exports" from the two countries to the EU, "asymmetric and gradual opening of markets to EU goods" and other measures facilitating trade between the EU and the two states (EU Commission, DG TRADE, undated 2). A comprehensive Economic Partnership Agreement covering the whole region is being discussed at the moment of writing (EU Commission, DG TRADE, undated 2). What is more, the EU is the biggest supporter worldwide of the "Aid for Trade" (AfT) scheme. The scheme crosscuts with ODA and aims to increase investments and finance infrastructural projects so that countries can develop their competitive capacities as trade partners (EU Commission, DG TRADE, undated 1). Niue, the Marshall Islands, Papua New Guinea, Fiji, the Solomon Islands, Vanuatu and East Timor have benefited in different degrees from the AfT (EU Commission, DG DEVCO, 2015).

Table 6.6 Eleventh EDF commitments towards Pacific countries, indicative allocation (€ million)

Cook Islands	1.40
East Timor	95.00
Fiji	28.00
Kiribati	23.00
Marshall Islands	9.10
Micronesia	14.20
Nauru	2.40
Niue	0.30
Palau	1.60
Papua New Guinea	184.00
Samoa	20.00
Solomon Islands	40.00
Tonga	11.10
Tuvalu	6.80

Source: Correspondence with EU delegation in Fiji

Humanitarian aid

As in the case of developmental assistance, humanitarian aid is strongly linked with human security even if the EU institutions and member-states do not officially and overtly make the linkage. Donated in order either to relieve post-crisis situations or to prepare for imminent disasters, it substantially contributes to freedom from fear. Unlike trade and development instruments that are accompanied by political conditionality, humanitarian assistance complies with basic principles of international humanitarian law: humanity, neutrality, impartiality and independence (EU Commission, DG ECHO, undated 1). The Directorate-General Humanitarian Aid and Civil Protection (DG ECHO) of the EU Commission manages the EU humanitarian aid, coming under the EU budget, and co-ordinates intergovernmental assistance channelled through the EU Civil Protection Mechanism (EUCPM). Table 6.7 notes humanitarian aid allocations and civil protection assistance following the activation of the EUCPM by the country in need, mostly due to natural disasters (floods, earthquakes, tropical storms, cyclones), to which the Pacific region is particularly prone.

At the same time, the Pacific countries are eligible for systematic funding through the Disasters Preparedness ECHO Programme (DIPECHO), which aims at increasing the resilience of disaster-prone countries worldwide (EU Commission, DG ECHO, undated 2). For the period 2009–11, €3.6 million has been granted to the Pacific region through DIPECHO (EU Commission,

Table 6.7 EU humanitarian aid and civil protection assistance to Pacific countries, 2010–15 (major cases)

Year	Humanitarian aid	Civil protection
2010	–	–
2011	–	–
2012	Fiji (floods)	Fiji (tropical cyclone Evan, request for assistance
2013	Pacific (cyclones, hurricanes, tropical storms)	Solomon Islands (earthquake)
2014	Solomon Islands (floods, landslides)	Solomon Islands (preparedness/ environmental mission)
2015	–	–

Source: EU Commission, DG ECHO, undated c

DG ECHO, undated 2). The most recent funds given by ECHO to the Pacific region are registered according to data availability in Table 6.8.

To sum up, the EU has tried to address humanitarian emergencies in the Pacific countries, depending on the latters' political willingness to request assistance from the EU (Table 6.7) and their eligibility for regular humanitarian aid through participation in the DIPECHO programme (Table 6.8). According to the available data, the EU has not so far refused humanitarian aid to a Pacific state that in times of great need, calamity and emergency knocks on Europe's door by activating the EUCPM.

Environmental and public health aid

The Pacific region is greatly concerned with climate change. Tuvalu, Kiribati and the Marshall Islands present common morphological features rendering them vulnerable to the rise of the sea level. All three countries consist of coral atolls with little arable land available; they have tropical climate with storms and typhoons; and deal with the scarcity of potable water on a daily basis. All three countries are to vanish if their low-level ground keeps on sinking under the sea levels rising due to climate change.[6] Such a disaster goes against everything that human security represents.

The EU has supported UN-led efforts against climate change. Both the EU and its member states signed and ratified the UN Framework Convention on Climate Change (UNFCC) (1992) and the ensuing Kyoto Protocol (1997), having also unilaterally proceeded to a declaration by which they commit themselves to a reduction of carbon dioxide emissions bigger than the one predicted by the Protocol. More recently, the EU set ambitious goals regarding the implementation of the UNFCC 2015 Paris Agreement,

Table 6.8 Disbursements of DG ECHO funds to Pacific countries, 2013 and 2014 (€ million)

Pacific countries	2013	2014
Cook Islands	0.04	0.00
East Timor	0.00	0.00
Fiji	0.59	0.10
Kiribati	0.04	0.00
Marshall Islands	0.13	0.03
Micronesia	0.07	0.00
Nauru	0.01	0.00
Niue	0.01	0.00
Palau	0.04	0.00
Papua New Guinea	1.09	1.46
Samoa	0.99	0.27
Solomon Islands	0.85	0.23
Tonga	0.09	0.06
Tuvalu	0.01	0.00
Vanuatu	0.84	0.18

Source: EU Commission, DG DEVCO, undated c. DH ECHO has not made publicly available disaggregated date for the fiscal year 2015. A total amount of €26 million is registered as humanitarian aid in 2015 for Southeast Asia and the Pacific.

intending further reductions of greenhouse emissions, more efficient usage of energy and more investments in renewable energy sources (EU Commission, DG CLIMA, 2016).

Concerning financing the fight against climate change, the European Investment Bank invested more than €90 billion during the period 2010–15 in climate action projects all over the world. Further, the EU and its member states are the leading sponsors of the Green Climate Fund (GCF) – contributing US$4.7 billion out of $10.2 billion of the total Fund. GCF has been especially established for helping the developing countries to lower the use of carbon energy without compromising their growth (EU Commission, DG CLIMA, 2015). Most importantly for the Pacific region, the EU and member states established the Global Climate Change Alliance for assisting least-developed countries and small island developing states to pursue environmentally friendly development, channelling more than €300 million up to 2015 for supporting fifty projects in roughly forty countries (EU Commission, DG CLIMA, 2015: 6).

There has been no environmental EU instrument, though, that targets exclusively climate change and environmental protection in the Pacific. The

EU Commission supports French efforts (worth €4 million) to manage climate change consequences in the region, especially the erosion of land (EU Commission, DG CLIMA, 2015: 14). The so-called RESCCUE project has been co-financed by the French Development Agency and the French Global Environment Facility (EU Commission, DG CLIMA, 2013).

On a similar note, the EU has not addressed public health needs in the Pacific in an exclusive manner. The region benefits on the one side from the EU's central role in global health governance, as the EU works closely with the World Health Organisation in the fight against pandemics (European Centre for Disease Prevention and Control, undated), and on the other from EU aid channelled to developing countries for achieving the health-related Millennium Development Goals (e.g., on maternal health, on child mortality) and for fighting communicable and non-communicable diseases (Council of the EU, 2010).

In both environmental and health issues, the Pacific countries (and the Asia-Pacific region in general) can indirectly benefit from the EU–ASEAN inter-regional co-operation that we elaborated above. The two partners have explicitly committed to "a greener partnership for a sustainable future", arranging inter-regional sectoral and policy dialogues on climate change, environment and sustainable development (EU Commission and High Representative, 2015: 9–10); and, more practically, the EU has allocated sources from its regional co-operation programme, the Asia Investment Facility and the SWITCH Asia Programme to support the environmental endeavours of ASEAN (EU Commission and High Representative, 2015: 9–10). On health issues, EU and ASEAN have promised to deepen their co-operation by means of a sectoral dialogue, which will take on board *inter alia* health security questions such as pandemics (EU Commission and High Representative, 2015: 6, 9).

Conclusion: what future for human security in EU foreign policy?

The chapter has shown a presence of the EU in the Asia-Pacific, which is not military as in the case of other players in the region (US, China, Australia). Even if the EU official discourse has conceptualised human security as primarily freedom from fear, the existing EU policy instruments rather relate to freedom from want. This shows up quite strongly here. The EU makes use of primarily developmental, trade, environmental and humanitarian instruments to provide human security to the region. Concentrating on the Pacific islands, the previous section has demonstrated that the EU sponsors infrastructural projects to sustainably boost the economies of the islands and it grants aid in times of calamity mostly due to natural disasters. Even though the chapter has presented empirical data to underpin these activities, it has not touched upon the question of effectiveness. Commitments and disbursements do not automatically demonstrate how effectively the EU funds are used. For example, is the humanitarian assistance of Table 6.8 sufficient to address the acute disasters wrought by nature in the Pacific as well as the climate change consequences? The question of how effective a human security provider in the Pacific the EU is still lingers for future scholarly investigations.

Two additional inferences can be drawn from the above narrative. The first has to do with the question of EU's actorness. By proving the EU to be a human security provider in the Asia-Pacific, the chapter underpins a long sequence of academic works arguing that the EU bears its own actorness (Jupille and Caporaso, 1998; Bretherton and Vogler, 2006; Blavoukos and Bourantonis, 2011; Kaunert and Zwolski, 2013; Wunderlich, 2012; Brattberg and Rhinard, 2012; Gehring et al., 2013). The EU's capacity to take decisions, mobilise capabilities (belonging to itself (from the EU budget) or to the member-states (for instance, the EDF or civil protection assistance)) and co-ordinate activities in such a remote region as the Pacific backs up the argument that the EU is an international security actor. The second inference relates to the significance of human security for EU foreign policy. For the time being, this is far from what the authors of Barcelona and Madrid reports have envisioned. Human security has not become the new strategic narrative of EU foreign policy. It has not vanished from the EU foreign policy nonetheless. Defined as both freedom from fear and freedom from want, human security remains the normative plane upon which EU foreign policy is designed and conducted. It might well be that human security as a conception gradually collapses into the EU's comprehensive approach towards security or even into the EU's recent emphasis on resilience. At least, this is what we can infer from the 2016 EUGS, which says that "The EU will foster human security through an integrated approach" (European External Action Service, 2016: 28).

Notes

1 For the EU–Japan strategic partnership, see also Chapter 8 by Atanassova-Cornelis below.
2 For a more detailed analysis of the security dimension of EU–ASEAN co-operation, see also chapter 9 by Wong below.
3 It should be mentioned that, just like China, ASEAN prefers to use the term NTS, seeing human security – owing to its affiliation to responsibility to protect (R2P) – as a concept incompatible with the organisation's strict focus on national sovereignty, territorial integrity and non-intervention.
4 The chapter follows the official EU definition of the Pacific as the region consisting of the following countries: Cook Islands, Federated States of Micronesia, Fiji, Kiribati, Nauru, Niue, Palau, Papua New Guinea, Republic of Marshall Islands, Samoa, Solomon Islands, East Timor, Tonga, Tuvalu and Vanuatu. This

is more of a functional and administrative definition rather than a strictly geographical one.
5   Notice here that part of the IfS is managed by EU Commission, DG DEVCO.
6   Academic discussions on the future statehood of sinking nation-states primarily concentrate on the legal dimension of the question from the perspective of international humanitarian law (Jacobs, 2005; McAdam 2012) or on environmental politics and how climate change affects national sovereignty and security (Bakker and Simperingham, 2012; Long and Wormworth, 2012; Barnett, 2009).

References

Acharya, Amitav. (2001). "Human Security: East versus West", *International Journal* 56 (3): 442–60.
Asia–Europe Meeting, ASEM. (2015). *Working Together for a Sustainable and Secure Future: 12th ASEM Foreign Ministers' Meeting, Chair's Statement*. www.aseminfoboard.org, accessed online 10 April 2016.
Association of Southeast Asian Nations, ASEAN. (2012). *Bandar Seri Begawan Plan of Action to Strengthen the ASEAN–EU Enhanced Partnership*. www.europarl.europa.eu/cmsdata/124481/129884.pdf, accessed online 10 April 2016.
Bakker, Jordan, Scott Leckie and Ezekiel Simperingham (eds). (2012). *Climate Change and Displacement Reader*. London: Routledge Press.
Barnett, Jon. (2009). "Climate Change and Human Security in the Pacific Islands: The Potential for and Limits to Adaptation", in J. Boston, P. Nel and M. Righarts, (eds). *Climate Change and Security: Planning for the Future*. Wellington: Institute of Policy Studies.
Blavoukos, Spyros, and Dimitris Bourantonis (eds). (2011). *The EU Presence in International Organisations*. Abingdon: Routledge.
Brattberg, Erik, and Mark Rhinard. (2012). "The EU as a Global Counter-Terrorism Actor in the Making", *European Security* 21 (4): 557–77. DOI: 10.1080/09662839.2012.688809.
Bretherton, Charlotte, and John Vogler. (2006). *The European Union as a Global Actor*. London: Routledge.
Christou, George. (2014). "The European Union's Human Security Discourse: Where Are We Now?", *European Security* 23 (3): 364–81.
Council of the EU. (2003). *A Secure Europe in a Better World: European Security Strategy*. Brussels. www.consilium.europa.eu/uedocs/cmsUpload/78367.pdf, accessed online 10 April 2016.
Council of the EU. (2008). *Report on the Implementation of the European Security Strategy: Providing Security in a Changing World*. Brussels. https://europa.eu/globalstrategy/en/report-implementation-european-security-strategy-providing-security-changing-world accessed online 10 April 2016.
Council of the EU. (2010). *Council Conclusions on the EU Role in Global Health*. Brussels. www.consilium.europa.eu/uedocs/cms_Data/docs/pressdata/EN/foraff/114352.pdf, accessed online 20 May 2016.
Council of the EU. (2013). *Main Aspects and Basis Choices of the CFSP*. Brussels.http://eeas.europa.eu/cfsp/docs/st14924_en.pdf, accessed online 20 April 2016.

Council of the EU. (2014). *Council Conclusions on the EU's Comprehensive Approach*. Brussels. www.consilium.europa.eu/uedocs/cms_Data/docs/pressdata/EN/foraff/142552.pdf, accessed online 10 April 2016.

Dorussen, Han, Ling, Jing, and Evangelos Fanoulis. (2016). "Civil Protection: Identifying Opportunities for Collaboration", in E. Kirchner, T. Christiansen and, H. Dorussen (eds). *EU–China Security Cooperation: Performance and Prospects*. Cambridge: Cambridge University Press.

Ehrhart, Hans and Kerstin Petretto. (2014). "Stabilizing Somalia: Can the EU's Comprehensive Approach Work?", *European Security* 23 (2): 179–94.

European Centre for Disease Prevention and Control, ECDC (ECDC). (undated). *Partnerships*. http://ecdc.europa.eu/en/aboutus/Partnerships/Pages/partnerships.aspx, accessed online 20 May 2016.

European External Action Service, EEAS. (2013). *Declaration by High Representative Catherine Ashton on Behalf of the European Union on the Reintroduction of the Death Penalty in Papua New Guinea*. Brussels. www.consilium.europa.eu/uedocs/cms_Data/docs/pressdata/en/cfsp/137377.pdf, accessed online 20 April 2016.

European External Action Service, EEAS. (2014). *Statement by the Spokesperson on the Parliamentary Elections in Fiji*. Brussels. http://eeas.europa.eu/statements/docs/2014/140917_01_en.pdf, accessed online 20 April 2016.

European External Action Service, EEAS. (2016). *Shared Vision, Common Action: A Stronger Europe. A Global Strategy for the European Union's Foreign and Security Policy*. https://eeas.europa.eu/top_stories/pdf/eugs_review_web.pdf, accessed 1 October 2016.

European External Action Service, EEAS. (undated). *EU Delegations' Web-sites*. http://eeas.europa.eu/delegations/index_en.htm, accessed online 10 April 2016.

European Strategic Partnerships Observatory, ESPO. (undated). *European Strategic Partnerships*. http://fride.org/project/28/european-strategic-partnerships-observatory, accessed online 10 April 2016.

EU–Asia Security Factsheet. (2012). http://eeas.europa.eu/archives/docs/asia/docs/eu_in_asia_factsheet_en.pdf, accessed online 10 April 2016.

EU Commission and High Representative. (2015). *The EU and ASEAN: A Partnership with a Strategic Purpose*. http://eur-lex.europa.eu/legal-content/EN/TXT/PDF/?uri=JOIN:2015:22:FIN&from=EN, accessed online 1 October 2016.

EU Commission, DG CLIMA. (2013). *European Union Climate Funding for Developing Countries in 2013*. http://ec.europa.eu/clima/events/docs/0086/funding_en.pdf, accessed online 20 May 2016.

EU Commission, DG CLIMA. (2015). *European Union Climate Funding for Developing Countries 2015*. http://ec.europa.eu/clima/publications/docs/funding_developing_countries_2015_en.pdf, accessed online 20 May 2016.

EU Commission, DG CLIMA. (2016). *Europe Readies Next Steps to Implement Paris Agreement*. http://ec.europa.eu/clima/news/articles/news_2016030201_en.htm, accessed online 20 May 2016.

EU Commission, DG DEVCO. (undated a). *Countries: Fiji*. http://ec.europa.eu/europeaid/countries/fiji_en, accessed online 20 April 2016.

EU Commission, DG DEVCO. (undated b). *Investment Facility for the Pacific*. https://ec.europa.eu/europeaid/regions/pacific/investment-facility-pacific-ifp_en, accessed online 20 May 2016.

EU Commission, DG DEVCO. (undated c). *List of Annual Reports*. Brussels. https://ec.europa.eu/europeaid/annual-reports_en, accessed online 20 April 2016.

EU Commission, DG DEVCO. (2015). *Aid for Trade: Report 2015*. http://trade.ec.europa.eu/doclib/docs/2015/september/tradoc_153808.pdf, accessed online 20 May 2016.

EU Commission, DG ECHO. (undated a). *Humanitarian Principles*. http://ec.europa.eu/echo/who/humanitarian-aid-and-civil-protection/humanitarian-principles_en, accessed online 20 May 2016.

EU Commission, DG ECHO. (undated b). *Disaster Risk Reduction*. http://ec.europa.eu/echo/what/humanitarian-aid/risk-reduction_en, accessed online 20 May 2016.

EU Commission, DG ECHO. (undated c). *Annual Reports*. http://ec.europa.eu/echo/who/accountability/annual-reports_en, accessed online 20 May 2016.

EU Commission, DG TRADE. (undated a). *Aid for Trade*. http://ec.europa.eu/trade/policy/countries-and-regions/development/aid-for-trade/, accessed online 20 May 2016.

EU Commission, DG TRADE. (undated b). *Countries and Regions: Pacific*. http://ec.europa.eu/trade/policy/countries-and-regions/regions/pacific/, accessed online 20 May 2016.

EU Commission, Service for Foreign Policy Instruments (FPIs). (2012). *Overview of Election Observation Missions – 2012*. http://ec.europa.eu/dgs/fpi/documents/activies_and_funding_4.pdf, accessed online 10 April 2016.

EU Commission, Service for Foreign Policy Instruments (FPIs). (undated a). *Key Documents*. http://ec.europa.eu/dgs/fpi/key-documents/index_en.htm, accessed online 10 April 2016.

Fanoulis, Evangelos, and Emil Kirchner. (2015). "Non-traditional Security Issues", in Jianwei Wang and Weiqing Song (eds), *China, the European Union and International Politics of Global Governance*. Basingstoke: Palgrave Macmillan.

Gebhard, Carmen, and Per Martin Norheim-Martinsen. (2011). "Making Sense of EU Comprehensive Security towards Conceptual and Analytical Clarity". *European Security* 20 (2): 221–41.

Gehring, Thomas, Sebastian Oberthür and Marc Mühleck. (2013). "European Union Actorness in International Relations: Why the EU Is Recognised as an Actor in Some International Institutions, but Not in Others", *Journal of Common Market Studies* 51 (5): 849–65.

Global Development Research Center. (undated). *Definitions of Human Security*. www.gdrc.org/sustdev/husec/Definitions.pdf, accessed online 15 March 2015.

Human Security Study Group. (2007). *A European Way of Security: The Madrid Report of the Human Security Study Group Comprising a Proposal and Background Report*. Madrid.

Jacobs, Rebecca. (2005). "Treading Deep Waters: Substantive Law Issues in Tuvalu's Threat to Sue the United States in the International Court of Justice", *Pacific Rim Law & Policy Journal* 14.

Jupille, Joseph, and James Caporaso. (1998). "States, Agency and Rules: The European Union in Global Environmental Politics", in C. Rhodes (ed.), *The European Union in the World Community*. Boulder: Lynne Rienner.

Kaldor, Mary, Mary Martin and Sabine Selchow. (2008). "Human Security: A European Strategic Narrative", in *International Policy Analysis*. Washington, DC: Friedrich Ebert Stiftung.

Kaunert, Christian, and Kaunert Zwolski. (2013). *The EU as a Global Security Actor: A Comprehensive Analysis beyond CFSP and JHA*. Basingstoke: Palgrave Macmillan.

Kaunert, Christian, and Sarah Léonard. (2011). "Introduction: European Security after the Lisbon Treaty: Neighbours and New Actors in a Changing Security Environment", *Perspectives on European Politics and Society* 12 (4): 361–70.

Kotsopoulos, John. (2006). "A Human Security Agenda for the EU?", *European Policy Centre Papers* 48. Brussels.

Long, Stephanie, and Janice Wormworth. (2012). "Tuvalu: Islanders Lose Ground to Rising Seas", in J. Bakker, S. Leckie and E. Simperingham (eds), *Climate Change and Displacement Reader*. London: Routledge.

Martin, Mary, and Taylor Owen. (2010). "The Second Generation of Human Security: Lessons from the UN and EU Experience", *International Affairs* 86 (1): 211–24.

Matlary, Janne Haaland. (2008). "Much Ado about Little: The EU and Human Security", *International Affairs* 84 (1): 131–43.

McAdam, Jane (ed.). (2012). *Climate Change, Forced Migration, and International Law*. Oxford: Oxford University Press.

Mold, Andrew (ed.). (2007). *EU Development Policy in a Changing World*. Amsterdam: Amsterdam University Press.

Study Group on Europe's Security Capabilities. (2004). *A Human Security Doctrine for Europe: The Barcelona Report of the Study Group on Europe's Security Capabilities*. Barcelona.

United Nations Conference on Trade and Development, UNCTAD. (2014). *The Least Developed Countries Report*. http://unctad.org/en/PublicationsLibrary/ldc2014_en.pdf, accessed online 10 April 2016.

UN Trust Fund for Human Security, UNFHS. (undated). *About Human Security*. www.un.org/humansecurity/about-human-security/human-security-all, accessed online 15 March 2015.

Wunderlich, Jens-Uwe. (2012). "The EU an Actor *Sui Generis*? A Comparison of EU and ASEAN Actorness", *Journal of Common Market Studies* 50 (4): 653–69.

Zhu, Tianxiang. (2015). "Different Versions of Interregionalism and ASEM's Multilateral Utility for Global Governance", in Jianwei Wang and Weiqing Song (eds), *China, the European Union and International Politics of Global Governance*. Basingstoke: Palgrave Macmillan.

PART III

Selected countries and groups

7 The European Union's partnership with China: navigating between trouble and promise

Gustaaf Geeraerts

Introduction

Since 2003 the EU and China have acknowledged each other as strategic partners. Slowly but steadily they have built a partnership, which constitutes probably one of the most structured relationships between two global powers in today's world system. Given the ongoing transformation of the international system in which the re-emergence of China is a major driver of change, the EU–China strategic partnership constitutes an important dimension in Chinese and European foreign policies. As the world's major trading entities, China and Europe affect each other deeply. They form the second-largest economic co-operation in the world and the sheer size of their markets gives them scope to mobilise plenty of resources for policies beyond their borders. At the same time, however, China's re-emergence and mounting influence are affecting Europe's relative position in the global distribution of capabilities, and also constitute a challenge to Europe's very identity and governance outlook. The EU and China make quite unlikely partners as their relationship reveals deep-seated conceptual differences concerning norms, visions of power, modes of international engagement and the organisation of the emerging world order (Michalski and Pan, 2017). Moreover, in the wake of the 2008–9 financial crisis and subsequent Great Recession, China and the EU have encountered growing friction in their economic and trade relationship, the fundamental link between them (Farnell and Crooks, 2016).

This chapter attempts to uncover a number of diverging and converging trends in the EU–China partnership. First, it discerns three diverging trends: (1) the changing global context of the relationship between the EU and China and how this process affects their relative positions in the global distribution of power and identities; (2) the limits of the EU as a transformative power and its implication for the EU's relationship with China; and (3) the creeping economic security dilemma between the EU and China. Next, it takes a look at two converging trends: (1) the high level of institutionalisation of the EU–China partnership and its potential for reciprocal socialisation; and (2) signs of mutual accommodation and convergence between the EU and China in their efforts to adapt themselves to the changing international system. The chapter concludes that the partnership between the EU and China is bound to be an intricate equilibrium between diverging and converging trends – at best an enlightened calibrating of national interests and global governance ambitions within a complex and transforming international environment that leads on to joint efforts at concerted order-shaping.

The changing global context of the EU's relationship with China

The world within which the EU and China have to deal with each other is changing. The unipolar moment is slowly fading and giving way to a more complex international system characterised by multi-layered and culturally diversified polarity or 'new multipolarity' (Geeraerts, 2011, 2013a). In this process, China's re-emergence and mounting influence – and that of other emerging countries for that matter – is not only having an impact on the Western developed nations' position in the global distribution of capabilities, it also constitutes a challenge to the values and organisational principles they stand for (Geeraerts, 2011; Kupchan, 2012). The successful economic growth of an idiosyncratic power as China is stretching the present international order, which chiefly mirrors the Western worldview of liberal democracy and free markets (Foot, 2009; Layne, 2012; Chen, 2016). While for more than half a century the United States, in tandem with Europe, has watched over the provision of global public goods such as monetary stability and free trade, and has propagated the practice of liberal democracy, good governance, human rights, international trade regulations, humanitarian intervention and state-building, recently both the US's and Europe's authority as political drivers of global governance stand to the test (Acharya, 2014; Kupchan, 2012). As much as the US, weighed by debt and deficits, is struggling to maintain its superpower status, the EU, faced with the Eurozone debt crisis – and more recently the refugee crisis in combination with the creeping challenge of the far right – is struggling to keep its act together. The EU remains unsure about its role in the world, "not least in terms of its security and its ability to do new trade deals. Brexit will diminish the EU's size and possibly its trade and security influence" Demertzis, Sapir and Wolff, 2017: 2).

Meanwhile, China has risen to become the world's largest economy in purchasing power parity terms (García-Herrero et al., 2017). Its stellar economic development has increased its economic and political influence well beyond its borders and is turning it into a more assertive player.

Increasingly Beijing is also developing different discourses of modernity and spelling out its own narratives of global governance (Breslin, 2013; Pan, 2012; Schweller and Pu, 2011). Part of these narratives question the present global governance regime's ability in providing economic and monetary stability as well as its authority in setting norms of good governance. China's successful re-emergence is putting the Western liberal order to the proof and raises the question whether Western liberal governance principles are here to stay or will be challenged by alternative models (Ikenberry, 2008; Kissinger, 2014; Acharya, 2014). This is all the more pertinent, as the contestation of Western hegemony is part of a broader historical movement. The so-called Rising Rest, represented by the BRICS countries (Brazil, Russia, India, China and South Africa), has stepped up its efforts to expand its international influence and demanded a reform of the prevailing liberal world order (Chen, 2016; Kupchan, 2012). The BRICS leaders made very clear in their joint statement of July 2014 that they "believe the BRICS are an important force for incremental change and reform of current institutions towards more representative and equitable governance, capable of generating more inclusive global growth and fostering a stable, peaceful and prosperous world" (Ministry of External Relations of Brazil, 2014). In general, the BRICS countries request better respect for state sovereignty, restriction of the use of force and unilateral intervention, and to obtain commensurate decision-making power in the main global and regional institutions. As such the emerging powers have been successful in questioning the principles and norms of the Western liberal order and thereby "overturned its hitherto unchallenged position as a normative paradigm of the international system" (Michalski and Pan, 2017: 16).

The changing constellation of world power is affecting the EU's international standing and appeal as a model of integration. The future is increasingly shaped by Asia, and China in particular. The growing economic weight of Asia and China's re-emergence as a major economic and political force pose a challenge to the EU's status as a transformative power in the international order. Indeed, Europe is going through a process of "decentring": the fact that most emerging countries – and China foremost among them – "are accumulating sovereignty or the means to stronger sovereignty, not sharing sovereignty as the European experience promotes, means that the European region remains quite exceptional in both its political dynamics and its strategic organization" (Kerr, 2012: 72). The BRICS' opposition to the liberal order poses a particular challenge to the EU's understanding of multilateralism as an organisational concept for world governance and the norms associated with it. Effective multilateralism is hard to practise "when powers such as China and Russia openly oppose the values and principles upon which it rests. For the BRICS countries, an unconditional inclusion in international organizations and multilateral regimes is not acceptable.

Therefore, they ask for some form of accommodation of the prevailing order to their concerns" (Michalski and Pan, 2017: 16, 17).

Meanwhile, as China continues to defend its national interests both by solidifying its bilateral relations and by working within existing and through creating new multilateral institutions, its growing capabilities as a foreign policy actor and rising role as an order-shaper (Chen, 2016) require the EU to adapt its strategic outlook and foreign policy capabilities (Geeraerts, 2013a). In this regard, the EU's new Global Strategy constitutes a timely effort to formulate a plan of action more adapted to challenges of the changing global environment and China's increasing role in it (EEAS, 2016). Still, the main challenge for the EU is to pool the fragmented capabilities of its member states into real levers for exerting influence if it is to be taken seriously as a strategic international actor by Beijing. Whilst the EU will continue to figure as one of the world's leading economies and most important entities in terms of external trade flows and Foreign Direct Investment (FDI), politically and militarily it performs far below its potential and in terms of comprehensive power is no match for China (Geeraerts, 2013b). At the end of the day, Europe has no strategic geopolitical or security stake in East Asia, no global power projection capacity and no unified foreign or defence policies. The EU is a significant global force only in trade and investment, to a lesser extent in the international financial system and "perhaps a bit through soft power" (de Jonquières, 2016: 1).

The limits of the EU as a transformative power

The countries of the European Community, later to become the EU, were a critical part of the American-led liberal order in the Cold War era. However, after the end of the Cold War, they were bound to take a somewhat distinctive path (Sperling and Kirchner, 1997). Indeed, "largely freed from the threat of the Soviet Union and facing fewer constraints from the United States, EC countries gave new impetus to the European integration process with the establishment of the European Union, strengthened the EU's foreign policy capacity in the form of the Common Foreign and Security Policy and tried to shape the European and world order based on the EU's own successful model" (Chen, 2016: 779). Whilst this enhanced order-shaping effort was inherently Western, as Europe shares with the United States the basic values of liberal democracy and market economy, it was also substantially European, in view of the unique and transformative nature of the European normative project (Manners, 2002, 2013). Decades of European integration led the EU to develop its typical postmodern and post-sovereign features. Within the confines of the Union, the EU gradually transformed the nation-state system into a regional bloc with strong supranational features, thereby creating in Europe a zone of peace and prosperity. This development led Cooper (2000: 22) to claim that the EU had evolved into a postmodern entity characterised by the breaking down of the distinction between domestic and foreign affairs; mutual interference in (traditional) domestic affairs and mutual surveillance; the rejection of force to resolve disputes and the consequent codification of rules of behaviour; the growing irrelevance of borders; and security based on transparency, mutual openness, interdependence and mutual vulnerability (Chen, 2016). In due course, the EU had developed an identity as a transformative power (Grabbe, 2006), founding its policies on values, institutions and co-operation rather than power politics. The ambition was to reshape the power paradigm to reflect a new kind of power in global politics, one that seeks to promote the norms and values on the international scene that are central to its identity and role as international actor (Michalski and Pan, 2017). As stated in its 2003 Security Strategy the EU aims at the "development of a stronger international society, well-functioning international institutions and a rule based international order" (CEU, 2003: 9). The rules underpinning this new international order are to be founded on Europe's liberal political norms, its views of an open global market and its preference for highly institutionalised multilateralism.

In this vein, relations with China and other emerging powers were largely constructed from the belief that the latter should adapt their international political norms to the European standards. Normative convergence figured as the starting point for developing relations with those countries. Europe's policy towards China was mainly one of conditional co-operation with normative convergence as its final aim. The EU was prepared to help the People's Republic of China (PRC), to invest in the development of the country, but in turn China was expected to meet a number of standards and demands. In this way, Europe expected to forge tighter links and strengthen its influence through ever-increasing economic interdependence and shared values. In this process, Europe saw itself as the model China should aspire to. The underlying assumption of this policy was the belief that "human rights tend to be better understood and better protected in societies open to the free flow of trade, investment, people, and ideas. As China continues its policy of opening-up to the world, the EU will work to strengthen and encourage this trend" (European Commission, 1995: 6).

The crucial question here is to what extent this approach could ever be successful. Beijing has never put democracy and respect for human rights at the top of its list of priorities (Geeraerts, 2016). In terms of foreign policy, it is unrealistic to think Beijing will ever comply with Europe's "postmodern" discourse. Following Robert Cooper's distinction between "modern states" and "post-modern states" (Cooper, 2000), China is to be categorised as a "modern state", for which "internationalism" is but one modus operandi serving the national interest (Geeraerts, 2013a). True to its credentials as a "modern state" the PRC never really was at a point where it was willing to meet European expectations. Chinese officials, scholars and pundits all tend to vindicate this when talking in private. It is crucial for the EU to be aware what power it has to sway policy in China. An important parameter in the EU's dealings with China is the strategic weight Brussels is capable of bringing to bear with Beijing. China perceives the EU foremost as an economic actor, far less as a political one.

On closer examination, there are grounds to be critical of the EU's leverage as a transformative power and to take on board its limitations (Grabbe, 2014). China may well recognise the advantages of co-operating with the EU and of learning from it in certain areas, but in line with its identity of a "rejuvenating nation" it is certainly not willing to accept the tutelage of the EU. China is not a prospective EU member, nor does it see itself as a weak nation, depending exclusively on the EU for support in its political and economic reform process. The most real incentive that the EU has to offer is access to its large market. The EU's success with China will to a large extent rest on mutual benefit in trade and investment, but also in areas of common interest such as environment, energy and regional security (García-Herrero et al., 2017). The degree to which China's interests can be expected to match those of the EU will largely determine the sustainability of the relationship.

When all the chips are down, the strength of the EU as a transformative power is dependent on the success of its economic and social model, as well as its capability of effective collective action. On these accounts, "the international status of the EU has suffered setbacks in the last decennium due to the onset of multiple crises, chiefly the sovereign debt crisis in the Eurozone, the refugee crisis and the British referendum on its continued membership of the EU" (Michalski and Pan, 2017: 4). The perception that the EU's economic governance model and its regulatory regime were not able to prevent the sovereign debt crisis seriously undermined the EU's credibility in promoting its economic and governance norms and principles (Liu and Breslin, 2016). In addition, the largely decentralised EU falls short in political capacity: it has difficulty in formulating coherent external policies, also in the economic realm (its major area of competence), which, combined with the grit of a centralised China to deal with individual EU member states rather than the EU as a whole, creates a major imbalance in political leverage (Liu and Breslin, 2016). The manifest lack of internal cohesiveness and consensus among the EU member states, together with the EU member states' propensity to seek bilateral agreements with China, is saddling the EU up with a collective action problem of sorts, which hampers its performance as a foreign policy actor and transformative power. Lastly, Europe's neighbourhood is now in its most precarious state since the end of the Cold War. Instead of having built a "ring of friends" around it, the EU is now surrounded by an "arc of instability" (Chen, 2016: 780).

A creeping economic security dilemma?

The post-Cold War period saw the growing importance of the EU's economic security (Sperling and Kirchner, 1998). In its 1993 White Paper, *Growth, Competitiveness, Employment – the Challenges and Ways Forward into the 21st Century*, the European Commission makes the point that,

> while traditional definitions of security have been closely linked to defence against military threats, the end of the Cold War and the rise of the globalisation process have led to the emergence of new, broader notions of security, among which economic security is one of the most important. According to the Commission, in this globalised world the EU's economic security must be protected. In this view Europe's economic security is understood as the long-term ability to preserve its relative economic position by maintaining macroeconomic stability, sustaining production capability, safeguarding competitiveness, securing market outlets and ensuring access to resources. (Casarini, 2006: 11)

On a more general level, economic security relates to the strategic ability of states to maintain and develop their socio-economic system of choice and safeguard their relative economic power position under conditions of anarchy (Geeraerts and Huang, 2016). In today's globalised world the economic dimension of security is gaining in importance. Increasingly, threats in this realm flow from the eroded policy autonomy of major states, which resonates the heightened interdependence in the real, financial, and monetary sectors of the global economy (Sperling and Kirchner, 1998). While interdependence has been a feature of economic globalisation all along, the rise of the emerging economies and China in particular has turned global economic interdependence into a different playing field altogether. The outsourcing of production and services from advanced to emerging countries, together with increasing economic exchanges among emerging economies themselves, have markedly diversified and complicated trade and investment patterns in the global economy. The 2008–9 financial crisis and subsequent Great Recession made clear not only how much the trade, fiscal and monetary policies of major economic players like China, the US and the EU had become intertwined but also how much their economic relationship had become unbalanced. In the interconnected global environment, economic power and prosperity, access to resources, and cutting-edge technologies are defining both power and vulnerabilities, turning competition in these areas more and more into a securitised game (Geeraerts and Huang, 2016).

Economic security is fundamentally different from military security (Ronis, 2011). Whilst military threats to national security are both specific and intentional, economic threats are both diffuse and systemic, they may be unintended or a secondary consequence of state action (Sperling and Kirchner, 1998). Examples would be the consequences of macroeconomic malfeasance by one or more major economic powers, the collapse of financial markets, major debt repudiation or a collapse of currency markets that might put in jeopardy the very survival of the state or upend the economic foundation of political stability. Economic security comprises two major elements. First, "economic security reflects a concern over sustaining economic welfare, over the ability of the state to protect the social and economic fabric of a society". Second, "economic security concerns the ability of the state to foster a stable international economic environment in order to extract the welfare gains of openness while minimizing the potentially negative consequences for national welfare flowing from a loss of policy autonomy" (Sperling and Kirchner, 1998: 230).

In the wake of the Great Recession and the Eurozone sovereign debt crisis, concerns about the EU's relative position in the global distribution of capabilities have increased. As the EU now accounts for a lower share of world trade, investment, currency holdings, defence expenditure and development assistance, this deeper shift appears to have stepped up apprehensions about the Union's relative decline and its future economic security (Youngs, 2014). These concerns have also trickled down in the relationship between the EU and China and engendered the growing politicisation of economic affairs. As Holslag (2015: 132) aptly observes: "Europe had been confident in its leading edge, while China, feeling behind in its position in global production networks, assumed that it had to catch up by building its own strong industries, strengthening influence over global trade flows, and promoting an indigenous knowledge network. As the balance of power started to shift with added fuel from the financial crisis, Europe came to take its wealth less for granted, to interpret development as a matter of security, and to consider defending its economy by political means."

Faced with the prospect of a slow economic recovery and the fallout of the sovereign debt problem, political forces in Europe asking for turning the distorted Sino-EU economic relationship into a level playing field have become much stronger. Through better market access, European exporters should be well placed to increasingly sell their products on the rapidly expanding Chinese consumer market and, in the process, remedy the EU's trade deficit with China (Leal-Arcas, 2012). While China continues to be regarded as a promising export market and destination for investment, the image of China as a fierce and unfair competitor have gained a strong foothold. A contentious issue here is the poor access to the Chinese services market. Unlike the other G20 countries, China is very restrictive about direct investment in modern services such as finance, telecom, media and logistics. Whilst total bilateral trade in goods reached €521 billion in 2015, trade in services is still about ten times lower at €63.7 billion and remains an area full of potential if China were to open its market more. Voices demanding that China should take up greater responsibilities in redressing bilateral trade imbalances and supporting a sustainable global economy are growing louder and sounding more determined. A growing part of the European business community feels thwarted about China's trade barriers, currency policy and lack of enforcement of intellectual property rights. Calls for more assertive trade policies and trade defence measures are resounding all the more loudly throughout the lobbying corridors in Brussels and the capitals of EU member states (de Jonquières, 2016).

The economic security concerns figure prominently in the Joint Communication *Elements for a Nnew EU Strategy on China*, which maps out the European Union's relationship with China for the next five years and definitely implies a "tit-for-tat" strategy of pragmatic conditional engagement (European Commission and High Representative of the Union for Foreign Affairs and Security Policy, 2016). Identifying major opportunities for the EU's relationship with China, the document stresses in particular the creation of jobs and growth in Europe as well as the promotion of a greater opening up of the Chinese market to European business. Opportunities mentioned include concluding a comprehensive agreement on investment, a Chinese contribution to the Investment Plan for Europe, and joint research and innovation activities, as well as connecting the Eurasian continent via a physical and digital network through which trade, investment and people-to-people contact can flow. At the same time, the communication complains about the lack of progress in giving the market a more decisive role in the economy in the key areas of concern to the EU. Recent legislative initiatives have introduced new restrictions on foreign operators in China, which go against market opening and the principles of reciprocity and a level playing field. Looking further ahead, it mentions the possibility of a deep comprehensive Free Trade Agreement, but makes this conditional on the successful conclusion of a comprehensive investment agreement between the two sides and the implementation of conclusive reforms levelling the playing field for domestic and foreign companies. In this regard, China must make significant, time-bound and verifiable cuts in industrial over-capacity, most urgently in the steel sector, to prevent negative consequences from unfair competition. Another "neo-mercantilist"-flavoured priority is the strengthening of the EU's Trade Defence Instruments, notably through the swift adoption of the Commission's Trade Defence Instruments modernisation proposal of April 2013. Meanwhile, the EU will continue to support China's economic and social reform programme through its many dialogues with China in the expectation that this will facilitate market-led reform, including by eliminating state-induced economic distortions and reforming state-owned enterprises.

The shift in the balance of economic power has clearly affected the EU's relative position vis-à-vis China and, in the process, put the relationship on a more realistic footing (Michalski and Pan, 2017; Li, 2016). While the EU has not lost in absolute terms, as its overall trade balance is still positive, it is facing economic difficulty in sustaining its high levels of welfare and consumption, and it is continuing to lose ground in terms of scale, innovation and job creation. Europe now recognises that the very fundamentals of its welfare, political integration and social stability are at stake (European Commission, 2010; EEAS, 2016). China, notwithstanding its stellar economic development, is equally confronting major challenges. Faced with a structural economic slowdown, its transition to a more sustainable pattern of development is complex and may lead to bouts of turbulence within China and more widely (Lardy, 2011; Pettis, 2011). Moreover, China's export-driven economic development has made it highly sensitive to the turbulences and growing uncertainties in the global economy (Geeraerts and Huang, 2016). So both the EU and China are confronted with a diminished sense of confidence in their economic future. According to Holslag (2015: 147) this "lack of confidence on both sides has turned economic affairs into a security issue". A major problem with this development is that it "legitimates governments on both sides to intervene more actively in their markets. Europe is exploring new ways to 'bring the state back in' via industrial policy, assertive trade strategies, and raw materials policies." It is also starting to adopt more neo-mercantilist narratives, especially when it comes to China. An economic security dilemma appears to be in the making: "still quite uncertain, but hard to reverse, especially if Europe continues to be confronted with painful economic reforms. Although neither Beijing nor Brussels has the intention to threaten the other side's interests, and considers its own intervention in economic affairs as a very defensive policy, each perceives the other's actions as provocative and offensive. Hence the risk of spiralling tensions may increase between Europe and China" (Holslag, 2015: 147)

Achieving mutual economic security will be a crucial test of both China's and Europe's ability to adjust themselves successfully to the emerging multipolar world and to secure their relative economic position in a changing and uncertain global economy. As trade and investment will remain a major driver of the bilateral relationship, the development of a more balanced economic relationship is necessary if they are to overcome the creeping economic security dilemma. Whether this will succeed will very much depend on domestic developments in China and the EU, especially both sides' ability to maintain crucial growth and tackle development challenges. Safeguarding economic security for both of them will hinge on an ability to maintain growth and productivity, create jobs and increasing the livelihood of citizens (Holslag, 2015). For their continuing prosperity, both are also mutually dependent on trade with one another, and thus have a shared interest in regional and global stability facilitating economic growth (Christiansen, 2016). Finally, economic security for both sides also means meeting common global challenges in the shape of access to resources and climate change (Bo, Biedenkopf and Chen, 2016; García-Herrero et al., 2017).

Institutionalisation as a source of resilience and a beacon of hope

While EU–China relations have at times been severely strained and substantial progress has been difficult to bring about, bilateral disputes and diplomatic frictions have never reached the point where further co-operation was no longer possible. One factor explaining this resilience is that since 2003 these relations have become "highly institutionalised through the establishment of a 'strategic partnership'" (Christiansen, 2016: 41). Such partnership can be understood as a co-ordinated framework for political co-operation, which in the case of the EU and China consists of an extensive web of bilateral dialogues. The most important dialogue mechanism is the EU–China annual summit, under the umbrella of which has developed a huge "dialogue architecture" (Christiansen, 2016: 41), bringing together Chinese and EU policy-makers.

The scope of these dialogues is wide and evolves around three pillars: political relations, economic relations and social relations (Liu and Breslin, 2016). Each of these pillars is headed by a specific EU–China High-Level Dialogue: High-Level Strategic Dialogue (2010), High-Level Economic and Trade Dialogue (2007), and High-Level People-to-People Dialogue (2012). Under each of these headings there are a number of distinct dialogues and a broad range of more specific working groups, which "are part and parcel of the executive diplomacy involving officials from European External Action Service (EEAS), the European Commission and the Chinese ministerial bureaucracies" (Christiansen, 2016: 41). While the nature of the bilateral dialogues is deliberative rather than decisional they provide a "platform for Chinese and EU policy-makers to exchange views on topics of mutual interest, to understand the different perspectives each side has, and to overcome potential problems" (Christiansen, 2016: 42).

Viewed from the perspective of liberal institutionalism (Keohane, 1984), the EU–China dialogue architecture provides a continual framework that "obliges both sides to meet one another regularly and creates an administrative routine around these meetings, involving agenda setting, chairing arrangements, review mechanisms and other procedural elements that normalise and regularise bilateral relations". This high degree of institutionalisation explains the resilience of the EU–China relationship even in the face of serious frictions, "as have been the case on several occasions (e.g., antidumping measures against Chinese made solar panels, extraterritorial application of the EU's Emissions Trading System) and indeed continuously (e.g., EU arms embargo imposed after Tiananmen Square)" (Christiansen, 2016: 43).

A clear signal of both sides' willingness to continue the institutionalised relationship is the 2013 agreement on an *EU–China 2020 Strategic Agenda for Cooperation* (EEAS, 2013). The document sets out a framework for deeper co-operation on four major issues: peace and security, prosperity, sustainable development, and people-to-people contacts. While it is very ambitious and cast in rather general terms, the 2020 agenda nevertheless indicates that processes of path dependence and (embryonic) reciprocal socialisation appear to be at work here. The EU–China partnership has created a structure in which learning takes place among civil servants at the functional levels as well as among political leaders and high-level diplomats (Michalski and Pan, 2017). It is the result of a sustained process of negotiation in which representatives of both sides engage in information exchange, signalling of perceptions and expectations, stipulation of mutually acceptable rules of the game, positioning and alignment of norms and standards, and regular stocktaking of results and problems based on joint agreed norms and standards. As such the partnership structure makes possible the kind of regular social interaction that bolsters the diffusion of knowledge, and shapes a context in which learning is likely to result in the construction of common practices. For such a process to be sustainable, intercourse is to be based on the principles of openness, mutual respect and reciprocity, as they make it possible to move beyond "we–they" distinctions and "in-group projection" – two features that still figure prominently behind the scenes. Critical tools in bringing about reciprocal socialisation are small informal groups and personalised interactions as they create the kind of interpersonal dynamics which are needed for true mutual learning and understanding. The major aim of the process is to reach consensus, not unanimity. When dealing with actors with such different identities as the EU and China (Geeraerts, 2011; Pan, 2012), a realistic goal is to reach a broad agreement on a series of strategic issues and principles, while at the same time allowing for a degree of deviation (Terhalle, 2011).

Reciprocal socialisation is a long-term process. Little can be expected in terms of substantive policy changes in the short run. However, it is the process in itself that is important. It is the process that can shape a substantive strategic partnership in the long run. Over time, as analyses and viewpoints are repeated and increasingly shared, officials are more likely to gravitate towards a common diagnosis of crucial problems in the Sino-EU relationship and their solution. An area of promise where broad consensus could be found is climate change. Both China and the EU are deeply concerned by the issue. The topic is of such importance that it cuts across many other aspects of the relationship. In this regard, the ongoing combination of the Belt and Road Initiative and the EU's Juncker plan for strategic investments within the EU–China Connectivity Platform offers real opportunities to build infrastructure in a sustainable way, and for both the EU and China to share their development experiences, standards and expertise to their mutual benefit as well as to the benefit of third parties. As such, it constitutes a practical experiment in reciprocal socialisation, which could evolve into a paragon of concerted order-shaping with regional and global implications.

The promise of concerted order-shaping?

The EU and China are very much in the same boat as they both face formidable challenges in their domestic and regional environment. The EU faces daunting challenges to revitalise the economy, create jobs, overcome extremism and cope with a large wave of refugees from a chaotic neighbourhood. China needs to come to terms with slowing economic development and at the same time ensure sustainable development and protect the environment. They both also "need to manage the system-shocks that their powers have generated in their own regions, to avoid unnecessary geopolitical rivalries with other regional powers in their neighbourhood and to check their ambitions for regional dominance" (Chen, 2016: 790). In the final analysis, this is a national responsibility, but in a world of complex interdependence it can be successfully taken up only in a stable and predictable international environment.

The bigger challenge for the EU and China, then, is to deal with a global governance system that is evolving from a multilateral system centred on the US into a more diffuse system resting on the three strong trading poles of China, the EU and the US. Against a background in which the US is increasingly drawing into question its commitments to free trade and the global commons, the question is whether the EU and China are willing and able to jointly support the multilateral system as the US steps back from its hegemonic role. The EU and China both clearly have an interest in supporting an open multilateral trading system, as success in this endeavour would largely determine the boundary conditions for tackling their domestic and regional challenges as well as overcoming the creeping economic security dilemma between them. Still, it is an open question whether they can act in a co-ordinated manner as the EU and the US have done in the past.

This is not a trivial question because the EU and China differ much more from each other, politically, economically and socially, than do the EU and US. At the end of the day, the EU and China have very different identities and their relationship reveals deep-seated conceptual differences concerning norms, visions of power and governance, modes of international engagement and the organisation of the emerging world order. The EU is a union of nation-states, a hybrid collective actor, which to this very day has the highest level of integration among all associations of states. As a substantially post-sovereign union, it welcomes mutual interference in domestic affairs, major transfers of sovereignty and strong rule-based international institutions in governing world affairs. In contrast, China is the largest sovereignist state in the world, which regards a strong sovereign state as a guarantor of its national independence and a precondition for national "rejuvenation". As a result, China prioritises the defence of state sovereignty and non-interference with domestic affairs, and prefers international co-operation based on intergovernmental consensus rather than the pooling of sovereignty under the heading of supranational governance.

The EU and China also have different political, economic and social systems, which leads

> the two players to view the best way to manage domestic governance differently, and also creates problems in EU–China co-operation in their efforts to shape the outside world. Europe in general has embraced political liberalism, seeing democracy, competitive elections, press freedom, vibrant civil society and human rights as basic components of internal good governance. In China, with its strong statist tradition and a twentieth-century revolution led by the Communist Party of China, a party-state has been in place since the founding of the PRC. Its political system prioritises party leadership in the society.
> (Chen, 2016: 784)

Since Deng's market reform and open-door policy, the party has become a driving force of China's modernisation and economic development.

In light of the important differences between the EU and China, the crucial question is: how can the two players possibly jointly support and reshape the multilateral system? Interestingly, Chen (2016: 788–9) points to two developments that are facilitating convergence between the EU and China in their order-shaping efforts and could lead to a more concerted relationship in the future. The first is the return of the developmental agenda in Europe and the move beyond developmentalism in China. With their advanced technology and economic competitiveness, European countries developed high-level welfare systems and came to place more emphasis on quality-of-life issues. However, the sovereign debt crisis and the subsequent problems faced by many EU countries have pushed the growth and development back on top of the agenda in the EU. As a result, the EU is becoming more modern, less postmodern and more like other countries in the world. Meanwhile, China is moving beyond developmentalism "to deemphasise growth and focus more on quality-of-life issues. For example, given the unbearable level of heavy smog hanging over major Chinese cities, the Chinese government is now under heavy domestic pressure to speed up the process of improving energy efficiency and expand the use of clean energy" (Chen, 2016: 789). These mutually converging tendencies are narrowing preference differences between the EU and China, and creating the boundary conditions for a better concerted relationship between them on wide-ranging bilateral and multilateral issues.

The second development is

> the new pragmatism in Europe and growing globalism in China. Facing internal problems and a turbulent neighbourhood, the EU is preoccupied with finding solutions to internal growth and cohesion problems, as well as the task of stabilizing its neighbourhood. As a result, the EU is becoming more pragmatic in its drive to transform the rest of the world and its relations with China. European countries all agreed to the 2010 International Monetary Fund (IMF) reform, which allowed some voting rights to be transferred mostly from Europe to China and other emerging countries. Trade disputes such as the solar panel disputes, though initially very confrontational, were eventually solved through a constructive compromise. Upon the deadline of 30 March 2015, 14 of the 28 EU Member States decided to be founding members of the China-sponsored AIIB, disregarding the explicit initial opposition from the United States government. (Chen 2016: 789)

The EU's new Global Strategy even goes as far as to suggest that "unless they undergo structural reforms to better reflect the changed world order, the traditional international financial institutions risk losing their unique status as agenda-shapers in their respective domains" (Ujvari, 2016: 2). This shows that the EU is coming to terms with the fact that, having grown disenchanted with the slow pace of reforms in the IMF, World Bank and World Trade Organisation, emerging powers – with China in the driver seat – have become more proactive in their attempts to step up their sway in international affairs.

Meanwhile, Chinese foreign policy has taken a more globalist orientations, and the country is now prepared to take on greater responsibility internationally. An important step is this regard was taken in 2005 "when China endorsed the World Summit document which embraced the idea of 'responsibility to protect', indicating that China is willing to accept that certain crimes committed at home are not immune to international intervention, which implies a loosening of its rigid view of state sovereignty. China has also supported a number of United Nations Security Council resolutions under Chapter 7 of the UN Charter, which include coercive measures such as sanctions and military interventions" (Chen, 2016: 789). What is more, ever since his speech at the World Economic Forum in Davos, Xi Jinping increasingly figures as the new advocate for economic openness and international co-operation in the world.

In short, signs of mutual accommodation and convergence between the EU and China in their efforts to adapt themselves to the changing international system appear to be unfolding. As they have both a keen interest in a sound management of the evolving decentred multilateral order, the EU and China have ample reason to explore concerted efforts to provide individual and joint contributions to the general global public good. The challenge for the two of them is to build on their past successes and make themselves "greater contributors to a more peaceful, prosperous and just world at large" (Chen, 2016: 790). Especially the EU–China Connectivity Platform offers a concrete possibility to engage in mutually beneficial projects of infrastructure construction, which would not only open up new ground for EU–China co-operation but also offer the opportunity for the two to join forces to promote stability and development in the vast areas in the Eurasian continent between them. Over time, as analyses and viewpoints evolve and become increasingly aligned, and successful co-operative projects start bearing fruit, participants on both sides are more likely to gravitate towards consensus and step up their engagement in concerted order-shaping. Globally, more convergence in their preferences would lead to a stronger concerted order-shaping partnership.

Conclusion

With the boundary conditions of their relationship shifting, co-operation between China and the EU has become anything but easier. While they have many interests in common, they are also competitors within the confines of a multilateral system under stress. Building a true strategic partnership will not come easily, as the previous sections have indicated. The differences in their respective systems and identities pose challenges on the road to concerted order-shaping, and policy-makers on both sides need to engage in reciprocal socialisation if they are to overcome them. As they have both a keen interest in a sound management of the evolving decentred multilateral order, signs of mutual accommodation and convergence between the EU and China in their efforts to adapt themselves to the changing international system appear to be unfolding. Still, the partnership between the EU and China is bound to be an intricate equilibrium between diverging and converging trends – at best an enlightened calibrating of domestic interests, and regional and global governance ambitions within a complex and transforming international environment that leads on to joint efforts at concerted order-shaping.

References

Acharya, Amitav. (2014). *The End of American World Order*. Cambridge: Polity.
Bo, Yan, Katja Biedenkopf and Zhimin Chen. (2016). *Chinese and EU Climate and Energy Security Policy*. Basingstoke: Palgrave Macmillan, pp. 102–24.
Breslin, Shaun. (2013). "China and the Gloabal Order: Signalling Threat or Friendship?", *International Affairs* 89 (3): 615–34.
Casarini, Nicola. (2006). "The Evolution of the EU–China Relationship: From Constructive Engagement to Strategic Partnership", in *Occasional Paper* 64. Paris: EU Institute for Security Studies.

CEU (Council of the European Union). (2003). "A Secure Europe in a Better World", *European Security Strategy*, Brussels.
Chen, Zhimin. (2016). "China, the European Union and the Fragile World Order", *Journal of Common Market Studies* 54: 775–92.
Christiansen, Thomas. (2016). "A Liberal Institutionalist Perspective on China–EU Relations". In Jianwei Wang and Weiqing Song (eds), *China, the European Union, and the International Politics of Global Governance*. Basingstoke: Palgrave Macmillan, pp. 233–51.
Cooper, Robert. (2003). *The Breaking of Nations: Order and Chaos in the Twenty-First Century*. Bedford Park: Atlantic Press.
de Jonquières, Guy. (2016). "The EU and China: Redressing an Unbalanced Relationship", *ECIPE Policy Brief* 1: 1–3. Available at http://ecipe.org/publications/the-eu-and-china-redressing-an-unbalanced-relationship/, accessed online 27 September 2017.
Demertzis, Maria, André Sapir and Guntram Wolff. (2017). "Europe in a New World Order", *Bruegel Policy Brief*. Bruegel. http://bruegel.org/wp-content/uploads/2017/02/Bruegel_Policy_Brief-2017_02-170217_final.pdf, accessed online 5 October 2017.
EEAS. (2013). *EU–China 2020 Strategic Agenda for Cooperation*. Brussels.
EEAS. (2016). *Shared Vision, Common Action: A Stronger Europe. A Global Strategy for the European Union's Foreign and Security Policy*.www.eeas.europa.eu/archives/docs/top_stories/pdf/eugs_review_web.pdf, accessed online 24 September 2017.
European Commission. (1995). *A Long-Term Policy for China–Europe Relations*. COM 279 final. Brussels: European Commission.
European Commission. (2010). *Europe 2020. A Strategy for Smart, Sustainable and Inclusive Growth*. COM(2010) 2020.
European Commission. (2013). *European Competitiveness Report 2013*. SWD(2013) 347 final.
European Commission and High Representative of the Union for Foreign Affairs and Security Policy. (2016). *Elements for a New Strategy on China*. JOIN(2016) 30 final.
Farnell, John, and Paul Urwin Crookes. (2016). *The Politics of EU–China Economic Relations: An Uneasy Relationship*. London: Palgrave Macmillan.
Foot, Rosemary. (2009). "China and the United States: Between Cold War and Warm Peace", *Survival* 51 (6): 123–46.
Fox, John and François Godement. (2009). *A Power Audit of EU–China Relations*. Brussels: European Council on Foreign Relations.
García-Herrero, Alicia, Kwok, K.C., Liu, Xiangdong, Summers, Tim and Yansheng Zhang. (2017). *EU–China Economic Relations to 2025: Building a Common Future*. London: Chatham House. www.chathamhouse.org/sites/files/chathamhouse/publications/research/2017–09–13-eu-china-economic-relations-2025-garcia-herrero-kwok-liu-summers-zhang-final.pdf, accessed 4 October 2017.
Geeraerts, Gustaaf. (2011). "China, the EU, and the New Multipolarity", *European Review* 19 (1): 57–67.
Geeraerts, Gustaaf. (2013a). "The Changing Global Context of China–EU Relations". *China International Studies* 42 (September/October): 53–69.

Geeraerts, Gustaaf. (2013b). "EU-China Relations", in Thomas Christiansen, Emil Kirchner and Philomena Murray (eds), *The Palgrave Handbook of EU–Asia Relations*. Basingstoke: Palgrave, pp. 492–508.

Geeraerts, Gustaaf. (2016). "China, the EU, and Global Governance in Human Rights", In Jianwei Wang and Weiqing Song (eds), *China, the European Union, and the International Politics of Global Governance*. Basingstoke: Palgrave Macmillan, pp. 233–51.

Geeraerts, Gustaaf, and Weiping Huang. (2016). "The Economic Security Dimension of the EU–China Relationship: Puzzles and Prospects", in Emil Kirchner, Thomas Christiansen and Dorussen Han (eds), *Security Relations between China and the European Union from Convergence to Cooperation?* Cambridge: Cambridge University Press, pp. 187–208.

Grabbe, Heather. (2006). *The EU's Transformative Power: Europeanization through Conditionality in Central and Eastern Europe*. Basingstoke: Palgrave Macmillan.

Grabbe, Heather. (2014). "Six Lessons of Enlargement Ten Years On: The EU's Transformative Power in Retrospect and Prospect", *Journal of Common Market Studies* 52 (Issue Supplement S1): 40–56.

Holslag, Jonathan. (2012). "Unravelling Harmony: How Distorted Trade Imperils the Sino-European Partnership", *Journal of World Trade* 46 (2): 221–38.

Holslag, Jonathan. (2015). "Explaining Economic Frictions Between China and the European Union", In Vinod K. Aggarwal and Sara A. Newland (eds), *Responding to China's Rise. US and EU Strategies*. Heidelberg: Springer, pp. 131–50.

Ikenberry, John. (2008). "The Rise of China and the Future of the West. Can the Liberal System Survive?", *Foreign Affairs* 87 (1): 23–37.

Keohane, Robert. (1984). *After Hegemony: Cooperation and Discord in the World Political Economy*. Princeton: Princeton University Press.

Kerr, David (2012). "Problems of Grand Strategy in EU–China Relations", in Jan van der Harst and Pieter Swieringa (eds), *China and the European Union. Concord of Conflict?* Maastricht: Shaker Publishing, pp. 69–88.

Kissinger, Henry. (2014). *World Order: Reflections on the Character of Nations and the Course of History*. London: Penguin Books.

Kupchan, Charles A. (2012). *No One's World: The West, The Rising Rest, and the Coming Global Turn*. Oxford: Oxford University Press.

Lardy, Nicholas R. (2011). *Sustaining China's Economic Growth after the Global Financial Crisis*. Washington: Peterson Institute for International Economics.

Layne, Christopher. (2012). "The End of Pax Americana: How Western Decline Became Inevitable", *The Atlantic*, 26 April.

Leal-Arcas, Rafael. (2012). "European Union–China Trade Relations: Difficulties, Possible Solutions, and the Way Forward", in Jan van der Harst and Pieter Swieringa (eds), *China and the European Union. Concord or Conflict?* Maastricht: Shaker Publishing, pp. 129–45.

Li, Mingjiang. (2016). "China–EU Relations: Rivalry Impedes Strategic Partnership", in Jianwei Wang and Weiqing Song (eds), *China, the European Union, and the International Politics of Global Governance*. Basingstoke: Palgrave Macmillan, pp. 13–29.

Liu, Hongsong, and Shaun Breslin. (2016). "Shaping the Agenda Jointly? China and the EU in the G20", in Jianwei Wang and Weiqing Song (eds), *China, the*

European Union, and the International Politics of Global Governance. Basingstoke: Palgrave Macmillan, pp. 95–113.
Manners, Ian. (2002). "Normative Power Europe: A Contradiction in Terms", *Journal of Common Market Studies* 40 (2): 235–58.
Manners, Ian. (2013). "Assessing the Decennial, Reassessing the Global: Understanding European Union Normative Power in Global Politics", *Cooperation and Conflict* 48 (2): 304–29.
Michalski, Anna, and Zhongqi Pan. (2017). *Unlikely Partners. China the European Union, and the Forging of a Strategic Partnership*. Singapore: Palgrave Macmillan.
Ministry of External Relations of Brazil. (2014). Sixth BRICS Summit – Fortaleza Declaration, 15 July. Available at http://brics6.itamaraty.gov.br/media2/press-releases/214-sixth-bricssummit-fortaleza-declaration, Accessed online 7 July 2015.
Pan, Zhongqi (ed.). (2012). *Conceptual Gaps in China–EU Relations. Global Governance, Human Rights and Strategic Partnerships*. Basingstoke: Palgrave Macmillan.
Pettis, Michael. (2011). "The Contentious Debate over China's Economic Transition", in *Policy Outlook* 25 (March). Carnegie Endowment for International Peace. https://carnegieendowment.org/files/china_econ_transition.pdf, accessed onlne 4 October 2017.
Ronis, Sheila R. (ed.). (2011). *Economic Security. Neglected Dimension of National Security?* Washington, DC: National Defense University Press.
Schweller, Randall, and Xiao Pu. (2011). "After Unipolarity: China's Visions of International Order in an Era of U.S. Decline", *International Security* 36 (1): 41–72.
Sperling, James, and Emil Kirchner. (1997). *Recastsing the European Order. Security Architectures and Economic Cooperation*. Manchester: Manchester University Press.
Sperling, James, and Emil Kirchner. (1998). "Economic Security and the Problem of Cooperation in Post-Cold War Europe", *Review of International Studies* 24: 221–37.
Terhalle, Maximilian. (2011). "Reciprocal Socialization: Rising Powers and the West", *International Studies Perspectives* 12 (4): 341–61.
Ujvari, Balzs. (2016). "The EU Global Strategy: From Effective Multilateralism to Global Governance that Works?", *Egmont Policy Brief* 76. pp. 1–4. www.egmontinstitute.be/content/uploads/2016/06/SPB76.pdf?type=pdf, accessed online 15 September 2017.
Youngs, Richard. (2014). *The Uncertain Legacy of Crisis: European Foreign Policy Faces the Future*. Washington, DC: Carnegie Endowment for International Peace.

8 Shifting constraints, evolving opportunities and the search for the "strategic" in the European Union and Japan bilateral partnership

Elena Atanassova-Cornelis

Introduction

For Europe (the European Union)[1] Japan represents the most institutionalised bilateral link in the Union's engagement with the Asia-Pacific.[2] Based on the shared values of freedom, democracy and the rule of law, the EU's relations with Japan have steadily evolved since the early 1990s. A major driving force is the deepening economic interdependence between the two. In 2016, Japan was the EU's sixth largest trading partner (after the US, China, Switzerland, Russia and Turkey). Trade with Japan accounted for 3.6 per cent of the EU's total trade, while the shares of the US and China were the largest, 17.6 per cent and 14.9 per cent, respectively (European Commission, 2016). The EU28, for its part, was in 2016 the second largest trading partner for Japan. Its share of Japanese trade was 12.4 per cent, following China's share of 25.8 per cent and ahead of the US share of 11.4 per cent (European Commission, 2017).

Over the past two decades the EU–Japan partnership has moved beyond the traditional focus on economics and trade to include a politico-security dimension. An important driver behind the expansion of the bilateral relations has been the mutual recognition of each other's growing significance in the international arena, as well as a shared comprehensive approach to tackling security challenges. Europe and Japan have entered the second decade of the twenty-first century with a new priority of raising their bilateral relations to the level of a formal strategic partnership. To this end, in 2013 Brussels and Tokyo embarked on parallel negotiations of a comprehensive Economic Partnership Agreement / Free Trade Agreement (EPA / FTA) and a Strategic Partnership Agreement (SPA). The agreements were finalised in early 2018 and officially signed at the EU–Japan Summit in Tokyo on 17 July 2018.

This chapter examines the evolving EU–Japan strategic partnership by focusing, in particular, on the security dimension of the bilateral relations. "Strategic" partnership refers here to one that is built on normative congruence and common interests between the partners, as well as that is multidimensional in terms of substance and scope (Reiterer, 2013). The following discussion first explores the mutual perceptions and the respective motivations of Europe and Japan for deepening their engagement since the early 1990s. It then examines the present geopolitical concerns of Tokyo and Brussels, as well as the opportunities and constraints for enhancing the bilateral security ties. This is followed by an overview since the 2000s of the EU–Japan summit agenda and the main areas of the bilateral security co-operation. Before concluding, the chapter offers some policy reflections on how to strengthen EU–Japan relations.

Japan in the EU's Asia policy

In 1994, the European Commission produced its first Asia strategy paper. The document stressed the need for the EU to "strengthen its economic presence" in, and "develop a political dialogue" with, Asia, to "make a positive contribution to regional security" and economic development, as well as to promote the consolidation of democracy, the rule of law and respect for human rights in the region (European Commission, 1994: 1–3). The last three objectives are core ones from the perspective of the EU's foreign policy and are shared by Japan. What was new was Europe's interest in moving beyond the economic dimension to include political and security interactions with that part of the world.

This envisaged expansion of Europe's involvement in Asia was closely linked to Brussels's positive assessment of Japan's changing foreign policy. Both the 1994 document and the Commission's 1995 paper *Europe and Japan: The Next Steps* emphasised the EU's appreciation of Japan's significant contribution to the economic development and stability of East Asia by means of "soft power", namel, through trade and investment, provision of Official Development Assistance (ODA) and participation in confidence-building measures (European Commission, 1994, 1995). It seems that already in the early 1990s Tokyo was regarded as being sufficiently *qualified* to become Brussels's strategic partner in Asia.

The progress in European integration from the early 1990s on and, related to it, the EU's willingness and ability to assume a larger global role have further stimulated Brussels to seek a deeper engagement with East Asia and Japan. The Union has sought to enhance its credibility as an international actor by establishing in 1992 a Common Foreign and Security Policy (CFSP) and by developing since 1999 the European Security and Defence Policy (ESDP), later called the Common Security and Defence Policy (CSDP) under the 2009 Lisbon Treaty. The Union has also sought to make its "external" face more visible through the creation of the position of High Representative for Foreign Affairs and Security Policy, currently held by Federica Mogherini,[3] and through the launch in 2011 of the European External Action Service, a *de facto* foreign ministry.

The Commission's 2001 Asia paper brought a whole new dimension into the Union's relations with the region, notably a security one. Europe would now "build global partnerships and alliances with Asian countries" (European Commission, 2001: 3). This included a strategic partnership with Japan (along with China and India) (European Council, 2003). Defining Japan as a "strategic partner" since 2003 (Council of the European Union, 2012), Brussels also regards Tokyo "unquestionably" as its "closest partner" in the region on the basis of the shared values of freedom, democracy and the rule of law (Solana, 2006). Japan's democratic political system is said to make it a *"natural* strategic partner" for Europe (Ferrero-Waldner, 2006, emphasis added).

The shared values have also been linked to the mutual perception of Europe and Japan as civilian powers (Van Rompuy, 2010) – namely, international actors that rely on soft power and focus primarily on economic policy instruments to exert international influence through, for example, provision of foreign aid and development policies. In considering Brussels's relations with Tokyo, Europe's conceptualisation of security in the 2003 European Security Strategy (ESS) deserves a special attention. The EU's approach stresses the comprehensive nature of security threats (i.e., going beyond the traditional or military dimension) and the variety of means (e.g. political, economic, civilian) needed to tackle them (European Council, 2003). It is in this context that the Union has developed "a holistic approach to crisis management", which encompasses both preventive strategies and post-conflict reconstruction, and is part of the overall framework of Brussels's comprehensive foreign policy that relies on diverse diplomatic and defence instruments (Reiterer, 2015). As the Council's *Guidelines on the EU's Foreign and Security Policy in East Asia* updated in 2012 points out, Europe is expected to expand its contribution to Asian-Pacific stability primarily by means of non-military security co-operation, support for regional integration and promotion of democratic values and the rule of law (Council of the European Union, 2012). As discussed below, most of these objectives are relevant for the EU's partnership with Japan, for the focus is largely on soft power and non-military foreign policy tools.

The EU in Japan's foreign policy

Tokyo's interest in deepening its relations with Brussels after 1989 was initially based on the economic opportunities emerging from the eastward enlargement of the Union and the EU's increasing economic power. At the same time, Europe's rise as an international political and security actor that prioritised soft power tools resonated well with Japan's promotion throughout the 1990s of a civilian power profile and its focus on non-traditional (or soft) security objectives.

Common approaches to security have emerged as a particularly important factor driving Japan's partnership with Europe. Since the postwar years Tokyo has embraced a comprehensive conceptualisation of security that goes beyond the traditional military dimension, and stresses economic, social, political and environmental foreign-policy objectives. As discussed earlier, the ESS advocates a similar approach to security. Until the late 2000s and in line with Tokyo's comprehensive conceptualisation of security, Japan's regional and global security strategy significantly relied on soft power (Atanassova-Cornelis, 2010a). This was reflected, for example, in Japan's ODA policies and involvement in post-conflict reconstruction activities.

As early as 1991 Japan's *Diplomatic Bluebook* explicitly called for strengthening Euro-Japanese relations (Ministry of Foreign Affairs, Japan, 1991). The document stressed that the shared political values, common security interests and both actors' growing international responsibilities formed a solid basis for transforming the bilateral relationship from an economic one to one more comprehensive in nature. This Japanese perception clearly mirrored Europe's approach towards Japan discussed earlier. The "indivisibility" of security, i.e. the concept that events in one region could affect other parts of the world, was clearly seen by Tokyo as an important factor for a strengthened partnership with Brussels.

In the *2003 Diplomatic Bluebook* Tokyo underscored its intention to "build a strategic partnership" with Brussels (Ministry of Foreign Affairs, Japan, 2003), which was a demonstration of the growing importance of the EU in Japan's foreign policy. Successive editions of the *Diplomatic Bluebook* since the second half of the 2000s refer to the EU as a strategic partner for Japan. They emphasise the similarities between the two actors, notably that both are major advanced democracies sharing common values, and their role and responsibility in fostering international stability and prosperity (see Ministry of Foreign Affairs, Japan, various issues, 2007–15). More recently, under Prime Minister Abe Shinzo (2012 to present), Europe is also seen as critical for Japan's pursuit of its security policy of "proactive contribution to peace", introduced in the 2013 National Security Strategy (NSS), as well as for the implementation of a foreign policy that "takes a panoramic perspective of the world map" (Ministry of Foreign Affairs, Japan, 2014: 22; 2015: 118). Appearing for the first time in the 2014 edition of the *Diplomatic Bluebook*, the so-called "panoramic" perspective emphasises the Abe Administration's strategic diplomacy towards different countries and world regions, including Europe, while upholding "universal values", notably shared by the EU.

In the NSS Japan's co-operation with both the EU and North Atlantic Treaty Organization (NATO) is stressed in reference to the establishment of "an international order based on universal values and rules" (Prime Minister of Japan and His Cabinet, 2013b). This alludes, among other things, to the global maritime order and to Japan's concerns over the rising tensions in the East and South China Seas, with a particular focus on Chinese behaviour. Similarly, the 2014 *Diplomatic Bluebook* of the Abe Administration explicitly refers to Japan's worries about "risk escalation" in the global commons, especially in the seas (Ministry of Foreign Affairs, Japan, 2014: 3). As Japan is promoting the establishment of "the rule of law at sea", Europe seems a natural partner for Japan.

All in all, the EU is presented as a partner that both appreciates Japan's expanded international security role and assists in the pursuit of Japan's global responsibilities, while also helping Tokyo to preserve the liberal international order. The Union, for its part, has stressed that it has "welcomed the prospect of Japan contributing more proactively to regional and global peace and security" (EU–Japan Summit, 2013) in line with Prime Minister Abe's proactive foreign policy. As observed by Reiterer (2015), the "comprehensive" and the "panoramic" perspectives that are advocated by the EU and Japan as their respective guiding foreign policy principles indicate a compatible vision and are likely to facilitate the building of a strategic partnership.

Geopolitical concerns of Japan and Europe

The present analysis makes it clear that the EU–Japan strategic partnership is driven by the mutual perceptions of "likemindedness" in terms of shared values and approaches to security, as well as by the growing awareness of one another's increasing role in the international arena. Added to this, as examined below, is the shared understanding of the necessity, and arguably urgency, of joint contributions for preserving the existing global order, including the respective security orders in the Asia-Pacific and Europe.

The Asia-Pacific exemplifies a region where hard power politics largely defines regional international relations. Since the late 2000s the thinking of Japanese strategists has been dominated by geopolitical concerns, especially by those associated with the People's Republic of China's (PRC) security behaviour in the region and the sustainability of the US military presence.

One of the aspects of China's rise as a great power, which has led to concerns across Asia and in the US (but much less so in Europe), has been the strengthening of its military power. Linked to this, as stated in the 2016 Pentagon report, has been Beijing's "willingness to tolerate higher levels of tension" in recent years in the pursuit of its territorial claims in the East and South China Seas (US Department of Defense, 2016: i). The 2013 strategy documents of the Abe Administration, i.e., the NSS and the National Defence Programme Guidelines (NDPG), depict the PRC's security behaviour (notably, China's military modernisation and its intensified activities in the seas and airspace around Japan) as an "issue of concern for the international community, including Japan" (Prime Minister of Japan and His Cabinet, 2013a, 2013b). The perception that the PRC attempts to change unilaterally "the status quo by coercion", disregarding international law and infringing upon the freedom of navigation has come to dominate the political discourse in Japan. As the Chinese navy is developing capabilities to control the "near seas" (within its so-called "first island chain") and anti-access or area-denial (A2/AD) strategy, Tokyo fears that China's military modernisation may potentially have broader regional objectives, notably ambitions for a future domination of maritime East Asia (Atanassova-Cornelis et al., 2015). Should the PRC acquire control of the East China Sea, it would be able to block trade routes there strategically critical for Japan; this, in turn, could have potentially devastating economic (and security) implications for this island nation. The PRC's behaviour in the South China Sea reinforces Tokyo's geopolitical concerns.

Japan's anxieties about China are further exacerbated by the growing uncertainties associated with the sustainability of the US security commitments to the Asia-Pacific in the mid to long term (Atanassova-Cornelis and Van der Putten, 2015). While Tokyo's worries about Washington's ability to remain engaged in Asian security lingered until the end of Obama's term in office, these have intensified under the Donald J. Trump Administration.[4] The US withdrawal from the TPP in early 2017, coupled with its persistent lack of clarity in China and Asia policies, has further reinforced Japanese (and Asian) perceptions of America's declining leadership.

Uncertainties about regional stability have also become a defining feature of the thinking of the EU's strategists. The 2014 Russian annexation of Crimea, the ongoing conflict in Ukraine and the refugee crisis of unthinkable proportions, itself a consequence of the instability in Syria, Libya and Afghanistan, have exposed the fragility of the European neighbourhood. In particular, these developments have intensified the debate in Brussels and in various European capitals regarding the existing means to prevent and respond to violations of international legal standards, and the possible partners to engage with in defending the established norms and rules (Raine and Small, 2015).

The EU's response to the conflict with Moscow has included imposing (and renewing in 2016) a series of economic sanctions on Russia, as well as seeking a reinforcement of NATO's deterrent capabilities and a stronger US security commitment. Tokyo has expressed solidarity with Brussels in defending rule-based order in Europe by imposing its own economic sanctions against Moscow. However, this move has had implications for Japanese diplomacy. Indeed, upon entering office at the end of 2012, Prime Minister Abe focused on seeking a resolution of the territorial issue with Russia as a major foreign-policy objective. The dispute over the Southern

Kurils or Northern Territories has prevented the two neighbours from concluding a peace treaty to formally end their Second World War hostilities. Prior to the developments in Ukraine, the bilateral relations under the Abe and Putin Administrations had seen good progress, with frequent high-level summits and government talks, stepped-up economic, energy and security co-operation, and co-ordination on North Korea. This mutual embrace was driven, to a significant degree, by shared concerns about China, and was part of Moscow's and Tokyo's respective diversification strategies in Asia (Hyodo, 2014; Atanassova-Cornelis and Van der Putten, 2015).

Japan's sanctions on Russia in the wake of the Crimean crisis were much limited in scope in comparison with the American and the European ones. Nevertheless, they did affect the bilateral ties negatively, as Moscow hardened its stance on the territorial issue. While showing solidarity with its European partners (and the US), Japan suffered diplomatic losses, demonstrating thereby "the common threat they [Japan and the EU] face when major powers seek to change the status quo by force or coercion" (Raine and Small, 2015: 9). At the same time, this also led to expectations on the part of Tokyo for a reciprocal European commitment to maintaining the integrity of the Asian security order, including in the East and South China Seas.

"Old and new" opportunities for EU–Japan co-operation

Throughout the 1990s and well into the late 2000s the main opportunities for Euro-Japanese security co-operation were those associated with the realm of non-traditional security. To a large extent, this reflected both actors' projection of a civilian power image, which was further linked to the area of development as both the EU and Japan were major providers of foreign aid. Joint promotion of sustainable development and the reduction of poverty, along with the increased mutual involvement in one another's region (Joint Declaration, 1991), may therefore be regarded as "old", now already established, areas of co-operation. These were mentioned as early as 1991 in the *Joint Declaration on Relations between The European Community and Its Member States and Japan* signed in The Hague. The above objectives were echoed in the 2001 Joint Action Plan, titled *Shaping Our Common Future*, which was a step further towards upgrading the political relations to a higher level of strategic partnership (Atanassova-Cornelis, 2010b). The promotion of respect for human rights, and joint involvement in conflict prevention and peace-building activities were singled out as priority areas (EU–Japan Summit, CB2001).

The shifting geopolitical environment in both the Asia-Pacific and Europe is emerging as an important driving force for Japan and the EU to consider "new" opportunities for co-operation and reconsider existing limitations. In particular, the return of geopolitics in Europe, at a time of China's more assertive behaviour in Asia, is yet another proof of the indivisibility of the global security order. Although Europe's security concerns about Russia are different in nature from Japan's security concerns about China, in both cases the issue at stake concerns challenges to established rules and norms of behaviour, and how to preserve the rule of law. This clearly presents an opportunity, and even necessity, for the EU and Japan to enhance their collaboration to jointly preserve rule-based order.

For example, as is Japanese trade, so is European trade heavily dependent on the safety of the South China Sea shipping lanes, through which US$5 trillion ship-borne trade passes each year. A major escalation of the maritime territorial disputes in the East Asian theatre is very likely to jeopardise the safety of Asia's Sea Lines of Communications (SLOCs), which are critical for both European and Japanese exports and imports, and hence for their respective economic prosperity. Looked at from a broader perspective, geopolitical stability in Asia is intertwined with the safety of the SLOCs passing through the Indo-Pacific, so the Indian Ocean may be regarded as a "natural geostrategic meeting point" between the two, offering various opportunities for co-operation (Simon, 2015). Accordingly, while Europe is indeed geographically distant from Asia, Asian-Pacific geopolitics does impact European interests in the region. In this context, a potential EU–Japan co-operation to maintain the broader maritime security order, ranging from joint anti-piracy operations to the strengthening of legal mechanisms for the resolution of territorial claims (Raine and Small, 2015), may be regarded as "new" opportunities. These should be built upon the already established co-operation in non-traditional security.

Reaching out to each other for support now seems a matter of urgency rather than necessity. Japan seeks to diversify its strategic partners due to uncertainties associated with China's regional ambitions and future US security commitments in Asia. The EU, for its part, tries to find reliable partners to support its foreign policy objectives regarding Russia, at a time of reduced defence spending in Europe, Brexit and Trump. To be sure, the nature of the emerging mutual regional involvement is rather different from what was envisaged in the 1991 Hague Declaration. Back in the 1990s, the focus of the bilateral co-operation was largely on the field of ODA. Since then Tokyo has provided foreign aid for the postwar reconstruction of the Western Balkans, while Brussels has extended humanitarian and development assistance to Asian countries, such as Cambodia, Thailand and North Korea. Although development does remain an important bilateral objective, realist-driven strategic considerations appear to be shifting the overall focus of the EU–Japan partnership. Notably, the return of geopolitics in Europe seems to be reinforcing the relevance of hard power for maintaining and defending regional order.

In this regard, as some of the "old" constraints associated with Japan's security role are now receding, the joint use of hard power (likely within a multilateral framework) is not inconceivable in the future. Under Abe, Japan has seen a growing defence budget for five consecutive years, as well as an overall expansion of the country's security role in terms of both geographical focus and security missions. In 2014, the Abe Cabinet reinterpreted Article 9 of the Constitution in order to allow a limited exercise of the right to collective self-defence under specific circumstances. This was in line with the conceptualisation shift of Japan's security role from the hitherto "one-country pacifism" to "proactive pacifism" – a shift that was introduced in 2013 by Abe's two main strategy documents, namely the NSS and the NDPG (Atanassova-Cornelis, 2017). In 2015, the Abe Administration enacted new security legislation, which enables the Self-Defence Forces (SDF) overseas to be dispatched overseas on a variety of international missions ranging from logistical support to peacekeeping activities such as security enforcement. These changes may potentially open a whole new array of opportunities for Japan's security co-operation with Europe beyond the Asian-Pacific theatre.

"Old and new" constraints on EU–Japan co-operation

The EU–Japan partnership continues to face some "old" constraints. Whereas Japan has become a more active security player, also beyond its alliance framework with the US, the EU's role as an independent (from NATO) and coherent foreign policy actor (in Asia) is still limited.

Shortly after the launch of the ESDP at the end of the 1990s the EU succeeded under this framework in developing both military and civilian crisis management capabilities, with an emphasis on the latter. What seemed a distant prospect in the 1990s became a reality in 2003 when the EU launched its first ever military operation, in Macedonia (taking over from a NATO force), and its first ever autonomous operation in Congo. Approximately a decade later, in 2014, the EU adopted a maritime security strategy and a framework for cyber defence policy in order to strengthen its CSDP. In 2013, the Union launched a civilian mission to support the training of the Malian armed forces (European Union Training Mission in Mali). It has been extended until 2018. In 2014–15 it deployed a military mission to restore public order in the Central African Republic (EUFOR RCA).

Although Europe has sought to reduce its dependence on American hard power through the CFSP and ESDP, the Union's military power projection capabilities outside NATO have remained limited (Hughes, 2007). With the notable exception of the long-range capabilities of France (the UK being excluded), Europe's forces are configured for continental missions and conflicts in the immediate neighbourhood (Lee, 2016). Moreover, NATO's relevance has increased little in the wake of the Ukraine crisis, at a time of steadily decreasing defence budgets of the EU member states and Brexit. Admittedly, the Asia-Pacific is not a main geographical area of Brussels's foreign policy. This is not likely to change in the foreseeable future. The ongoing crises in Europe's immediate neighbourhood have reinforced the priority of the EU's security interests and missions on the geographical areas that are "closer to home", notably Central and Eastern Europe, the Mediterranean and Africa. This, in turn, means fewer diplomatic, economic and military resources for involvement in Asia.

In addition to the EU's hard power and geographical limitations of its foreign policy, Europe has no permanent troop deployments in Asia either. To be sure, some EU member states (the UK excluded) do have limited military presence and engagement in the region. Examples are France's small naval deployments in the Indian Ocean and the South Pacific, and the military ties between some EU member states and key Asian players, including Japan and China (Casarini, 2013). European countries are also major suppliers of weapons to the region, especially in Southeast Asia, with their arms sales being second only to those of the US.

As for Europe's security concerns in East Asia, the 2012 *Guidelines on the EU's Foreign and Security Policy in East Asia* makes it clear that the EU recognises the diversity of threats to regional security. Importantly, these include the Korean peninsula and the South China Sea – theatres of geostrategic importance for both Europe and Japan. However, the EU's limited hard power capabilities, even more so after the UK leaves the EU, mean that the Union is unable to play a substantial role in Asia's critical security theatres. This limitation places constraints on the EU–Japan strategic partnership, and dampens Japan's enthusiasm for engaging Europe in the security area.[5] Furthermore, as the UK was traditionally one of the most important partners of Japan among the EU member states,[6] Britain's exit from the Union might reduce even further Europe's strategic significance to Japan.

The maritime disputes in the East and South China Seas, in particular, are placing "new" constraints on EU–Japan co-operation, notably from the perspective of Brussels's own relations with Beijing. The ever growing importance of the EU's trade ties with the PRC, the Union's second largest trading partner, has meant that a lot of European resources in recent years have been dedicated to the development of the EU–China partnership. This has also meant that Brussels has sought to avoid policies that might jeopardise this partnership.

The 2012 *Guidelines* stressed a "principled neutrality" position of the Union on maritime territorial disputes in Asia and encouraged dispute resolution in accordance with international law (Council of the European Union, 2012: 19). The EU's general reluctance to be more outspoken on these issues largely reflects the "China factor" in Europe's Asia policies. Indeed, many Asian observers tend to agree that fears of negative implications for European business interests in the PRC are the actual driver of Brussels's perceived "timidity" (Berkofsky, 2014). This also seems to reinforce the longstanding argument that for the EU in Asia economic interests trump geopolitical ones.[7] The Union's primarily trade-based approach towards Asia, largely driven by the "China opportunity" perception, hinders Europe's relevance for Japan as a strategic partner; indeed, despite the shared democratic values between the two (Atanassova-Cornelis, 2015).

Finally, there are well-known institutional limitations on the part of the EU that continue to impose "old" constraints on Brussels's partnership with Tokyo. These concern Europe's inability to "speak with one voice" and be a more coherent foreign-policy actor. From a Japanese perspective, the continuing arms sales to China by some European countries (despite the EU's arms embargo) are illustrative of the problem: not only do these developments underscore Europe's rather one-sided approach towards China as an "economic opportunity" (with little consideration of Asian geopolitics) but they also demonstrate a divided EU.

Not surprisingly, these EU-associated limitations have often dampened Tokyo's expectations for forging meaningful international initiatives with the Union, resulting in Japanese policy-makers' preference for dealing bilaterally with the individual EU member states (Reiterer, 2006; Tsuruoka, 2008). Despite the attempts made by the Lisbon Treaty to address these shortcomings, forging a common EU position on various (Asia-related) issues remains a challenge for Brussels. Furthermore, the involvement by some EU member states in the region's military-strategic affairs through arms sales or enhanced bilateral military ties with Asian countries tends to "sideline the EU level and sends mixed signals" regarding Europe's role in Asian security (Casarini, 2013: 189). As an actor made up of 27 sovereign states, each with their own bilateral interests in Asia, the EU, therefore, prefers to circumvent sensitive regional issues and "keeps silent" on those "that might complicate interests of key European states" (Lee, 2016: 10).

Summit agenda and main areas of security co-operation[8]

Since the 1991 Joint Declaration Japan and the EU have come a long way in institutionalising their relations. Bilateral consultations at the highest level have been taking place on a regular basis. These include annual bilateral summits between, on the one hand, the President of the European Council and the President of the Commission and, on the other, the Japanese Prime Minister. As an aspect of EU–Japan "declaratory politics", the annual summit seeks to evaluate the results of co-operation and indicate the new priority initiatives to be pursued.

The specific summit priorities in the security dimension of EU–Japan relations have closely followed the most salient global and regional issues, and evolved in response to the two actors' expanded international role discussed earlier. For example, in the 2000s, the dominant topics included counter-terrorism (2002), reconstruction of Iraq and the war on terror in Afghanistan (2004), the arms embargo on China (2005) and from 2007 climate change, energy security, development and human security (especially in Africa) (EU–Japan Summit, various years). The 2010 Summit was significant as a stepping stone to the future strategic partnership in that it pointed to a "more action-oriented" co-operation in the future, based on "common positions and joint projects" (EU–Japan Summit, 2010). To this end, the following areas for bilateral co-operation were singled out: capacity building in Afghanistan, counter-piracy off the coast of Somalia and the Gulf of Aden, and Japan's interest in contribution of non-military personnel to civilian missions within the CSDP framework. The 2011 Summit announced the intention to embark on the two parallel negotiations of an EPA/FTA and SPA, which started in 2013.

In the 2013 Summit regional geopolitical issues in Asia and Europe were given a particular attention. Notably, there is a strong emphasis in the Joint Statements on the tensions in "East Asia's maritime areas". Without directly mentioning China, successive documents explicitly stress that unilateral actions or coercion should be avoided, that disputes should be resolved peacefully and in accordance with international law, and that freedom of navigation and overflight should be guaranteed (EU-Japan Summit, 2013, 2014, 2015). The 2015 statement, for example, mentions that Japan and the EU are "concerned by any unilateral actions that change the status quo and increase tensions" in the East and South China Seas, which is an implicit criticism of Chinese behaviour. The EU's tensions with Russia are emphasised as well: it is argued that Tokyo and Brussels "remain determined never to recognise the illegal annexation of Crimea by the Russian Federation" (EU–Japan Summit, 2015).

As for the EU–Japanese security co-operation, it has largely developed in the area of soft security. This has reflected both actors' reliance on soft power and projection of a civilian power image in the international arena, especially characteristic of Japan's security policy until the late 2000s (Atanassova-Cornelis, 2010b). Joint initiatives have been pursued at both global and regional levels.

The area of development has been a natural area of convergence between Brussels and Tokyo due to the emphasis on soft power tools in their respective foreign policies, namely through the provision of ODA. The EU is the world's largest ODA and humanitarian aid donor. The objectives of Europe's development policy include poverty reduction and sustainable economic development, which are inherently linked to the Union's main foreign policy goals of promoting democracy, the rule of law and respect for human rights

(Keukeleire and MacNaughtan, 2008). For Japan, given its imperialistic past in Asia, the utilisation of ODA became a main diplomatic instrument in the country's pursuit of a peaceful foreign policy during the Cold War years (Atanassova-Cornelis, 2010a). Tokyo became a primary ODA donor, in particular, to Southeast Asian states and China, and was the driving force behind the economic development and modernisation of East Asia during the Cold War. As for bilateral co-operation in the area of global development, since 2010, for example, Japan and the EU have been holding a Development Policy Dialogue. The dialogue seeks to achieve a better bilateral co-ordination on aid and development effectiveness, and places a special emphasis on regional development issues in Africa and Asia.

Another "old" area of the bilateral security co-operation that deserves special attention is conflict prevention and peace-building. This area, too, reflects the emphasis that Japan and the EU have for a very long time placed on economic and non-military instruments of power in their foreign policies. As mentioned earlier, the EU has since the 1990s developed a holistic approach to crisis management, which encompasses both pre- and post-conflict mechanisms. Its holistic approach seeks to shape the political, legal, socio-economic and security structures in the countries concerned in order to tackle conflicts at their root and, ultimately, promote a peaceful environment (Keukeleire and MacNaughtan, 2008). Japan, for its part, considers peace-building, which is defined as one of the priority issues in its ODA Charter, to be a core area for Japan's international engagement. Tokyo's activities have included dispatching SDF on United Nations peacekeeping operations and providing financial support to peacekeeping operations training centres in Asia and Africa, as well as human resource development of civilian experts in the field of peacebuilding (Ministry of Foreign Affairs, Japan, 2014, 2015).

Tokyo and Brussels have co-operated in non-military crisis management and post-conflict reconstruction on the basis of their shared view of the need for a comprehensive approach in this area. Some of their initiatives since the 2000s include joint promotion of the peace process in Sri Lanka, as well as the rebuilding of the Western Balkans, especially Bosnia-Herzegovina and Kosovo. More recently, the two have co-operated in capacity-building missions in Mali and Congo, and for security improvement in Niger. Co-operation in Ukraine and Somalia has been identified as a next step (EU–Japan Summit, 2015).

The EU–Japan security co-operation is expected to be enhanced with the SPA – a legally binding, political document. This new agreement seeks to give the existing partnership a truly "strategic" orientation. From an EU perspective, a strategic partnership is characterised by a normative congruence, is built upon common interests and is multidimensional – it includes both politico-security and economic objectives, and has a strong regional/global impact (Reiterer, 2013). From a Japanese perspective, what undermines Brussels's value as a strategic partner to Tokyo is Europe's hitherto predominant focus on trade and economics in its foreign policy (and hence on China), as well as the EU's inability and unwillingness to get involved in Asian geopolitical issues. Accordingly, for Tokyo, the likelihood of the EU–Japan partnership having a truly "strategic" impact in the Asia-Pacific, a region characterised by power politics, is rather low. This, however, does not deny the importance for Japan of the soft security dimension of the bilateral co-operation, especially at the global level.

Policy reflections: Whither EU–Japan co-operation?

On the basis of already established areas of co-operation, the EU and Japan should, in the first place, try to build a partnership narrower in scope yet action-oriented in security. The signing of the two agreements of the SPA (and EPA/FTA) in July 2018 is a welcome development, for the SPA will prioritise fewer policy areas for joint actions, thereby streamlining the bilateral co-operation. More broadly, the EU's focus in Asia should be more on security issues rather than on economic and trade matters, while its foreign policy priorities should be limited to a few selected areas, in which it can be sure to deliver concrete results (Reiterer, 2016). Without any doubt, this policy recommendation applies to the EU's relations with Japan. In addition to SPA, Brussels and Tokyo should consider a Framework Participation Agreement (FPA) along the lines of the EU's agreement with South Korea. This is likely to provide a further boost to the security ties, for an FPA would enable the SDF's participation in CSDP's civilian (and possibly military) missions and operations.

Secondly, what concerns specific areas of bilateral security co-operation, maritime security, notably capacity-building and anti-piracy, should be prioritised. Admittedly, Japan's increased willingness to play a security role in geographical areas that are of geostrategic importance to Europe is a critical factor for this. For example, from 2012 to 2017 the SDF were engaged in the UN peacekeeping operations in South Sudan helping to construct roads, bridges and other infrastructure, as well as providing medical assistance. Following the passage of the 2015 security legislation, the SDF were allowed to come to the aid of other countries' troops or UN staff under attack. Japan also has a base in Djibouti in East Africa, and has been involved in capacity-building in Somalia and its neighbouring countries. Therefore, EU–Japan co-operation in Somalia is a promising future area for collaboration and should be explored as soon as possible. This should go hand in hand with a broader bilateral objective to bring stability to the region. Notably, Japan and Europe should explore opportunities for jointly strengthening the capacities of the coast guards and internal security services of the countries of the Horn of Africa (Simon, 2015). Concomitantly, EU–Japan maritime security co-operation off the coast of Somalia and in the Gulf of Aden should be deepened. The basis for this already exists. It is in this geostrategic theatre that Japan and the EU in 2014 carried out their first joint counter-piracy exercise between deployed units of the EU's Naval Force Somalia–Operation ATALANTA and SDF. The SDF involvement since 2009 in anti-piracy operations in the area, seeking to ensure the safe passage of civilian vessels, made this joint mission possible.

Thirdly, future EU–Japan co-operation in the Asia-Pacific should be based on the premise that maritime security order is inseparable from the regional and global order. If Japan and the EU want to preserve the integrity of their respective regional orders, the joint promotion of the rule of law should be considered as an absolute necessity rather than merely a choice. From this perspective, Tokyo and Brussels should co-operate for the strengthening of legal mechanisms for the resolution of territorial claims.

In regard to the East and South China Seas, the EU, with its commitment to the rule of law, should exercise leadership in proposing initiatives that are likely to be supported by Japan and other like-minded partners. For example, the EU could establish a multilateral declaratory policy regime along the lines of the 2002 Declaration of Conduct in the South China Sea, but with a broader geographical scope and with a clear reference to international law (Lee, 2016). The EU could also organise a conference and invite the co-signatories of ASEAN's TAC, including Japan, to examine the application of Tactical Air Control's (TAC) principles in the context of the South China Sea (Reiterer, 2016). Without any doubt, if the EU wants to enhance its credibility as a partner for countries like Japan, Brussels should take the lead in "translating the promotion of the rule of law into action" (Reiterer, 2016). This will help maintain the liberal international order that is a shared value by Japan and the EU.

Finally, and related to the above, the Union should seek to enhance its attractiveness as a strategic partner to Japan in order to ensure Tokyo's support on many critical, for Brussels, political and security issues. This means that the Union should embrace a broader view of the region beyond the hitherto China-centric vision, as well as actively support the integrity of regional order in Asia. As security issues are increasingly interconnected, and if Europeans do not expect their partners in Asia to remain "neutral" on the Ukraine crisis, the EU, too, is expected to support "those in Asia who oppose any change of status quo by force or coercion" (Kundnani and Tsuruoka, 2014). Accordingly, Brussels should not circumvent "sensitive" issues but move from being a "passive" observer to a more "involved" player.

The EU seems to have embraced a more critical, albeit still restraint, position regarding the PRC's behaviour in the East and South China Seas. For example, in 2013 in the wake of China's establishment of an Air Defence Identification Zone (ADIZ) in the East China Sea, Brussels stressed that this development "heightened the risk of escalation and contributed to raising tensions in the region" (Ashton, 2013). Although the statement came five days after the ADIZ's declaration by the PRC, this rather strong language regarding Beijing's policies was unusual for the EU, which typically preferred to avoid antagonising China. In March 2016, the Union issued a Declaration on the South China Sea, calling on "all claimants to refrain from militarisation in the region, from the use or threat of force, and to abstain from unilateral actions", as well as urging dispute resolution "in accordance with international law including United Nations Convention on the Law of the Sea and its arbitration procedures" (Council of the European Union, 2016). At the same time, after several days of internal disagreements among the EU member states, Brussels succeeded in issuing only a carefully worded statement on the South China Sea ruling handed down in July 2016 by the Permanent Court of Arbitration in The Hague. There was no mention of China and the Union merely "acknowledged" the court's decision. This did raise questions in Tokyo and in various Asian capitals regarding Europe's ability and willingness to support the integrity of the rule-based international order.

Conclusion

Over the past two decades the security co-operation between the EU and Japan has evolved to become an important aspect of the bilateral partnership and has added a "strategic" dimension to it. Shared values and comprehensive security approaches, as well as the two partners' growing efforts to undertake joint actions in pursuit of common foreign policy goals testify to this evolution.

"New" opportunities for EU–Japan co-operation have emerged, as the geopolitical environment in both Europe and Asia has changed, and as some of the "old" constraints have receded. Japan has expanded its security role and has enhanced its value as a partner to Europe in global security missions. This has been paralleled by the growing realisation in both Brussels and Tokyo that mutual support is imperative for preserving rule-based order. These are now the major drivers behind the current move to forge a stronger EU–Japan partnership. At the same time, important constraints remain, especially those associated with Tokyo's focus on Asian-Pacific geopolitics and on the "China threat", as well as with the EU's limited strategic impact as a foreign-policy actor in Asia. Therefore, it seems that, although geopolitics is an important factor driving the EU–Japan partnership and there is a promising bilateral security co-operation at the global level, it is at the regional level in Asia – where power politics is dominant – that the limitations of the EU–Japan relations may be observed the most.

The EU and Japan are "natural" strategic partners – yet more at the rhetorical level rather than in practice, for the international significance of their partnership remains limited, especially in Asia. If Europe and Japan are able to recognise the existing limitations and to build on the established strengths of the bilateral relations, they will surely succeed in making their partnership a truly strategic one. If not, the search for the "strategic" will continue.

Notes

1 In this chapter, Europe refers to the European Union as a regional entity, but excludes the UK following the 2016 Brexit vote (except when explicitly referring to EU28). The discussion does not examine the bilateral relations between the individual EU member states and Japan, which have not been replaced by the Japan–EU partnership.
2 Asia, Asia-Pacific and East Asia are used interchangeably throughout the text. The region is conceptualised as including the sub-regions of Northeast Asia (Japan, China, Taiwan and the two Koreas) and Southeast Asia (ASEAN 10).
3 She concurrently serves as Vice-President of the European Commission.
4 Author's interviews and private conversations with Japanese scholars and officials in Tokyo and Brussels, in 2015 and 2017.
5 Author's interviews and private conversations with Japanese scholars and officials, Tokyo, 2015.
6 In 2013, Japan and Britain signed the "UK–Japan Defence Equipment Co-operation Framework" and an "Information Security Agreement". This established a legal framework for closer bilateral co-operation on defence and security.
7 Author's interviews and private conversations with Japanese scholars and officials, Tokyo, 2015.
8 This section is by no means exhaustive. It selectively examines some areas of the EU–Japan security co-operation.

References

Ashton, C. (2013). *Declaration by the High Representative Catherine Ashton on Behalf of the EU on the Establishment by China of an "East China Sea Air Defence Identification Zone"*. http://www.consilium.europa.eu/uedocs/cms_Data/docs/pressdata/EN/foraff/139752.pdf/, accessed online 28 November 2017.

Atanassova-Cornelis, Elena. (2010a). "Foreign Policy Instruments and Factors for Policy Change: Japan's Security 'Normalisation' Reconsidered". *Asian Journal of Social Science* 38 (2): 277–304.

Atanassova-Cornelis, Elena. (2010b). "The EU–Japan Strategic Partnership in the 21st Century: Motivations, Constraints and Practice", *Journal of Contemporary European Research* 6 (4): 478–95.

Atanassova-Cornelis, Elena. (2015). "Constraining or Encouraging? US and EU Responses to China's Rise in East Asia", *Central European Journal of International and Security Studies* 9 (4): 6–27.

Atanassova-Cornelis, Elena. (2017). "Evolving Japanese Security Strategy", in D. Vanoverbeke, T. Suami, T. Ueta, F. Ponjaert and N. Peeters (eds), *Developing EU–Japan Relations in a Changing Regional Context*. London: Routledge, pp. 71–5.

Atanassova-Cornelis, Elena, and Frans Paul van der Putten. (2015). "Strategic Uncertainty and the Regional Security Order in East Asia", *E-International Relations*. www.e-ir.info/2015/11/24/strategic-uncertainty-and-the-regional-security-order-in-east-asia/, accessed online 28 November 2017.

Atanassova-Cornelis, Elena, Ramon Pacheco Pardo, and Eva Pejsova. (2015). *Pride and Prejudice: Maritime Disputes in Northeast Asia*. Paris: EU Institute for Security Studies (EUISS). www.iss.europa.eu/publications/detail/article/pride-and-prejudice-maritime-disputes-in-northeast-asia/, accessed online 12 April 2017.

Berkofsky, Axel. (2014). "The European Union in Asian Security: Actor with a Ppunch or Distant Bystander?", *Asia-Pacific Review* 21 (2): 61–85.

Casarini, Nicola. (2013). "The Securitisation of EU–Asia Relations in the Post-Cold War Era", in T. Christiansen, E. Kirchner and P. Murray (eds), *The Palgrave Handbook of EU–Asia Relations*. Basingstoke: Palgrave Macmillan, pp. 181–97.

Council of the European Union. (2012). *Guidelines on the EU's Foreign and Security Policy in East Asia*. http://eeas.europa.eu/asia/, docs/guidelines_eu_foreign_sec_pol_east_asia_en.pdf/, accessed online 15 June 2017.

Council of the European Union. (2016). *Guidelines on the EU's Foreign and Security Policy in East Asia*. www.consilium.europa.eu/en/press/press-releases/2016/03/11-hr-declaration-on-bealf-of-eu-recent-developments-south-china-sea/, accessed online 11 March 2018.

EU Commission. (1994). *Towards a New Asia Strategy*. Communication from the Commission to the Council. Brussels: COM (94) 314 final, 13 July.

European Commission. (1995). *Europe and Japan: The Next Steps*. Communication from the Commission to the Council. Brussels: COM (95) 73 final, 8 March.

European Commission. (2001). *Europe and Asia: A Strategic Framework for Enhanced Partnerships*. Communication from the Commission. Brussels: COM (2001) 469 final, 4 September.

European Commission. (2016, 2017). "EU Bilateral Trade and Trade with the World",. *DG Trade statistics*. http://ec.europa.eu/trade/policy/countries-and-regions/, accessed online 11 March 2018.

European Council. (2003). *A Secure Europe in a Better World: European Security Strategy*. Brussels.

EU–Japan Summit. (2001a). *Shaping Our Common Future: An Action Plan for EU–Japan Cooperation*. www.eeas.europa.eu/japan/docs/actionplan2001_en.pdf/, accessed online 12 December 2017.

EU–Japan Summit. (2001b). *Joint Press Statement*. http://eeas.europa.eu/top_stories/2015/201115_eu-japan_summit_en.htm; http://www.consilium.europa.eu/, accessed online 15 December 2017.

EU–Japan Summit. (2013). *21st EU–Japan Summit: Joint Press Statement*. www.consilium.europa.eu/uedocs/cms_Data/docs/pressdata/en/ec/139641.pdf, accessed online 7 September 2018.

Ferrero-Waldner, Benita. (2006, April). "New Visions for EU–Japan Relations", in *Speech by the European Commissioner for External Relations and European Neighbourhood Policy at the Opening of the Joint EU–Japan Symposium*. Brussels (Vol. 6).

Hughes, Christopher C.W. (2007). "Europe and Japan F the Challenges of Peace and War: Declining Prospects for Cooperation in the Management of US Hegemony?", in T. Ueta, E. Remacle and F. Ponjaert (eds), *Japan–European Union: A Strategic Partnership in the Making. Studia Diplomatica: The Brussels Journal of International Relations*, LX (4): 55–72.

Hyodo, Shinji. (2014). "Russia's Strategic Concerns in the Arctic and Its Impact on Japan–Russia Relations", *Strategic Analysis* 38 (6): 860–71.

Joint Declaration on Relations between the European Community and Its Member States and Japan. (1991). The Hague. www.mofa.go.jp/region/europe/eu/overview/declar.html/, accessed online 12 February 2018.

Keukeleire, Stephan, and Jennifer MacNaughtan. (2008). The Foreign Policy of the European Union. Basingstoke: Palgrave Macmillan.

Kundnani, Hans, and Michito Tsuruoka. (2014). "The Illusion of European 'Neutrality' in Asia", *European Geostrategy*. www.europeangeostrategy.org/long-posts/, accessed online 25 September 2017.

Lee, John. (2016). "An EU-led Convention on East Asian Maritime Conduct", in Daniel Twinning (ed.), *Defending a Fraying Order: The Imperative of Closer U.S.–Europe–Japan Cooperation*. Washington, DC: The German Marshall Fund of the United States, pp. 9–16.

Ministry of Foreign Affairs, Japan. (various years 1991, 1993, 200–15). *Diplomatic Bluebook*. http://www.mofa.go.jp/policy/other/bluebook/, accessed online 15 November 2017.

Prime Minister of Japan and His Cabinet. (2013a). *National Defense Program Guidelines for FY2014 and Beyond*. http://japan.kantei.go.jp/96_abe/documents/2013/index.html, accessed online 17 December 2017.

Prime Minister of Japan and His Cabinet. (2013b). *National Security Strategy*. http://japan.kantei.go.jp/96_abe/documents/2013/index.html/, accessed 19 December 2017.

Raine, Sarah, and Andrew Small. (2015). *Waking up to Geopolitics: A New Trajectory to Japan–Europe Relations*. The German Marshall Fund of the United States. http://www.gmfus.org/publications/waking-geopolitics-new-trajectory-japan-europe-relations/, accessed online 22 March 2017.

Reiterer, Michael. (2006). "Japan and the European Union: Shared Foreign Policy Interests", *Asia Europe Journal* 4 (3): 333–49.

Reiterer, Michael. (2013). "The Role of 'Strategic Partnerships' in the EU's Relations with Asia", in T. Christiansen, E. Kirchner and P. Murray (eds), *The Palgrave Handbook of EU–Asia Relations*. Basingstoke: Palgrave Macmillan, pp. 75–89.

Reiterer, Michael. (2015). "EU Security Interests in East Asia: Prospects for Comprehensive EU–Japan Cooperation Beyond Trade and Economics", *NFG Policy Paper* 6, February. Freie Universität Berlin.

Reiterer, Michael. (2016). "Asia as Part of the EU's Global Security Strategy: Reflections on a More Strategic Approach", in O. Gippner (ed.), *Changing Waters: Towards a New EU Asia Strategy*. London: LSE IDEAS, pp. 62–70.

www.lse.ac.uk/ideas/Assets/Documents/reports/LSE-IDEAS-Changing-Waters-Towards-a-New-EU-Asia-Strategy.pdf, accessed online 7 September 2018.
Simon, Luis. (2015). "How Japan Matters to Europe", *European Geostrategy*. www.europeangeostrategy.org/2015/01/japan-matters-europe/, accessed online 22 February 2017.
Solana, Javier. (2006, April). "The EU's Strategic Partnership with Japan", in *Speech by Javier Solana, EU High Representative for Common Foreign and Security Policy*. Tokyo. www.consilium.europa.eu/uedocs/cms_data/docs/pressdata/en/discours/89298.pdf, accessed online 7 September 2018.
Tsuruoka, Michito. (2008). "Expectations Deficit in EU–Japan Relations: Why the Relationship Cannot Flourish?", *Current Politics and Economics of Asia* 17 (1): 107–26.
US Department of Defense. (2016). *Military and Security Developments Involving the People's Republic of China 2016*. Annual Report to Congress. www.defense.gov/Portals/1/Documents/pubs/2016%20China%20Military%20Power%20Report.pdf/, accessed online 3 January 2018.
Van Rompuy, Herman. (2010, April). "A Changing EU and a Changing Japan in a Changing World", in *Speech by the President of the European Council, Kobe University. Japan.: www.consilium.europa.eu/media/27966/113067.pdf, accessed online 7 September 2018.*

9 The European Union's security strategy in the ASEAN region

Reuben Wong

> The EU has a military dimension as well: our economic face is the one most Asians (and also most Europeans!) are more familiar with. … We are one of the major investors in this continent, both in qualitative and quantitative terms, and the biggest development donor. … But our engagement with Asia goes well beyond trade, investment, and aid. It's political. It's strategic(al). And it needs to develop more also in the security field. (Federica Mogherini, High Representative of EU CFSP, VP, European Commission, 2015)[1]

Introduction: The EU in Asian security

As regional integration projects, the European Union (EU) and the Association of Southeast Asian Nations (ASEAN) perceive regionalism as a means to promote and achieve peace and stability in their respective regions (Allison, 2015). On the basis of a common recognition of the value of integration and aspiration of being active players either in their respective regions (as in the case of ASEAN and the EU) or globally (as in the case of the EU), the EU has sought to promote integration to ASEAN through a series of predominantly economic co-operation programmes, and ASEAN regards the EU as an important point of reference (Wong, 2012; Allison, 2015). Inherently, the differences between the EU's and ASEAN's founding motivations and norms of interaction – the EU as aspiring towards greater supranationalism and the ASEAN focusing strictly on inter-governmentalism and the norms of non-interference – have traditionally limited the EU's influence on ASEAN to the economic domain (Allison, 2015).

In 1997, Paul Stares and Nicolas Régaud argued that the European Union had distinct security interests in the Asia-Pacific, and that the EU needed the will to co-ordinate and deploy member states' military capabilities towards the defence of these trade, humanitarian and human security-interests in the region (Stares and Régaud, 1997). They were perhaps too optimistic and ahead of their time. In the intervening twenty years, the EU has developed a military capability kicked off by the Anglo-French summit in Saint-Malo in December 1998. A European Security and Defence Policy (ESDP) was established, and ESDP operations involving European soldiers and hardware were deployed since 2003 to civilian, military and mixed missions around the world. Yet the impact of European military projection was limited mainly to Central and Eastern Europe, the Mediterranean and the Middle East, and southern Africa. Aside from the Aceh Monitoring Mission in Indonesia in 2005–6 and European arms sales in Asia, most scholars and defence analysts considered the EU a non-player in Asia-Pacific security, since the EU is generally not regarded a security actor in the traditional sense, much unlike the US and China (Yeo and Matera, 2015). The US is predominantly viewed as the guarantor of stability and security in the region, with a rising China challenging the postwar security system built by the US after Japan's surrender and the retreat of European colonial powers (Katzenstein, 2005; Proszowska, 2016: 66).

Stares and Régaud's thesis that the EU would need to project military power in East Asia, fell short primarily because a necessary precondition – the securitisation of EU–Asia relations – did not happen. As the engine of global economic growth shifted from the Atlantic to the Asia-Pacific region, along with the integration of Asian economies into the global trade and production chains, the increasing volatility in the Asian region in terms of the brewing US–China geopolitical rivalry and insufficient capabilities of the Southeast Asian states to handle emerging non-traditional security threats could potentially endanger the achievement of Europe's economic security, thus providing a solid basis for renewed EU interest in Asia (Proszowska, 2016: 57). An earlier attempt to establish a region-wide Free Trade Agreement (FTA) with ASEAN was scuttled in the mid-2000s, but the EU has established or is busy establishing bilateral FTAs with countries in East Asia, including ASEAN countries like Singapore, Vietnam and Thailand (Robles, 2008; Wong, 2012; Mckenzie and Meissner, 2017).

The uncertainties that emerged with the onset of numerous crises over the last two decades in both regions – the Asian financial crisis in 1997, the global financial crisis in 2007 that in turn triggered the Euro crisis, the recent refugee crisis and, more recently, terrorist threats – have demonstrated the insufficiency of the EU being active only in the economic arena. Compared to the EU's activity in the economic front, the EU is much less active in Asian security. But its interest in raising its security profile has begun to overlap with the priorities and demands of the ASEAN countries in Southeast Asia, as both are keen on a stable environment in the face of competition between the US and China (Reiterer, 2014; Allison, 2015; Yeo and Matera, 2015; Wong and Brown, 2016; Mckenzie and Meissner, 2017). Given the EU's experience in dealing with non-traditional security threats such as climate change, development goals, cybersecurity and counter-terrorism, the EU is placed in a unique position to craft out a niche role in the Asia-Pacific that will carry more political weight (Reiterer, 2014, 2016).

This chapter evaluates the EU's attempts to raise its economic and security profile in Asia. It argues that the EU's pursuit of its economic and security goals in ASEAN is in line with its larger strategy in the Asia-Pacific. But the EU is consistently unable to increaseyits visibility in the Asia-Pacific, or present itself as a credible partner for ASEAN alongside the US and China. In this chapter, I explore how the EU can pursue its security interests not just as an end unto itself but rather, as a means towards facilitating a stable and harmonious environment for trade and investment with – and ultimately, development of – ASEAN as a regional bloc.

This argument is divided into four parts: first I lay out the similarities and differences between the EU and ASEAN in their norms and regional processes; second I explore an overview on the EU strategies and policies towards the ASEAN region over the recent decades; third I discuss how co-operation could develop in non-traditional security (NTS); and finally I suggest how the EU's security strategy in ASEAN could be rethought and improved.

Different regionalisms

The EU and ASEAN share the view that integration is a process that may lead to the end goal of peace and stability in their respective regions (Allison, 2015: 79). For the EU's "half-century's worth of experience in regional integration", ASEAN has always been proactively referring to the EU as a point of reference and as an inspiration with respect to its own institutional development. (European Commission, 2003: 15; Allison, 2015: 130) But it is important to note that the norms and end goals of regionalism in the regions are quite different. In Western Europe, there were strong sentiments to build supranational institutions to avoid the past mistakes of international wars by building a common European framework for ever closer co-operation. Meanwhile in Southeast Asia, newly independent and decolonised states sought to strengthen their state structures by invoking norms of sovereignty, and non-interference, values and norms of interaction greatly limit the areas of co-operation where the EU's norm diffusion could be welcomed by ASEAN (Acharya, 2004; Allison, 2015).

The European Union: An "ever-closer union"

The EU – which evolved from the 1951 European Coal and Steel Community that was formed to address the needs of a postwar Europe and to discourage overtly negative nationalistic sentiments – tends towards the pooling of sovereignty and creation of supranational mechanisms as a way to maximise peace, stability and welfare within the European region (Olsen, 2007; Jetschke and Murray, 2012; Allison, 2015; Onestini, 2015). Besides the founding aspiration towards supranationalism, the hallmark of the European Integration project includes its development of dispute settlement mechanisms – such as the creation of the supranational European Court of Justice – to ensure that member states comply with the common implementation of legally binding EU laws.

In spite of heightened anti-supranational sentiments in many states in Europe, it is inherent that the aspiration towards achieving the normative ideals of peace and stability – to be achieved through the creation of an integrated economic community – in the aftermath of the Second World War continues to influence the majority of later EU institutional developments, policy-making and subsequent implementation (Allison, 2015). As a result of the norms that initially established the European community, the EU member states are arguably more receptive to, or at least tolerant of, regional efforts in co-operating on issues within sensitive domains such as security.

In fact, this aspiration towards achieving normative ideals of peace and security as a supranational entity is well reflected by the EU's decision-making mechanism. The EU applies the principle of subsidiarity, where decisions should be, and tend to be, taken at the level where it is most effective to do so (Kennes, 2015). Where it is recognised that it will be more effective for certain policies to be taken at an EU-wide level (i.e. policies concerning issues of a transnational nature), common policies are instituted. Policies regarding trade and competition which affect the economic prosperity of the bloc and the success of its internal market, for example, are some of the policies of which decision-making competence is delegated solely to the EU (Kennes, 2015). In recent decades, EU decision-making has also gradually evolved towards an increasing use of the Quality Majority Voting mechanism for issues that are less politically sensitive, moving away from arduous unanimous voting expectations (Kennes, 2015). Thus, recent incidents within Europe – such as terrorist attacks and the refugees crisis as a result of instability in the neighbouring Syria, Iraq and Afghanistan – have seen renewed efforts at co-operation in the security domain in their aftermath, such as the creation of an EU anti-terrorism team under Europol in addition to the Common Foreign and Security Policy (CFSP), and the approval by the European Parliament of a mandate to share air passenger data between security forces in the European Union (Jacobsen, 2016; Fioretti, 2016). A recent development has even eased, and sped up communications among citizens of the EU member states: the EU has abolished roaming charges, allowing its EU citizens to travel

Inter-governmentalism and sovereignty

In contrast to the EU, the focus of the regional integration project in ASEAN lies predominantly in smoothing political difficulties between its member states, rather than the explicit promotion of any fully fledged economic, political or security integration (Narine, 2016). Moreover, the key driving force to the founding of ASEAN was a response to the external environment of the Cold War – the fear of the expansion of the Communist bloc in Asia, and the fear of interference from external powers. The founding members of ASEAN were wary of the heightened Cultural Revolution propaganda by Chinese Red Guards and feared that Communist insurgencies and revolutions could take place within their borders (Storey, 2011; Mahbubani and Sng, 2017). Indeed, the psychological impact of the former American President Dwight Eisenhower's Domino Theory[2] created a prevailing climate of fear, to which, at that time, Singapore's former Foreign Minister S. Rajaratnam remarked to ASEAN colleagues, "if we do not hang together, we will hang separately" (Mahbubahni and Sng, 2017). In the wake of multiple Communist victories in Indochina,[3] ASEAN was thus founded in 1967, in hopes of a stable internal and external environment for the newly independent states conducive to focus on domestic development. In the post-Cold War period, sovereignty continues to be regarded by an ASEAN scarred by differing colonial experiences as key to the survival of viable states, the principle of non-interference remains the defining attribute that governs the relationships among the ASEAN member states.

The familiar structure – an intergovernmental one – of ASEAN's regional project thus frequently results in the commitment of regional citizens and elites to the ASEAN community being diluted by their own commitment "to more parochial identities and interests" (Narine, 2016). ASEAN's way of decision-making, which is as yet solely based on consultation and consensus, generally means that unanimity among member states, regardless of their varied and differing cultural and political characters, has to be achieved before significant strides in decision-making could be achieved (Kennes, 2015).

The expectation of the pooling of sovereignty necessary to building supranational institutions as part of the regionalisation project is therefore largely inconceivable to the ASEAN member states; and where crises which mandate closer co-operation in search for a regional solution does emerge, effective supranationalism is likely to move at an arduous, glacial pace, if not being avoided at all. Where co-operation in the security domain is traditionally viewed as an unacceptable impinge on national sovereignty, the topic is much more sensitive to broach in ASEAN than in the EU.

EU strategies towards ASEAN

ASEAN–EU co-operation commenced as early as in the 1970s, shortly after ASEAN was created in 1967; informal group-to-group talks took place as early as 1972, and these informal dialogues were formalised in 1977, with regular senior officials and ministerial meetings (Yeo, 2010; Kennes, 2015). What initially started off as institutional contact gradually developed into co-operation with political and economic considerations, as the EC was intent on improving its foreign-policy profile and reducing the influence of the Soviet Union in the region (Flers, 2010). However, although both regions condemned Vietnam's invasion of Cambodia in 1975, it highlighted the conflicting principles present in both communities, where ASEAN's emphasis on non-interference as its guiding principle was in stark contrast to the EC's approach of pooling sovereignty amongst member states (Flers, 2010).

Economic and political contact between ASEAN and the EC broadened during the 1980s, following a co-operation agreement between both regions signed in Kuala Lumpur on 7 March 1980. The 1980s represented a positive period in EC–ASEAN relations given that the Cold War brought about a convergence of interests, which, coupled with the withdrawal of US troops from Vietnam in 1975, presented the EC with an opportunity to play a more active role in the region (Forster, 2000). As a result of the Cold War, the EC also lent its support to ASEAN, many of which were authoritarian states, albeit pro-West and anti-Communist. However, although the EC and ASEAN strengthened their relations during this period, member states of ASEAN were mostly at the receiving end of developmental aid provided by the EC, leading to a weaker bargaining position during negotiations between the regions (Flers, 2010).

With the fall of the Soviet Union in 1991, the end of the Cold War in the 1990s meant that there was no longer any shared adversary between EC and ASEAN. Relations between both regions declined during this period as the EC shifted its foreign policy agenda upon its transformation into the EU. With Communism no longer deemed as an existential threat, the EU placed the defence of "EU Values", which included the promotion of democracy and human rights, at the forefront of its foreign-policy approach (Forster, 2000). The conditions imposed by the EU to promote these objectives were deemed divisive and unfair by member states of ASEAN. This episode highlighted the conflicting values inherent in the EU and ASEAN, with EU values coming up against the "Asian values" propagated by ASEAN leaders such as Mahatir Mohamad and Lee Kuan Yew. Relations between the EU and ASEAN deteriorated, with ASEAN rejecting the sanctions applied by the EU on China in response to the Tiananmen incident, and plunged even further when ASEAN rejected the stand of the EU and allowed Myanmar, a target of EU sanctions, to accede to ASEAN in 1996 (Forster, 2000; Mahbubani and Sng, 2017).

EU–ASEAN relations took a turn for the better only during the late 1990s as the EU adopted a pragmatic approach towards its dealings with ASEAN due to the vast economic opportunities available in the region. In view of ASEAN's economic dynamism, the EU unveiled a communication paper titled *Towards a New Asia Strategy*, which revealed then the fundamentally economic approach of the EU towards Asia (Yeo, 2010). Further, proposed by then Singapore Prime Minister Goh Chok Tong, the Asia–Europe Meeting (ASEM), an informal institutionalised forum attended by the heads of state and government from Europe and Asia biennially, aimed to function as a strategic umbrella for all areas of contact and establish networks at the non-governmental level (Forster, 2000). The ASEM was perceived as a substitute for renegotiating the EU–ASEAN Co-operation Agreement, which stalled as a result of straining ties between the two communities, and was also seen as an instrument to expand the EU's presence in the region. The apparent success of the ASEM was due to its non-legally binding and informal nature and it managed to redefine regional contact, provide a way out of an intractable membership problem, extend cooperation to new areas and provide a distinct opportunity to engage Asia and Europe through a multi-layered relationship (Forster, 2000). The context of competing EU–US economic and security interests in Asia also meant that ASEM and ASEAN–EU dialogue is more significant for the EU, given its exclusion from the East Asian Summit and Asia-Pacific Economic Community, to influence economic and security issues in its favour (Winand, 2012: 181–4).

Political changes in the ASEAN region were to open up further spaces for new engagement, following the wave of democratisation in Indonesia, in the wake of Suharto's resignation (Yeo, 2010). Such spaces of opportunities started becoming more clearly delineated, as the events of 11September 2001, and further threats of international terrorism, highlighted the need for greater involvement on non-traditional issues such as terrorism, piracy, even money laundering, and pollution. In 2003, the EU demonstrated its interest in playing a niche role focusing on Asia's non-traditional security when the European Commission issued its Communication, which called for the revitalising of EU's relationship with ASEAN and the broader region. With three of its six strategies highlighted in the communication focusing on non-traditional security, the new phase of the EU–ASEAN relationship cannot be regarded as driven only by economic interests (Yeo, 2010). Inevitably, that the EU chose to support ASEAN's endeavours in eradicating terrorism, piracy and organised crime, as well as tackling issues in regards to human rights and migration, reflected the EU's increasing recognition that mutual prosperity lies in the region's ability to remain politically stable, both ASEAN-wide as well as within individual member states.

Developing non-traditional security co-operation

> Terrorism, organised crime and illegal migration undermine the rule of law, discourage investment, and hinder development. Similarly, economic and trade development can best flourish in countries that not only encourage economic freedom but also respect human rights and the rule of law, practise good governance and rule democratically. (European Commission, 2003)

> Create a more dynamic and resilient ASEAN, capable of responding and adjusting to emerging challenges through robust national and regional mechanisms that address food and energy security issues, natural disasters, economic shocks, and other emerging trade-related issues as well as global mega trends. (ASEAN Secretariat, 2015)

Presently the EU and ASEAN enjoy an extensive relationship in trade. ASEAN is the EU's third largest trading partner outside Europe, whereas the EU is ASEAN's second largest trading partner (Eurostat, 2016). Moreover, the EU remains the largest investor in ASEAN countries, accounting for 22 per cent of Foreign Direct Investment inflow into the region, with EU companies investing an average of €19 billion annually in ASEAN.

Despite this extensive relationship in trade in interregional terms, it has been difficult to achieve an EU–ASEAN FTA due to variations in EU's trade exchanges with ASEAN states on a bilateral basis. This has resulted in the temporary abandonment of the interregional negotiations on a trade agreement (Meissner, 2016: 330). While it could be unfair to compare the EU–ASEAN FTA to other FTAs signed by ASEAN with other Asian countries due to significant differences in issues areas such as the inclusion of intellectual property rights, the inability to conclude an EU–ASEAN FTA in the context of these other FTAs meant that the EU was not able to score a political victory vis-à-vis China in proving that the EU could be a reliable partner for ASEAN in times of economic challenges. Although the EU–ASEAN FTA negotiations suffered a setback, ASEAN's goal of achieving an ASEAN single market under the ASEAN Economic Community (AEC) would rebuild the momentum towards restarting the negotiation process, an objective which the EU has not abandoned entirely.

Progress made by ASEAN and the EU in trade has been difficult to replicate in security matters. Although the 2002 Bali terror bombings had the result of raising the issue of transnational terrorism as grounds for deepening EU–ASEAN relations, subsequent developments were mostly restricted to non-binding, general letters of intent (Heiduk, 2016). Likewise, the 2007–12 Plan of Action subsequently proposed by EU and ASEAN to provide guidelines for policy implementation were mostly limited to dialogue facilitation and exchange of best practices on topics such as landmines and weapons, with little focus on counter-terrorism and human trafficking (Heiduk, 2016). Subsequent renewal of the Plan of Action remained focused on dialogue forums and exchange of best practices through seminars and workshops, with the ASEAN Regional Forum providing a more prominent platform for security affairs (Heiduk, 2016). It is generally thought that the concluding of an FTA would be indispensable, politically, for a breakthrough in more complex issues in security (Moeller, 2007: 478–9).

Economic co-operation between the EU and ASEAN

Since the aftermath of the twin crises in Southeast Asia – the Asian financial crisis and the transboundary haze crisis of 1997 – recognition of the significance of economic integration in ASEAN has been increasingly acknowledged, and significant progress in this direction is epitomised in the decision for the establishment of the AEC in 2003 (albeit only formally established in 2015) and the creation of the ASEAN Charter in 2007 (Severino, 2007; Chia, 2011; Allison, 2015; ASEAN, 2015). In addition, the Chiang Mai Initiative Multilateralisation as a supplementary effort on top of existing international financial arrangements and aiming to "address balance of payment and short-term liquidity difficulties in the region", eased closer efforts at economic integration among the Asia-Pacific states; Allison, 2015).

Post-crises, ASEAN is therefore arguably more integrated economically, even though Yeo argues that more could be done to see the building of an ASEAN that is more cohesive and "ready for business"; in other words, to maximise the potential of the regional bloc in contributing to a stable and vibrant economic environment that both ASEAN and the EU can benefit from (Yeo, 2016). Indeed, statistics provided by both the ASEAN Secretariat and Eurostat reveals a clear economic stake the EU has in ASEAN, both with individual member states and ASEAN as a bloc: The EU was ASEAN's third largest trading partners in 2014, comprising 10 per cent of ASEAN's total trade, and the EU is ASEAN's largest source of Foreign Direct Investment, accounting for 21 per cent of the region's total amount of inward investment (ASEAN, 2015b); conversely, the main destination for EU exports in 2013 was Asia and – albeit the EU recording a trade deficit with ASEAN in 2014 – ASEAN still accounts for 5 per cent of the total extra-EU exports, and ASEAN's economic potential is expected to further broaden (Eurostat, 2016; Yeo, 2016).

Where the EU is primarily seen as an economic actor in ASEAN, ASEAN sees the EU as a valuable reference point predominantly from an economic perspective, and has been receptive towards establishing partnership programmes with the EU that will encourage further productive economic integration in ASEAN. Following the European Commission's communication of *A New Partnership with Southeast Asia* in 2003, three co-operation programmes – the ASEAN Programme for Regional Integration Support from 2003 to 2010, the ASEAN Regional Integration Support by the EU and the Regional EU–ASEAN Dialogue Instrument (READI) – were launched at the subsequent ASEAN–EU ministerial meetings specifically for the purpose of focusing on EU–ASEAN co-operation on economic integration and support for the development of the AEC (Allison, 2015; Yeo, 2016).

The nature of non-traditional security

Non-traditional security (NTS) is a term that denotes threats that are non-military in nature. The range of possible sources of NTS is vast, encompassing threats emanating from agents (as in terrorist attacks) and processes (for instance climate change). NTS threats may or may not *originate* from one single state – for instance, Indonesia was responsible for the environmental crisis that besieged ASEAN in 1997 – but they usually cause transboundary *effects*. The fact that NTS threats do not respect borders in terms of the consequences they produce means that it is impossible for any individual actor or state to develop a comprehensive solution autonomously. This means that co-operation at multiple levels – from local to regional and inter-regional – is imperative (Wong and Brown, 2016).

Given that security is a domain traditionally dealt with from state-centric perspectives, especially in the case of ASEAN, it is essential for NTS to be framed as a human-centric domain, namely one that is approached from the "human security" perspective. Conceptually, the referent object is individual humans, rather than states which have conventionally enjoyed centrality in discussions of that which is to be secured. To frame NTS threats as such carries significant weight with regard to transboundary co-operation, for to ensure and secure human security means that individuals, regardless of nationality, are to be protected from threats that cannot be controlled by one state alone, inevitably requiring regional co-operation (Wong and Brown, 2016).

For an ASEAN governed by norms of non-interference, and whose creation is undergirded by the understanding that sovereignty is a non-negotiable public good, NTS is an promising area where co-operation and integration could be deepened and where the EU can provide valuable insights to, and hence craft, a security niche for itself in the Asia-Pacific region (Maier-Knapp, 2012; Onestini, 2015; Wong, 2015; Yeo and Matera, 2015; Narine, 2016; Wong, 2016). NTS, as a concept, remains vague but extensive, allowing Southeast Asian states to subsume most types of challenges to the region, and sticking to the central role of the state as both the object and provider of security. As such, the EU's dilemma lies in the NTS concept possessing the possibility of undemocratic and illiberal abuse of the concept that runs contrary to the values of the EU, but it remains a rare opportunity for the EU to raise its politico-security profile in sectors of heightened sensitisation caused by NTS crises endangering state and human security (Maier-Knapp, 2012). The fact that geopolitical and security issues have always been priorities for ASEAN also means that co-operation in the NTS domain has the potential to be extensive and fruitful (Chia, 2011; Allison, 2015). However, the EU frequently lacks on-site presence, and its actorness or perceived visibility was minimal in proportion to its efforts. Since the success of the Aceh Monitoring Mission, the EU has been seen only as a crisis manager and peacebuilder, rather than a security actor per se.

The Commission's *New Asia Strategy* in 1994 demonstrates that the EU's recognition of a shift in economic power to Asia goes back over two decades. Since then, political and even security instruments have been used to advance EU interests in this part of the world. However, the major limiting factor to a real strategic "pivot" to Asia has been the EU's unwillingness and inability to deploy "hard" security instruments in the region (Wacker, 2014). The members of the Five-Power Defence Arrangements (FPDA) – the UK, Australia, New Zealand, Malaysia and Singapore – have been holding regular joint military exercises since the FPDA was established in 1971. Essentially a series of bilateral defence relationships, the FPDA provides for defence co-operation and for an Integrated Air Defence System for peninsular Malaysia and Singapore. There is otherwise no permanent European military presence in the region except for small French bases in the South Pacific and in the Indian Ocean (Stares and Régaud, 1997). This scanty European security presence makes many Asians sceptical of the utility of a greater role for the EU in regional security discussions beyond the ASEAN Regional Forum (ARF) where the EU is already present; the Shangri-La Dialogue (attended by "Big 3" member states rather than the EU since 2002); and the Council for Security Co-operation in the Asia-Pacific (CSCAP), where the EU made a return in June 2014 after a ten-year absence.

In designing projects that accommodate the values and needs of Southeast Asian governments, theoretically, the EU's profile in ASEAN is enhanced. But this may also strengthen certain power and normative structures that run contrary to the EU's normative agenda in its external relations, undermining the EU's identity and actorness on NTS challenges (Maier-Knapp, 2012). This is in recognition of the crisis-centric nature of NTS that renders the EU a passive actor in ASEAN's security as EU's justification for an expanded role largely depends on the number of securitised and sensitised sectors, above the issue of whether the EU could exploit these opportunities to enhance its profile. As such, the NTS concept has kept the EU engaged in ASEAN and Asia, but the utilisation of NTS has also imposed certain restrictions on the

EU's potential role in Asian security, and it would require a paradigm shift in the EU's conception of NTS or even the EU's foreign-policy thinking to further secure the EU's security profile in ASEAN and Asia.

Moving forward and conclusion

The European Union has held and pursued economic interests distinct from those of the US with regards to the major actors in Asia. But pursuing an economics-first policy makes for an unbalanced presence in Asia. The EU's "market power" and its share of world trade is still impressive, but this proportion will slide as a percentage of world trade with the rise of other trading powers (like the BRICS countries Brazil, Russia, India, China, South Africa).

But if the EU hopes to count or be consulted in shaping security outcomes in Asia, then it has to step up to a more visible and active role in Asian security: in the important security fora, and in creative partnership with Asian states themselves (Wong and Tay, 2014). The EU must ensure that the High Representative participates annually in the ARF, and that appropriate high-level defence representatives take part in "Track I" security fora like the Shangri-la Dialogues and "Track II" fora like CSCAP. The EU has used its soft power resources to good effect in the past. These could be channelled towards working more closely with ASEAN partners to build greater human security in the region.

In terms of Common Security and Defence Policy, the EU can boast only one significant military operation in East Asia: monitoring the resolution of hostilities between the Indonesian government and the Aceh independence forces in the Aceh Monitoring Mission, in 2005–6. Of course, it has played a very useful security role in conflict resolution and crisis management areas: co-mediating and hosting the Paris Peace Agreements that ended the Vietnamese occupation of Cambodia (1991), and helping with police training in the democratic transition in Myanmar (2013–14) to name other examples. But it was absent in high-profile international efforts for the search for MH370, the search and location of QZ8501 in 2014, and the important regime-building ARF DiREx exercises which even Russia takes part in. Search and Rescue and Humanitarian Assistance/Disaster Relief efforts are important opportunities for countries and organisations to showcase their political and civil-military co-ordination prowess, and for governments to boost their image, building goodwill abroad (Pejsova, 2015). The EU should increase its contribution to such activities in ARF and in the Asia–Europe Meeting (ASEM).

A more cohesive EU response might be suitable if the EU wants to be seen as an actor in itself and not simply an inchoate sum of its parts. In response to the December 2004 Indian Ocean tsunami, the European

Commission gave over £123 million in humanitarian aid and over £350 million to long-term reconstruction. Individual member states, led by Germany and the UK, were among the most generous international donors. Although the combined EU effort in disaster relief in the 2004 case exceeded U$2b (European Commission, 2014; Guardian, 2014), the psychological impact of the EU's contribution would have been much larger if the EU and its member states had a more consolidated response to disaster relief.

Stares and Régaud's 1997 argument, made before the EU launched a defence capability and many years before it even had a diplomatic service, was prescient in recognising that the EU needed to play an enhanced role in Asian security. Since then, China has launched a massive "Belt and Road" initiative that reaches across central and Southeast Asia into the Middle East and Europe; and US–China tensions in the South China Sea have picked up steam. At the same time, ASEAN has furthered its institutionalisation as a regional organisation with an ASEAN Charter (2007), and attempts to go beyond its own founding norms of strict non-interference in the domestic affairs of member states. In such a dynamic region, it simply does not suffice for the EU to dismiss security in Asia as a US concern. With rising Asian states competing with the EU for resources and trade in Africa, and increasingly, bringing their interests right to the EU's "home" turf in the Atlantic region, the EU is, by default, already implicated in Asian security concerns and competition, whether these concern security in food, energy resources, minerals, raw materials, commodities or climate change.

Notes

I am indebted to Jiayu Hong and Pipeng Tan for their research assistance.

1 Speech by High Representative / Vice-President Federica Mogherini at the IISS Shangri-La Dialogue 2015, 31 May, in Singapore. See https://eeas.europa.eu/headquarters/headquarters-homepage/6254/speech-by-high-representativevice-president-federica-mogherini-at-the-iiss-shangri-la-dialogue-2015_en.
2 The domino theory suggests that once a country falls under the influence of communism, neighbouring countries will be likely to fall as well. The theory alludes to a comment attributed to former American President Dwight Eisenhower, "You have a row of dominoes set up, you knock over the first one, and what will happen to the last one is the certainty that it will go over very quickly. So you could have a beginning of a disintegration that would have the most profound influences" (Eisenhower, 1954, cited in The Pentagon Papers, 1971, cited in Mahbubani and Sng, 2017).
3 The territory formerly known as "Indochina" corresponds to the present-day countries of Myanmar, Thailand, Vietnam, Cambodia, Laos and peninsular Malaysia. This term, however, was more often used to refer to the French colony of Indochina, which consists of states known today as Vietnam, Cambodia and Laos.

References

Acharya, Amitav. (2004). "How Ideas Spread: Whose Norms Matter? Norm Localisation and Institutional Change in Asian Regionalism", *International Organisation* 58 (2): 239–75.
Allison, Laura. (2015). *The EU, ASEAN and Interregionalism*. New York: Palgrave Macmillan.
ASEAN. (1976). *Treaty of Amity and Cooperation*. http://asean.org/treaty-amity-cooperation-southeast-asia-indonesia-24-february-1976/, accessed online 9 September 2018.
ASEAN–EU. (2012). *Bandar Seri Begawan Plan of Action to Strengthen the EU–ASEAN Enhanced Partnership (2013–2017)*. www.europarl.europa.eu/cmsdata/124481/129884.pdf, accessed online 9 September 2018.
ASEAN Secretariat. (2015a). *ASEAN Economic Blueprint 2025*. Jakarta: Indonesia, Publication Division, ASEAN Secretariat, www.asean.org/storage/images/2015/November/aec-page/AEC-Blueprint-2025-FINAL.pdf, accessed online 9 September 2018.
ASEAN Secretariat. (2015b). *ASEAN Economic Community at a Glance*. Jakarta: Publication Division, the ASEAN Secretariat, www.asean.org/storage/2015/12/aec/AEC-at-a-Glance-2015.pdf, accessed online 9 September 2018.
Chia, Siow Yue. (2011). "Association of Southeast Asian Nations and Economic Integration: Development and Challenges", *Asian Economic Policy Review* 6 (1): 43–63.
Ciorciari, John. (2012). "Institutionalising Human Rights in Southeast Asia", *Human Rights Quarterly* 34 (3): 695–725.
European Commission. (2003). *A New Partnership with South-East Asia*. COM 399/4, Brussels. http://trade.ec.europa.eu/doclib/docs/2004/july/tradoc_116277.pdf, accessed online 9 September 2018.
European Commission. (2014). "Remembering the Indian Ocean tsunami, ten years on", 26 December, https://ec.europa.eu/echo/news/remembering-indian-ocean-tsunami-ten-years_en, accessed online 1 September 2018.
Eurostat. (2016). "EU Trade and Investment Statistics with the Association of South East Asian Nations (ASEAN)", *Eurostat: Statistics Explained*. Brussels. https://ec.europa.eu/eurostat/statistics-explained/index.php/EU-ASEAN_cooperation_-_key_trade_and_investment_statistics, accessed online 9 September 2018.
European Union. (2017). *Roaming in the EU: Roaming like at Home*. Europa.eu: Your Europe. https://europa.eu/youreurope/citizens/consumers/internet-telecoms/mobile-roaming-costs/index_en.htm, accessed online 9 September 2018.
Fioretti, Julia. (2016). "EU Parliament Approves Deal on Sharing Air Passenger Data after Militant Attacks", *CNBC by Reuters*.
Flers, Nicole Alecu de. (2010). *EU–ASEAN Relations: The Importance of Values, Norms, and Culture (EUC Working Paper, No. 1)*. Singapore: EU Centre.
Forster, Anthony. (2000). "Evaluating the EU–ASEM Relationship: A Negotiated Order Approach", *Journal of European Public Policy* 7 (5): 787–805.
Guardian. (2014). "Where did the Indian Ocean tsunami aid money go?" 26 December, https://www.theguardian.com/global-development/2014/dec/25/where-did-indian-ocean-tsunami-aid-money-go, accessed online 1 September 2018.

Heiduk, Felix. (2016). "Externalizing the EU's Justice and Home Affairs to Southeast Asia: Prospects and Limitations", *Journal of Contemporary European Research* 12 (3): 717–33.
Jacobsen, Henriette. (2016). "EU Justice Ministers Step Up Intelligence Sharing after Brussels Attacks". *Euractiv*. www.euractiv.com/section/global-europe/news/eu-justice-ministers-step-up-intelligence-sharing-after-brussels-attacks/, accessed online 9 September 2018.
Jakobsen, Peter Viggo. (2009), "Small States, Big Influence: The Overlooked Nordic Influence on the Civilian ESDP", *JCMS: Journal of Common Market Studies* 47 (1): 81–102.
Jetschke, Anja, and Philomena Murray. (2012). "Diffusing Regional Integration: The EU and Southeast Asia", *West European Politics* 35 (1): 174–91.
Katzenstein, Peter J. (2005). *A World of Regions: Asia and Europe in the American Imperium*. Ithaca: Cornell University Press.
Kennes, Walter. (2015). "Chapter 21: ASEAN and the EU: An Evolving and Solid Development Partnership", in Louis Brennan and Philomena Murray (eds), *Drivers of Integration and Regionalism in Europe and Asia: Comparative Perspectives*, London: Routledge, pp. 366–84.
Mahbubani, Kishore, and Jeffery Sng. (2017). *The ASEAN Miracle: A Catalyst for Peace*. Singapore: Ridge Books.
Maier-Knapp, Naila. (2012). "The EU and Non-Traditional Security in Southeast Asia", in D. Novotny and C. Portela (eds), *EU–ASEAN Relations in the 21st Century*. Basingstoke: Palgrave Macmillan, pp. 26–42.
Mckenzie, Lachlan, and Katharina L. Meissner. (2017). "Human Rights Conditionality in European Union Trade Negotiations: The Case of the EU–Singapore FTA" (July 2017), *JCMS: Journal of Common Market Studies* 55 (4): 832–49.
Meissner, Katharina Luise. (2016). "A Case of Failed Interregionalism? Analyzing the EU–ASEAN Free Trade Negotiations", *Asia-Europe Journal* 14 (3): 319–36.
Moeller, Joergen Oerstroem. (2007). "ASEAN's Relations with the European Union: Obstacles and Opportunities", *Contemporary Southeast Asia* 29 (3): 465–82.
Narine, Shaun. (2016). "ASEAN and the Response to Regional Crisis", in S. Saurugger and F. Terpan (eds), *Crisis and Institutional Change in Regional Integration*. Abingdon: Routledge.
Olsen, Johan P. (2007). *Europe in Search of Political Order: An Institutional Perspective on Unity/Diversity, Citizens/Their Helpers, Democratic Design/Historical Drift and the Co-existence of Orders*. Oxford: Oxford University Press.
Onestini, Cesare. (2015). "How Do We Assess Cooperation between Regional Organisations? EU and ASEAN as an Example of Region-to-Region Cooperation", in L. Brennan and P. Murray (eds), *Drivers of Integration and Regionalism in Europe and Asia Comparative perspectives*. Abingdon: Routledge, pp. 252–70.
Pejsova, Eva. (2015). "Asia: Disasters as Opportunities?", *EUISS Issue Alert* 16. Paris: EUISS. www.iss.europa.eu/uploads/media/Alert_16_SAR.pdf, accessed online 9 September 2018.
Proszowska, Dominik. (2016). "Facing the American 'Pivot' to Asia: EU's Role in the Power-Balancing Game in East and Southeast Asia from a Neorealist Perspective", *Stosunki Międzynarodowe i Geopolityka* 1 (6): 53–72.
Reiterer, Michael. (2014). "The EU's Comprehensive Approach to Security in Asia", *European Foreign Affairs Review* 19 (1): 1–21.

Reiterer, Michael. (2016). "Asia as Part of the EU's Global Security Strategy: Reflections on a More Strategic Approach", in *LSE Ideas: Changing Waters: Towards a New EU Asia Strategy*. London: LSE Ideas, pp. 62–70.
Robles Jr, Alfredo C. (2008). *The Asia–Europe Meeting: The Theory and Practice of Interregionalism*. New York: Routledge.
Severino, Rodolfo. (2007). "The ASEAN Developmental Divide and the Initiative for ASEAN Integration", *ASEAN Economic Bulletin* 24 (1): 264–92.
Stares, Paul, and Nicolas Régaud. (1997). "Europe's Role in Asia-Pacific Security", *Survival* 39 (4): 117–39.
Storey, Ian. (2011). *Southeast Asia and the Rise of China: The Search for Security*. New York: Routledge.
Wacker, Grant. (2014). "Good Suggestions, but the EU Can Do Even More", 7 January, http://europesworld.org/2014/01/07/the-eus-role-in-shaping-asias-security/#.U5a4o_m1bYg, accessed online 9 September 2018.
Winand, Pascaline. (2012). "The EU, ASEAN and the Challenges of the 21st Century: Conclusions and Recommendations", in D. Novotny and C. Portela (eds), *EU–ASEAN Relations in the 21st Century*. Basingstoke: Palgrave Macmillan, pp. 179–92.
Wong, Reuben. (2012). "Model Power or Reference Point? The EU and the ASEAN Charter", *Cambridge Review of International Affairs* 25 (4): 669–82.
Wong, Reuben. (2015). "Creeping Supranationalism: The EU and ASEAN Experiences", in L. Brennan and P. Murray (eds), *Drivers of Integration and Regionalism in Europe and Asia Comparative Perspectives* (Abingdon: Routledge Research in Comparative Politics series), pp. 235–51.
Wong, Reuben. (2016). "Crisis and Regional Integration: Human Rights and Environmental Governance in ASEAN", in S. Saurugger and F. Terpan (eds), *Crisis and Institutional Change in Regional Integration*. Abingdon: Routledge.
Wong, Reuben and Scott Brown. (2016). "Stepping up EU–ASEAN Cooperation in Non-Traditional Security", in *Changing Waters: Towards a New EU Asia Strategy*. London: LSE, pp. 79–85. London: LSE Ideas.
Wong, Reuben, and Simon Tay. (2014). "Asian Institutions and the Pivot", in Hans Binnendijk (ed.), *A Transatlantic Pivot to Asia: Towards New Trilateral Partnerships*. Washington, DC: Center for Transatlantic Relations, pp. 109–24.
Yeo, Lay. (2010). "The EU as a Security Actor in Southeast Asia", in *Panorama: Insights into Asian and Political Affairs*. Singapore: Regional Programme Political Dialogue Asia, Konrad Adenauer Stiftung.
Yeo, Lay. (2016). "EU Strategy towards Southeast Asia and ASEAN", in *Changing Waters: Towards a New EU Asia Strategy*. London: LSE Ideas, pp. 6–12.
Yeo, Lay Hwee. (2014). "The EU's Role in Security and Regional Order in East Asia", in Peter Shearman (ed.), *Power Transition and International Order in Asia*. Abingdon: Routledge, pp. 44–57.
Yeo, Lay Hwee, and Margherita Matera. (2015). "The EU and ASEAN – Seeking a New Regional Paradigm", in L. Brennan and P. Murray (eds), *Drivers of Integration and Regionalism in Europe and Asia: Comparative Perspectives*. Abingdon: Routledge Research in Comparative Politics series), pp. 270–89.

10 The European Union in Australia and New Zealand

Nicole Scicluna

Introduction

The relationship between the EU, on the one hand, and Australia and New Zealand, on the other, reveals a paradox. The links between both of these South Pacific nations and the nations of Europe are deep, multifaceted and longstanding. Australia and New Zealand are former British colonies. Their political and legal institutions are modelled to a large extent on Westminster, their political values and culture flow largely from British sources. Following European settlement and the large influx of British and Irish migrants from the late eighteenth century onwards, both countries have been considerably enriched by immigration from other parts of Europe, particularly in the post-Second World War period. As a result, the vast majority of Australians and New Zealanders have European heritage, with those of British and Irish ancestry comprising the largest group.

Thus, both Australia and New Zealand have rich connections to the member states of the EU. Yet their relationship to the EU itself is relatively recent, comparatively shallow and marked on both sides by indifference, apathy and occasionally even antagonism. Indeed, as one analyst remarked in the late 1990s, "Australia and New Zealand are among the few countries in the world for which the EU has become less rather than more important since the 1980s" (Piening, quoted in Murray, Elijah and O'Brien 2002: 395). Why is this so? Owing to the British and European heritage of Australia and New Zealand, as well as their status as highly industrialised liberal democracies, the two countries share much with the EU in terms of values – democracy, rule of law, human rights, peaceful co-operation; and interests-maintenance of regional and international peace and security, promotion of multilateral institutions, promotion of free trade. Ostensibly, then, "normative power Europe" should resonate in Australia and New Zealand. Moreover, there is a significant economic component to the relationship. The EU was Australia's second largest trading partner in 2014 (DFAT, 2017) and New Zealand's fourth largest trading partner in 2013

(MFAT, 2013). This has yet to result in a Free Trade Agreement (FTA) between the EU and either New Zealand or Australia, although negotiations are under way with both countries.

This chapter, therefore, is animated by the following question: why, given the commonalities and historical linkages described above, is the relationship between the EU, on the one hand, and Australia and New Zealand, on the other, relatively weak, limited and low-key? The chapter is structured as follows. I will start by giving an overview of the EU's relationship to Australia and New Zealand, respectively, focusing on trade, diplomacy and bilateral agreements. I will then briefly recapitulate the literature on the EU as a normative power, in order to use this as a conceptual framework to assess the EU's influence in Australia and New Zealand. There follows a discussion of attempts by the EU to assert its normative values – firstly, by including political conditionality in all agreements with third countries, and, secondly, through international climate change negotiations. As we shall see, the EU's ability to influence the policy positions of New Zealand and Australian governments has been limited and inconsistent. Finally, I offer two possible (and not mutually exclusive) reasons for this limited influence: the impact of internal and external crises on the EU, and the Britain factor – which predates, but has been considerably complicated by, the June 2016 Brexit vote.

I conclude that the EU's relations with Australia and New Zealand are likely to remain a relatively low priority for all sides, despite increasing EU engagement with the Asia-Pacific region.

The EU in Australia and New Zealand: framing the relationship

Trade

Trade is a core component of the relationship between the EU and both Australia and New Zealand. The EU is Australia's second largest trading partner, behind only China. According to statistics from the Australian Department of Foreign Affairs and Trade (DFAT), total two-way goods and services trade between Australia and the EU in 2014 was worth AU$83.9 billion (more than 12 per cent of Australia's total trade). The EU is also Australia's largest market for the export of services. Nevertheless, Australia's trade with Europe is not evenly spread. Of Australia's top ten trading partners in 2014, only two were EU member states – the UK (ranked number seven) and Germany (ranked number ten) (DFAT, 2017). Thus, bilateral ties with individual states remain important for Australia, even though these cannot lead to formal trade relations. This is because trade is a supranational competence of the EU, meaning that only the European Commission is empowered to negotiate trade agreements on behalf of EU member states and to represent the bloc in international fora, such as the World Trade Organisation (WTO). This may lead to a lesser priority being accorded to countries, like Australia or New Zealand, which may be important trading partners for individual European countries, but are less significant for the bloc as a whole.

Further to this point, the trade relationship between Australia and the EU is highly unequal. This is unsurprising, given the discrepancy between the former – a nation of 24 million with a commodity-driven economy – and the latter – the world's largest economy and a market of 500 million people. Australia is only the EU's 15th largest export destination, taking 1.7 per cent of EU exports, and 34th largest source of imports, with 0.5 per cent of EU imports coming from Australia (DFAT, 2016).

Trade with the EU is also of great importance to New Zealand. In 2012, the EU accounted for 12.6 per cent of New Zealand's total trade, making it the country's third largest trading partner, after Australia (18.2 per cent) and China (15.5 per cent).[1] Once again, the trading relationship is strikingly unequal. New Zealand, with a population of less than five million, is the EU's 54th largest trading partner, accounting for only 0.2 per cent of EU trade in 2012. As is the case with Australia, New Zealand's trade with EU member states is concentrated in a handful of countries. In 2012, New Zealand exported a total of NZ$6.56 billion worth of goods and services to the EU and, of this, NZ$2.33 billion (35.5 per cent of the total) went to the UK. Germany is also a significant bilateral trading partner, receiving NZ$1.11 billion worth of exports (17 per cent of the total) in 2012 (MFAT, 2013: 14).

Despite its large scale, the economic relationship between the EU and Australia and New Zealand is not without its difficulties. In particular, agriculture has been a longstanding source of contention. Since the 1960s, the EU has operated a protectionist Common Agricultural Policy (CAP), which subsidises European farm producers and suppresses non-European competition. In 1986, Australia spearheaded the creation of the Cairns Group of agricultural exporters, of which New Zealand was a founding member. The group's mission is to oppose farm subsidies and other trade-distorting measures, and it currently has twenty members. Thus, the trade-distorting impact of the CAP has been a major – and negative – focal point of Australia–EU and New Zealand–EU relations, often dominating the bilateral agenda to the detriment of other issues where co-operation might have been more fruitful (Murray, Elijah and O'Brien, 2002: 398–402).

As with other dimensions of the Australia–New Zealand–EU relationship, trade will be complicated by Brexit, though in ways that may well end up being beneficial to Australia and New Zealand. Both Australia and the UK have expressed a willingness to push forward as quickly as possible with a new free trade agreement, though this cannot be concluded until the UK has left the EU. At any rate, for both Australia and New Zealand it will be important to pursue a dual-track strategy: cultivating strong economic links with the EU, while also seeking to establish a post-Brexit trade relationship with the UK as soon as possible.

Diplomatic representation

Prior to the entry into force of the Lisbon Treaty, the EU was represented in third countries by European Commission Delegations, which were not fully fledged embassies (not being entitled to speak on behalf of the EU member states) and which operated in parallel with the embassies of the individual member states. The European Commission Delegation to Australia was established in 1981, while the EU's New Zealand office was established in 2004 (before which the EU was represented in New Zealand by the delegation in Canberra). In September 2016, the first resident EU Ambassador to New Zealand was appointed.

One innovation of the Lisbon Treaty, which was signed in 2007 and entered into force on 1 December 2009, was the creation of an EU foreign diplomatic service. The European External Action Service (EEAS), as it is called, reports to the High Representative for Foreign Affairs and Security Policy, a position also created by the Lisbon Treaty with a view to better co-ordinating the EU's external policy. Following Lisbon's entry into force, all of the Commission delegations were renamed 'EU Delegations' as of 1 January 2010. At the same time, 54 of the then-existing 136 delegations, including the one in Canberra, were upgraded to embassy-like status, meaning their heads were empowered to speak on behalf of the union as a whole, where authorised to do so by the member state governments acting in the Council (Rettman, 2010).

Nevertheless, the EU's common foreign policy remains highly intergovernmental, and opportunities for the High Representative and, by extension, the EU delegations in third countries, to "speak on behalf of Europe" remain rare. The delegations in Australia and New Zealand, therefore, are mainly engaged in public diplomacy with a view to promoting and disseminating information about the EU, and encouraging the further development of bilateral relations. On more meaty economic and political issues, the delegations continue to play second fiddle to the embassies of the individual EU member states. Corroborating its primarily ceremonial role, the website of the EU delegation to Australia (2016) notes that it "does not however deal with trade promotion or other issues which have traditionally been handled by the Member State embassies, consulates, trade commissioners or national tourism offices".

The legal framework

Despite the importance of trade with the EU to both Australia and New Zealand, neither has yet concluded an FTA with the EU. New Zealand and the EU announced their commitment to begin negotiations on a future deep and comprehensive FTA in October 2015 (European Commission, 2015), while Australia and the EU made a similar announcement in November 2015 (Minister for Trade and Investment, 2015). In April 2017, the European Commission and the Australian trade minister concluded their preliminary discussions on the scope of a future trade agreement, though, at the time of writing, formal negotiations have not yet begun (European Commission, 2017). Similarly, FTA discussions between the EU and New Zealand are yet to formally commence.

In the meantime, the EU was preoccupied with other large-scale trade deals. Firstly, the Commission had been busily finalising an FTA with Canada, known as the Comprehensive Economic and Trade Agreement. Negotiations on that deal began in 2009, and the final agreement was signed only in October 2016, after almost being derailed by a last-minute rejection in the regional parliament of Wallonia (Rankin, 2016). Secondly, the Commission and other EU stakeholders were engaged in negotiations over the massive Transatlantic Trade and Investment Partnership agreement with the United States. The future of this agreement, however, was thrown into serious doubt by the election of Donald Trump, partly on an anti-free-trade platform, in November 2016. Similarly, for Australia and New Zealand, the key priority had been the US-led Trans Pacific Partnership (TPP), a twelve-member FTA, which was signed in February 2016, but derailed in January 2017 after the newly inaugurated Trump announced the US's withdrawal (Smith, 2017). Whether the protectionist attitudes of the new American administration lead to Australia and New Zealand placing a higher priority on trade relations with the EU (or vice versa) remains to be seen.

At any rate, there are non-trade-focused international law agreements that frame the EU's relationship with each of Australia and New Zealand. The first formal EU–Australia agreement – titled the Joint Declaration on Relations between the EU and Australia – was signed in 1997. Twenty years later, the two parties have concluded a Framework Agreement, which was signed on 7 August 2017. This agreement replaces the 2008 EU–Australia Partnership Framework, and marks a significant upgrade of the bilateral relationship. Indeed, the fact that relations have improved from the low point of the aborted 1997 Framework Agreement (discussed below) is indicated by the inclusion in the new agreement of the standard political clauses (e.g. commitment to human rights) that proved so controversial in the 1990s. The new Framework Agreement aims to facilitate and promote co-operation across multiple sectors, including trade, research and innovation, counter-terrorism, education and culture, and migration (European Commission, 2016). Its conclusion has been accompanied by other exercises in public diplomacy, including the first ever EU–Australia leadership forum, which was held in Sydney in June 2017.

The formal relationship between the EU and New Zealand is of a similar duration to that between the EU and Australia. The EU and New Zealand concluded their own Joint Declaration on Relations in 1999, which was superseded by the 2007 Joint Declaration on Relations and Cooperation. Most recently, EU High Representative, Federica Mogherini, and her New Zealand counterpart signed the Partnership Agreement on Relations and Co-operation in October 2016.

Normative power Europe: implications for the EU's foreign policy

The EU is neither a conventional body, in terms of its internal organisation, nor a conventional actor, in terms of its engagement in international relations. These two dimensions are interrelated, and both are relevant to an assessment of how the EU acts, and how it is perceived, in Australia and New Zealand. Internally, the EU is characterised by a horizontally and vertically differentiated approach to governance. Legislative functions are split between the Council, comprising the relevant ministers of the member states, and the European Parliament, which is directly elected by European citizens. National parliaments play a subsidiary role in EU law-making, mostly via the influence they exercise over national ministers. The European Commission functions partly as an executive and partly as a bureaucracy, and also represents the EU and its member states abroad, most notably in relation to trade, foreign aid and competition policy. EU governance is decentralised and heterarchical. The EU's coercive enforcement capacity is rather limited, and so EU laws and policies are carried into effect by national authorities (Weiler, 1994). As a result, EU decision-making is deliberative, consensus-oriented and backed by a dense framework of law and normative values, rather than hard coercive power.

These internal characteristics shape the EU's self-identity and its behaviour as an actor on the international stage. The proliferation of internal decision-making fora finds its counterpart in a preference for multilateralism in international relations. The EU's constitutional basis in the pooling of member states' sovereignty is matched by a desire to promote a post-Westphalian international rule of law. The concept of Normative Power Europe (NPE) was popularised by Ian Manners (2002), who wished to move beyond traditional categories of military power and civilian power – without disregarding those categories – in better understanding the "ideational impact of the EU's international identity/role" (Manners, 2002: 238). Manners defined the EU's normative power in terms of its "ability to shape conceptions of 'normal' in international relations" (Manners, 2002: 239–40).

The EU's promotion of itself as a normative power is partly a case of making a virtue of necessity, given that it lacks military capacity (Kagan, 2003). But it is also partly a self-conscious choice. Thus, NPE is not only a scholarly construct; it has been enthusiastically propagated by EU officials and other proponents of the European integration project (Diez, 2005).

The propagation of NPE serves multiple purposes. Internally, it bolsters the EU's claim to be a "community of values", which in turn serves as the kernel of a common identity to which Europeans can subscribe, in addition to their national identities. The EU constitutes itself as a community of values (and, therefore, more than just a common market) through the projection of those values on the global stage. Normative or "soft"-power Europe is often contrasted with the hard-power US – the latter depicted as prone to unilateralism and overly reliant on the use of force. Such comparisons were prominent around the time of the Iraq war (see e.g. Habermas and Derrida, 2003; Garton Ash, 2007), which coincided with (ultimately unsuccessful) efforts to give the EU a constitution.

In addition to the internal identity-building function, the propagation of NPE has an external dimension. The EU has a strong interest in trying to shape the world in its own image. During the Gulf War, the Belgian foreign minister, Mark Eyskens, famously described the EU as an "economic giant, a political dwarf and a military worm" (quoted in Manners, 2010: 75). Nearly twenty years later, it is still true that the EU is a major trading power, but a weak actor in the security and defence realms. It would, therefore, best be served by a world order based on strong multilateral institutions and a strong international rule of law and so its foreign policy promotes such a world order.

For the purposes of this chapter, the external dimension of NPE – that is, how the concept of NPE shapes the EU's engagement with the outside world – is of most relevance. The concept may be used to assess the ways in which the EU seeks to promote its values and normative leadership in and towards New Zealand and Australia. Has the EU been successful in exporting its norms and values? Have Australia and New Zealand been receptive to EU leadership? In fact, it seems that normative-power Europe holds limited sway over Australia and New Zealand, as the examples below suggest.

Can the EU export its values via bilateral agreements?

The EU's political conditionality takes the form of positive inducements (Von Stein, 2013), whereby preferential market access is linked to the other state's acceptance of certain standards of human-rights protection and promotion of democracy (see Karen Smith (1998) for a detailed discussion of the EU's conditionality policies and their evolution). Such human-rights conditionality forms a major part of the EU's development aid programmes, for example with the African, Caribbean, and Pacific countries with which the EU concluded the Lomé and Cotonou agreements (Riedel and Will,

1999). However, the EU also routinely includes such clauses in its free trade and partnership agreements.

The EU prefers positive to negative conditionality, i.e. offering the "carrot" of aid and market access, rather than threatening the "stick" of sanctions (Smith, 1998). Nevertheless, its human-rights promotion activities may still be perceived as an unacceptable encroachment upon state sovereignty. This was certainly the case with the aborted 1997 EU–Australia framework agreement, which failed when the conservative government of then Prime Minister John Howard refused to accept the EU's standard political clauses regarding respect for human rights and democratic principles (Murray, Elijah and O'Brien, 2002: 408).

This is a notable example of a failure by the EU to impart its normative values via bilateral diplomacy on an ostensibly likeminded partner. Nevertheless, it must also be understood in the context of John Howard's well-known Euroscepticism and preference for conducting Australia–EU relations largely via bilateral engagement with individual member states. Since Howard left office in 2007, significant progress has been made in improving relations, as evidenced by the recent conclusion of a comprehensive framework agreement.

Climate change negotiations as an opportunity for normative power Europe

The EU sees itself as a leader in international efforts to combat human-made climate change. It seeks to lead both by example (e.g. through its pioneering emissions trading scheme) and through diplomacy in global fora (e.g. taking a leading role in organising climate change conferences). Climate change is a paradigmatic example of a global challenge that cannot be effectively addressed either unilaterally or through coercive, hard power. It is therefore a good test case for the influence of NPE, especially on ostensibly likeminded liberal democracies, such as Australia and New Zealand. In terms of both setting an example for others and providing leadership and direction in international fora, the EU's efforts have produced mixed success (Parker and Karlsson, 2010). The EU's emissions trading scheme (ETS), launched in 2005, remains the largest ETS in the world, covering the 28 member states plus Iceland, Liechtenstein and Norway. However, it has suffered from internal problems, such as an initial oversupply of carbon credits that led to a collapse in the price (Muûls et al., 2016). There is also the question of whether the EU ETS has offered a model for countries like Australia and New Zealand to follow.

The EU also has a mixed record when it comes to exerting leadership in international climate change forums (Parker, Karlsson and Hjerpe, 2017). It was instrumental in securing the survival of the 1997 Kyoto protocol after the US pulled out. Yet the EU's very self-conscious efforts to drive the post-Kyoto agenda at the 2009 Copenhagen summit were much less successful. The EU tried to increase international ambition at that summit by pledging to increase its emissions reductions from 20 per cent to 30 per cent if other important emitters signed up. However, this pledge fell on deaf ears and the EU seemed particularly isolated in its efforts to push for a legally binding agreement. In the end, the EU could not bridge the significant gaps between developing and developed states, nor did it see eye to eye with other major developed emitters, notably the US. Significantly, the last-minute deal that saved the Copenhagen summit from ending without any official statement whatsoever was negotiated and announced by the US and China. The EU – despite its leadership ambitions – was sidelined. Instead, Copenhagen seemed to confirm the importance of the "G2" (US and China) for global governance. Finally, at the most recent international climate change summit, held in Paris in 2015, the EU was more successful in having its goals reflected in the final agreement. As Oberthür and Groen (2017: 13) explain, the outcome at Paris was partly a product of the EU's shift to a "leadiator" strategy, which emphasised coalition-building, especially with ambitious and progressive developing countries. This strategy, however, has had less of an impact on Australia and New Zealand.

As a major energy exporter, Australia is a laggard in efforts to combat climate change. It has looked more to the US than to Europe for leadership on this issue, and has also pointed to China's failure to take significant steps to lower greenhouse gas emissions as an excuse not to act. The Labor government of Kevin Rudd announced the creation of an ETS in December 2008. However, its implementation was deferred following the failure of the legislation to pass through parliament. The Gillard Labor government did eventually put a price on carbon in 2012, but the so-called Carbon Pricing Mechanism was repealed after the opposition Liberal/National coalition returned to power in 2013. By that time, the policy, widely known as the "carbon tax", had become politically toxic, meaning it is unlikely to be reintroduced in the near future (Rootes, 2014).

New Zealand has had an ETS since 2008, and successive governments have regarded the scheme as the most cost-effective way of meeting New Zealand's international commitments to greenhouse gas reduction, first under the Kyoto protocol and later the Paris climate change agreement. At the time of its introduction, it was the first ETS in the world designed to cover all sectors of the economy. Again, some have criticised the scheme for pricing emissions too cheaply and for making it too easy for emitters to buy carbon credits rather than reducing their emissions. The New Zealand and EU schemes are not linked and are incompatible on points such as the use of international carbon credits to offset emissions (Leining and Kerr, 2016).

Therefore, EU diplomacy has had a limited impact on the climate change policies of Australia and New Zealand, despite common rhetorical commitments to greenhouse gas reduction. To some extent, this is a product of longstanding limitations on the EU's ability to act coherently and with consistent purpose as an actor on the world stage. There are other factors that shape the influence of normative-power Europe, including the economic crisis that has dogged the Euro area since 2010 and the impending departure of the UK, an event that has particular significance for EU relations with Australia and New Zealand.

Explaining the limited influence of "Normative-power Europe" in Australia and New Zealand: impact of the EU's crises

The EU's ability to act effectively on the global stage – and to have itself *perceived* by other states as an effective actor – has long been inhibited by confusion over "who speaks on behalf of Europe". As noted above, the Lisbon Treaty addressed this problem, but did not resolve it, via the introduction of the EEAS and the High Representative for Foreign Affairs and Security Policy.

Indeed, the significance of the Lisbon changes to external policy was somewhat muted by the history of their implementation. The long and winding road to Lisbon's eventual ratification is indicative of the EU's persistent weakness as a unified actor on the international stage. The High Representative position had its genesis in the failed EU constitution, a project years in the making that was eventually abandoned in 2005, after the draft constitution was rejected in referendums in France and the Netherlands. In the draft constitution, the key external affairs position was labelled "foreign minister". This statelike nomenclature was abandoned in the Lisbon Treaty, though the substance of the position remained the same.

If the change was merely symbolic, we may ask whether it really matters. In fact, political symbolism matters a great deal. In abandoning the constitutional form and trappings of its failed predecessor, the Lisbon Treaty also stepped back from the ambitious project to create a robust and coherent European identity (Scicluna, 2015: 59–62). It is in this sense that the Lisbon Treaty has been described as a "smashed vase". Although it contains most of the pieces of the original, it is not quite the same and, furthermore, it "records and recalls the drama" that preceded it (Claes and Eijsbouts, 2008: 2). The consequences of this setback necessarily flow through to the realm of foreign policy and the EU's attempts to exert its normative power in its dealings with other states and international organisations.

Thus, ten years after the Lisbon Treaty was signed in the Portuguese capital, the EU still does not have much of a common foreign and security policy over which the High Representative may preside. Foreign policy cooperation in the EU remains intergovernmental and reliant on unanimity. States are the key actors when it comes to the "high politics" of security and defence. Those areas of external relations that are supranationalised

– such as trade policy – are governed by the Commission. This creates coherence and consistency problems in terms of the EU's engagement with third parties – the Union's economic and diplomatic instruments are not always perfectly co-ordinated; and the interests of individual member states often do not coincide perfectly with the "European interest" represented by the Commission (Smith, 1998).

Therefore, the EU's weakness as a political actor long predates the economic crisis that has plagued the EU, particularly the Eurozone, for the last several years. Nevertheless, the Euro crisis has exacerbated EU foreign policy weakness in two ways. Firstly, the crisis has fuelled external perceptions of the EU as a power in decline – riven by divisions and incapable of acting decisively. Secondly, the crisis has forced EU institutions and member states to turn inwards, diverting considerable attention and resources away from foreign-policy goals and towards seemingly never ending internal crisis management.

In relation to the first point, studies from 2011 show that Australian media coverage of the EU that year was dominated by the Euro crisis (Polonska-Kimunguyi and Kimunguyi, 2015). Unsurprisingly, this coverage was overwhelmingly negative, the key narrative being that of a fragmenting Union, unable to co-operate to the extent necessary to solve serious systemic problems. The debt crisis also tended to be framed as fanning the flames of interstate rivalry (e.g. Germany versus Greece), damaging the EU's image as a unitary actor and, perhaps, reinforcing the preference of Australian governments for conducting diplomacy with EU member states on a bilateral basis.

The Britain factor

Australia's and New Zealand's relationships to the EU cannot be understood without an appreciation of those countries' ties to the UK, the former colonial power. New Zealand was incorporated into the British Empire via the Treaty of Waitangi in 1840, was granted dominion status within the empire in 1907 and gradually increased its degree of self-rule during the twentieth century. British colonisation of Australia formally began with the establishment of the New South Wales colony in 1788. In 1901, the six Australian colonies joined together to create an independent federal state, though Britain retained a degree of legislative and judicial influence that tapered off over the succeeding decades. Both New Zealand and Australia are still part of Britain's Commonwealth and both retain the British monarch as their head of state.

Britain's global outlook – including both its "special relationship" to the US and its ties to the Commonwealth – had been cited by political leaders as reasons for abstaining from participation in the postwar European Coal and Steel Community, and later the European Economic Community (EEC)

(Bogdanor, 2005). In a speech in 1952, Foreign Secretary Anthony Eden justified his opposition to Britain's participation in continental integration initiatives in the following terms:

> Britain's story and her interests lie far beyond the continent of Europe. Our thoughts move across the seas to the many communities in which our people play their part, in every corner of the world. These are our family ties. That is our life: without it we should be no more than some millions of people living on an island off the coast of Europe, in which nobody wants to take any particular interest. (Quoted in Bogdanor, 2005: 692)

Nevertheless, by the 1960s, Britain's economic situation and position as a major power had declined to such an extent that successive governments – Harold Macmillan's Conservatives in 1963 and Harold Wilson's Labour government in 1967 – attempted to realign Britain towards Europe through membership of the European Community (EC). Both applications were vetoed by French President Charles de Gaulle and it was only after he left office that the UK joined the EC in 1973 under the Conservative government of Edward Heath. Given the close bonds between each of Australia and New Zealand and the UK, the latter's EC accession was met with much apprehension (Murray and Benvenuti, 2014: 435–8).

It also caused real economic loss – for example, of agricultural export markets, as Britain was obliged to accede to the EC's regime of protectionist farm subsidies. Kenyon and van der Eng (2014: 228–9) note that the Common Agricultural Policy (CAP) "was the cause of 20 years of trade tension and conflict between Australia and the EU" following the UK's accession. Moreover, the sense of frustration and exclusion engendered by Britain's participation in the single market was compounded in the twenty-first century by the UK's crackdown on non-EU migration – a consequence of the country's inability to restrict intra-EU migration – which has wound back the preferential access that Commonwealth citizens previously enjoyed.

Finally, for cultural as well as linguistic reasons, Australian and New Zealand perceptions of the EU are often refracted through a British lens. For example, Polonska-Kimunguyi and Kimunguyi (2015) note that the Europe correspondents of Australian media outlets are based in London, rather than Brussels. Therefore, British Euroscepticism influences New Zealand and Australian attitudes towards the EU as a supranational political entity. This is especially evident on the conservative side of politics and public opinion, and it played out in the reaction to the Brexit vote, which I discuss below.

The Brexit vote: reaction and impact

On 23 June 2016, the British electorate voted to leave the EU by a margin of 51.9 per cent to 48.1 per cent. The unexpected result sent shockwaves throughout Europe and beyond. The vote itself had no immediate legal impact, and it was only in March 2017 that the British government of Theresa May triggered Article 50 of the Lisbon Treaty, officially notifying Brussels of the UK's intention to leave the EU. As of September 2017, negotiations on the terms of the UK's departure are in their very early stages (though these must be completed by March 2019), and negotiations on post-exit EU–UK relations have not yet begun.

In Australia, some ideological support and sympathy for Brexit was evident, especially from the Murdoch press and the conservative side of politics. Former prime minister John Howard had backed the leave campaign and welcomed the result on the grounds that it was right for the British people and government to take back sovereign control of key policy areas such as immigration. In an interview with the *Financial Times*, he described the integration project as "fundamentally flawed", saying that "its best days are probably behind it and there will be increasing tensions [over migration]. Britain can't control its borders – it is ridiculous to say it can." He endorsed the leave case in unequivocal terms: "If I were British, which I'm not, I'd vote to leave. You have lost your sovereignty" (Smyth, 2016).

Again, that view was more prevalent on the conservative side of politics, and even then it was far from uniform. Nevertheless, such Eurosceptic sentiments reflect the fact that the ideological or political dimension of the European integration project has traditionally not resonated very strongly in Australia and New Zealand. Just as Britons saw the EEC/EU as mostly (or ideally) an economic project, so did their former colonies. Therefore, the general dismay that greeted Brexit in Australia and New Zealand mainly focused on economic concerns (as opposed to concern at the fate of the European construct). And a lot of that dismay is about uncertainty about the future.

The consequences of Brexit – for the EU, the UK and for third countries – will be far reaching. As far as Australia and New Zealand are concerned, Brexit will affect their relations with the EU in two main ways. Firstly, and more directly, the UK's departure means the loss of Australia's and New Zealand's main bilateral partner within the EU. Both countries will now need to develop a dual-track strategy – pursuing close economic and political ties with the EU as well as with post-Brexit Britain. Secondly, and at a more general level, Brexit will affect the EU's "actorness" in ways that are yet to play out. The loss of a member state whose commitment to the supranational project has never been wholehearted (Bogdanor, 2005) may well leave the EU27 more unified. However, at the same time the Union's international profile will necessarily be diminished by the loss of one of its largest and most powerful member states.

While Australia and New Zealand both potentially stand to benefit from closer trade relations with the UK post-Brexit, the UK's departure from the EU will undoubtedly complicate the bloc's relationship with the two Pacific nations. Australia and New Zealand risk being relegated to a lower priority as the EU and the UK negotiate their own future trade relationship. At the very least, Brexit adds an element of instability and uncertainty to EU–Australia–New Zealand relations. As Jacqueline Lo and Annmarie Elijah (2017) summarised the Australian perspective: "Just as the long shadow of British accession and its ramifications for Australia–EU relations appear to have given way to cooperation – perhaps genuine goodwill – the UK has once again called the terms of Australian relations with the EU28 into question with the proposed split. It is, at best, inconvenient."

Conclusion

The EU has good economic and strategic reasons to pivot towards the Asia-Pacific, but this is unlikely to translate into a higher priority being accorded to relations with Australia and New Zealand. Instead, its focus is likely to remain on bilateral relations with China and other significant regional players such as Japan (with which the EU is negotiating an FTA) and South Korea (with which the EU has an FTA). Co-operation with ASEAN, the major regional organisation, may also provide a focal point for the EU's diplomatic activity.

Indeed, China's rise has made it the dominant power in the Asia-Pacific. This has huge economic, political and strategic implications for other countries in the region. China is Australia's largest and New Zealand's second largest trading partner (after Australia).[2] China also commands considerable attention from extra-regional powers, including the EU, for which it is the second largest trading partner, after the United States (European Commission, 2015). In short, engagement with China is a high priority of all three of the EU, New Zealand and Australia, and somewhat overshadows further development of relations along the EU–Australia and EU–New Zealand axes.

Still, relations between the EU and each of Australia and New Zealand are solid. Moreover, as detailed above, there is scope for the further development of economic and broader strategic ties through the conclusion of framework and partnership agreements, and through future negotiation of FTAs. Trade is likely to remain the backbone of both relationships – despite sharing a lot in terms of values and culture, "normative power Europe" has not resonated very strongly in the liberal democracies of the South Pacific. In terms of global governance, Australian and New Zealand governments have tended to look more to traditional allies such as the US and the UK for leadership, rather than the EU. Strong historical and contemporary links between Australia and New Zealand, on the one hand, and the UK, on the other, also mean that the EU–Australia and EU–New Zealand relations are sensitive to changes in the UK's own engagement with the continent.

Notes

1 If the ASEAN-10 is treated as a regional bloc, the EU was pushed into fourth place in terms of volume of merchandise trade in 2013 (MFAT, 2013: 6). The EU Delegation to New Zealand (2016) notes that, "[w]hile the EU remains an important trading partner for New Zealand, New Zealand's trade focus is increasingly on the countries of the Asia-Pacific rim".
2 A study of elite perceptions in New Zealand indicated a growing view that Europe is in decline and that Asia is increasingly important to the country's economic future (Kelly, 2015).

References

Bogdanor, Vernon. (2005). "Footfalls Echoing in the Memory. Britain and Europe: The Historical Perspective", *International Affairs* 81 (4): 689–701.
Claes, Monica, and Willem Eijsbouts. (2008). "The Difference", *European Constitutional Law Review* 4 (1): 1–19.
Delegation of the EU to Australia. (2016). "The Role of the EU Delegation", *Delegation of the European Union to Australia*, http://eeas.europa.eu/archives/delegations/australia/about_us/delegation_role/index_en.htm, accessed online 19 May 2018.
Delegation of the EU to New Zealand. (2016). "Political and Economic Relations", *Delegation of the European Union to New Zealand*, http://eeas.europa.eu/delegations/new_zealand/eu_new_zealand/political_economics_relations/index_en.htm, accessed online 19 May 2018.
DFAT. (2016). "European Union Fact Sheet", *Australian Government Department of Foreign Affairs and Trade*, http://dfat.gov.au/trade/resources/Documents/eu.pdf, accessed online 12 June 2016.
DFAT. (2017). "Australia's Trade at a Glance", *Australian Government Department of Foreign Affairs and Trade*, http://dfat.gov.au/trade/resources/trade-at-a-glance/Pages/default.aspx, accessed online 12 June 2016.
Diez, Thomas. (2005). "Constructing the Self and Changing Others: Reconsidering 'Normative Power Europe'", *Millennium: Journal of International Studies* 33 (3): 613–36.
European Commission. (2015). "Statement of the Presidents of the European Council and the European Commission and the New Zealand Prime Minister", *European Commission Press Release Database*, Brussels, 29 October, http://europa.eu/rapid/press-release_STATEMENT-15–5947_en.htm, accessed online 2 September 2018.
European Commission. (2016). "Joint Proposal for a Council Decision on the Signing, on Behalf of the European Union, and Provisional Application of the Framework Agreement between the European Union and its Member States, of the one Part, and Australia, of the Other Part", *EUR-Lex*, JOIN/2016/08 final - 2016/0113 (NLE), Brussels, 14 April, http://eur-lex.europa.eu/legal-content/EN/TXT/?uri=CELEX%3A52016JC0008, accessed online 19 May 2018.

European Commission. (2017). "EU and Australia One Step Closer to Launching Trade Negotiations", *European Commission Press Release*, Brussels, 6 April, http://trade.ec.europa.eu/doclib/press/index.cfm?id=1643, accessed online 2 September 2018.
Garton Ash, Timothy. (2007). "Europe's True Stories", *Prospect Magazine*, 25 February.
Habermas, Jürgen, and Derrida, Jacques. (2003). "February 15, or What Binds Europeans Together: A Plea for a Common Foreign Policy, Beginning in the Core of Europe", *Constellations* 10 (3): 291–7.
Kagan, Robert. (2003). *Paradise and Power: America and Europe in the New World Order*. London: Atlantic Books.
Kelly, Serena. (2015). "New Zealand Elite Perceptions on the EU: A Longitudinal Analysis", *Baltic Journal of European Studies* 3 (3): 153–74.
Kenyon, Donald, and Pierre van der Eng. (2014). "Defining the Relationship between Australia and the European Union: Is the Framework Treaty Enough?", *Australian Journal of International Affairs* 68 (2): 225–42.
Leining, Catherine, and Suzi Kerr. (2016). "Lessons Learned from the New Zealand Emissions Trading Scheme", *Motu Economic and Public Policy Research*, Working Paper 16–06, pp. 1–40.
Lo, Jacqueline, and Annmarie Elijah. (2017). "The EU–Australia Relationship: Plus ça Change ...", *Australian Institute of International Affairs*, 5 June, www.internationalaffairs.org.au/australianoutlook/australia-european-union-continuity-change/, accessed online 2 September 2018.
Manners, Ian. (2002). "Normative Power Europe: A Contradiction in Terms?", *Journal of Common Market Studies* 40 (2): 235–58.
Manners, Ian. (2010). "Global Europa: Mythology of the European Union in World Politics", *Journal of Common Market Studies* 48 (1): 67–87.
MFAT. (2013). "Analysis of NZ Merchandise Trade Data – Year Ended June 2013", Ministry of Foreign Affairs and Trade, www.mfat.govt.nz/assets/Economic-stats-data/Trade-Statistics-Analysis-Analysis-of-NZ-Trade-Data-June-2013-Jun-2013.pdf, accessed online 2 September 2018
Minister for Trade and Investment. (2015). "European Union FTA Talks Progress", Minister for Trade and Investment, 16 November, http://trademinister.gov.au/releases/Pages/2015/ar_mr_151116.aspx, accessed online 2 September 2018.
Muûls, Mirabelle, Jonathan Colmer, Ralf Martin and & Ulrich Wagner. (2016). "Evaluating the EU Emissions Trading System: Take it or Leave It? An Assessment of the Data after Ten Years", Grantham Institute Briefing paper 21, www.imperial.ac.uk/media/imperial-college/grantham-institute/public/publications/briefing-papers/Evaluating-the-EU-emissions-trading-system_Grantham-BP-21_web.pdf, accessed online 2 September 2018.
Murray, Philomena, Annmarie Elijah and Carolyn O'Brien. (2002). "Common Ground, Worlds Apart: The Development of Australia's Relationship with the European Union", *Australian Journal of International Affairs* 56 (3): 395–416.
Murray, Philomena, and Andrea Benvenuti. (2014). "EU–Australia Relations at Fifty: Reassessing a Troubled Relationship", *Australian Journal of Politics and History* 60 (3): 431–48.
Oberthür, Sebastian, and Lisanne Groen. (2017). "Explaining Goal Achievement in International Negotiations: The EU and the Paris Agreement on Climate Change",

Journal of European Public Policy, DOI: 10.1080/13501763.2017.1291708: 1–20.
Parker, Charles, Christer Karlsson and Mattias Hjerpe. (2017). "Assessing the European Union's Global Climate Change Leadership: From Copenhagen to the Paris Agreement", *Journal of European Integration* 39 (2): 239–52.
Parker, Charles, and Christer Karlsson. (2010). "Climate Change and the European Union's Leadership Moment: An Inconvenient Truth?", *Journal of Common Market Studies* 48 (4): 923–43.
Polonska-Kimunguyi, Eva, and Patrick Kimunguyi. (2015). "Communicating the European Union to Australia: The EU Information Strategy and Its Reception Down Under", *Baltic Journal of European Studies* 3 (3): 127–52.
Rankin, Jennifer. (2016). "Belgian Politicians Drop Opposition to EU–Canada Trade Deal", *The Guardian*, 28 October.
Rettman, Andrew. (2010). "EU Commission 'Embassies' Granted New Powers", *EU Observer*, 21 January, https://euobserver.com/foreign/29308, accessed online 2 September 2018.
Riedel, Eibe, and Martin Will. (1999). "Human Rights Clauses in External Agreements of the EC", in Philip Alston, Mara R. Bustelo and James Heenan (eds), *The EU and Human Rights*. Oxford: Oxford University Press.
Rootes, Christopher. (2014). "A Referendum on the Carbon Tax? The 2013 Australian Election, the Greens, and the Environment", *Environmental Politics* 23 (1): 166–173.
Scicluna, Nicole. (2015). *European Union Constitutionalism in Crisis*. London: Routledge.
Smith, David. (2017). "Trump Withdraws from Trans-Pacific Partnership amid Flurry of Orders", *The Guardian*, 24 January.
Smith, Karen E. (1998). "The Use of Political Conditionality in the EU's Relations with Third Countries: How Effective", *European Foreign Affairs Review* 3: 253–74.
Smyth, Jamie. (2016). "Former Australian Premier John Howard Backs Britain to Lleave EU", *The Financial Times*, 7 April.
Von Stein, Jana. (2013). "The Engines of Compliance", in Jeffrey L. Dunoff and Mark A. Pollack (eds), *Interdisciplinary Perspectives on International Law and International Relations: The State of the Art*. New York: Cambridge University Press.
Weiler, Joseph. (1994). "A Quiet Revolution: The European Court of Justice and Its Interlocutors", *Comparative Political Studies* 26 (4): 510–34.

Index

African, Caribbean and Pacific states (ACP) 1, 101, 129, 130–1
ASEAN Regional Forum (ARF) 4, 17, 29, 67, 69, 124, 192, 194
Asia-Europe Meeting (ASEM) 3–4, 17, 29, 39–40, 43–5, 124–7, 190
Association of Southeast Asian Nations (ASEAN)
  economic relationships 3–4, 12–13, 17, 27, 40, 75–6, 84, 191–3
  governing norms 188–9, 193
  historical development of 62, 188–1
  institutional weakness of 46, 51, 84
  non-traditional security (NTS) 190–1, 193–5
  regionalism 48, 84–5, 188, 193
  strategic relationships 12–13, 17, 27, 29, 31, 40, 67, 69, 124–7, 136, 189–91
Australia/New Zealand 200–5, 210–13

Barcelona report (2004) 121–2
Belt and Road Initiative (BRI) 78, 90, 156, 196
bilateral trade agreements 48–9, 78
  see also free-trade agreements; trade
Brazil, Russia, India, China and South Africa (BRICS) 6, 147
Brexit 30, 51, 74, 92, 146, 173, 202, 211–13

China
  challenges to 157, 159
  economic relationships 6, 48–9, 78–9, 88, 90–1
  economic security of 154–5
  as emerging global power 5–6, 9, 18, 27, 86–7, 146–8, 159–60
  inter-regionalism 46, 48
  as a security threat 168–9
  sovereignty 149–50
  strategic relationships 12, 28, 145, 155–6
  unfair trade practices by 152–3
climate change 13, 134–5, 207–9
  see also sustainable development
Common Agricultural Policy (CAP) 202, 211
Common Foreign and Security Policy (CFSP) 1, 65–6, 96, 148, 165
Common Security and Defence Policy (CSDP) 165, 172, 195
Conference on Security and Co-operation in Europe (CSCE) see Helsinki Process
crisis management 126, 166, 172–3, 176, 195

development aid 129–30
diplomacy see public diplomacy
Directorate-General Humanitarian Aid and Civil Protection (DG ECHO) 133, 135 *table*

Directorate-General International
  Co-operation and Development
  (DG DEVCO) 129–30
Disasters Preparedness ECHO
  Programme (DIPECHO)
  133–4

East Asia 39, 42–3, 45, 46
East Asia Summit (EAS) 29, 67
economic relationships
  challenges to 5–6, 51, 79–80, 84
  factors in 73–4
  inter-regional 3–4, 12–13, 17, 27,
    40, 43–4, 67, 74–9, 83–4,
    88–92, 127–30, 132, 133–6,
    191–3
  intra-regional 5–6, 51, 84–6, 89
  state of current 74–6, 80–3
  see also bilateral agreements;
    free-trade agreements
economic security 151–5, 171
EU Global Strategy for Foreign and
  Security Policy (EUGS)
  challenges to 30–2, 148
  economic policies under 27–8
  implementation of 20–1, 30–1
  priorities for 20, 31
  regional strategies under 28–9
  security policies under 18–19, 24–6,
    70
  strategic context of 18–21, 66
European Community (EC) 148–9,
  189, 211
European Development Fund (EDF)
  130, 132 *table*, 133 *table*
European Economic Community (EEC)
  61–2
European External Action Service
  (EEAS) 18, 100–1, 203
European Security and Defence Policy
  (ESDP) 122, 165, 172, 185
European Security Strategy (ESS) 65–6,
  121, 123, 166

Five-Power Defence Arrangements
  (FPDAs) 194
foreign direct investment (FDI) 75, 78,
  148, 192

Foreign Policy Instruments (FPIs)
  128–9
free-trade agreements (FTAs) 4, 27, 43,
  47, 51, 76–7, 85–8, 185, 191,
  203–4
  see also bilateral trade agreements;
    trade

globalisation 8, 40, 62, 74, 92, 151
global strategy (EU) 1–2, 3, 7–8, 18,
  18–21, 39–40, 91–2, 159
  external challenges 18, 70
  internal challenges 6, 8, 45–6, 70,
    74, 90, 146, 150, 157, 159
  as international actor 21, 64–6, 137,
    148, 159–60, 165, 205
*Guidelines on the EU's Foreign and
  Security Policy in East Asia* 17,
  67, 166, 173

hard power 68, 70, 89–90, 173, 194
Helsinki Process 60, 62, 66
human rights, environmental and
  public health aid 21, 26–7, 89,
  133–6, 206–7
Human Security Doctrine for Europe
  (Barcelona report) 121–2

inter-regionalism
  establishing 40–1, 44–7, 51
  external influences 46, 48–50, 86–7
  regional identity 4–5, 41–3, 45, 46,
    48–9, 51–2

Korean peninsula 28–9, 49–50, 52

Lisbon Treaty (2009) 18, 30, 42, 45,
  101, 203

Maastricht Treaty (Treaty of the
  European Union) 1, 45, 65, 96
multilateralism 7, 21, 30, 46, 65, 147,
  205

National Security Strategy (NSS)
  167–8
New Zealand *see* Australia/New
  Zealand

Index

non-traditional security (NTS) 190–1, 193–5
normative power 6–7, 99, 148–50, 205–6
Normative Power Europe (NPE) 205–6, 209–10
North Atlantic Treaty Organisation (NATO) 19, 61, 169, 173

official development assistance (ODA) 129–30, 131 *table*, 175–6
"One Belt, One Road" 6, 49, 78–9

Paris Agreement (2015) 30, 69, 134–5
Partnership Co-operation Agreements (PCAs) 77, 124
political relationships
 challenges to 5
 inter-regional 12, 27, 127–8, 148–50
 intra-regional 5, 174, 195–6
"principled pragmatism" 7, 22, 30, 159, 190
public diplomacy
 defining 96–7
 instruments of 101–4, 127–8
 inter-regional 11, 31, 96
 intra-regional 100
 as managing perceptions 113–15
 as a "marketing" tool 117
 as raising awareness 104–13
 "track-two" diplomacy 68

reciprocity/reciprocal socialisation 79, 88, 145–6, 153, 156, 160
Russia 63, 169–70, 175

security
 challenges to providing 62–3
 hard power 68, 70, 89–90, 173, 194
 human 11–12, 29, 120, 121, 122–3, 126–8, 136–7, 193
 maritime 51, 69, 168, 178–9
 non-traditional (NTS) 190–1, 193–5
 soft power 30, 89–90, 166–7, 175–6

 threats to 49–50, 51, 52, 68, 69–70, 89, 168–9, 171, 173
 under EUGS 18–19, 24–6
security partnerships 59, 60–4, 68–9, 70–1, 175–7, 177–9, 184–5, 191–2, 195–6
socialisation, reciprocal/reciprocity 79, 88, 145–6, 153, 156, 160
soft power 66–7, 89–90, 166–7, 175
sovereignty 100, 150, 158, 187–90, 193
strategic partnership agreement (SPA) 164, 176, 177
strategic relationships 3–4, 10, 17, 18, 29, 31, 67, 69, 124–7, 136, 145, 164, 166–8, 189–91
 challenges to 172–4, 176–7, 179–80
 inter-regional 164–5, 170–2, 174–5
sustainable development 19, 20, 22, 23
 see also climate change
Sustainable Development Goals (SDGs) 23, 27

Towards a New Asia Strategy (1994) 1, 43, 96, 97, 165, 190, 194
trade
 challenges to 5–6, 48, 51, 67, 69–70, 73, 77–8, 84, 152–4, 168–9, 171, 173, 202
 extent of inter-regional 4, 27–8, 43–4, 47, 75, 77, 79, 130–3, 191–2, 201–2, 204
 intra-regional 84–5, 88, 164
 policies 11, 28, 48–9, 75, 78
 security for 89–90
 see also bilateral trade agreements; free-trade agreements
Trans-Pacific Partnership (TPP) 6, 27–8, 49, 73, 204
trans-regionalism *see* inter-regionalism
Treaty of Amity and Co-operation in Southeast Asia (TAC) 67
Treaty of Friendship, Co-operation, and Mutual Assistance (Warsaw Pact) 61
Treaty of Lisbon *see* Lisbon Treaty

Treaty of the European Union
    (Maastricht Treaty) 65
Trump, Donald 25, 40
  EU's relationship with 50
  isolationist policies of 31, 49–50, 88

UN Framework Convention on
    Climate Change (UNFCC, 1992)
    134

United States (US)
  Asian policy 49–50, 60–1, 86–7
  isolationism 27–8, 29, 30–1, 49–50,
    69, 74, 87, 88, 157, 169
  "pivot to Asia" 5, 18, 39, 63, 75

Warsaw Pact (Treaty of Friendship,
    Co-operation, and Mutual
    Assistance) 61

EU authorised representative for GPSR:
Easy Access System Europe, Mustamäe tee 50,
10621 Tallinn, Estonia
gpsr.requests@easproject.com

www.ingramcontent.com/pod-product-compliance
Lightning Source LLC
Chambersburg PA
CBHW071831230426
43672CB00013B/2817